T0330308

FACES OF PRECARITY

Critical Perspectives on Work, Subjectivities and Struggles

Edited by
Joseph Choonara, Annalisa Murgia and
Renato Miguel Carmo

BRISTOL
UNIVERSITY
PRESS

First published in Great Britain in 2022 by

Bristol University Press
University of Bristol
1-9 Old Park Hill
Bristol
BS2 8BB
UK
t: +44 (0)117 374 6645
e: bup-info@bristol.ac.uk

Details of international sales and distribution partners are available at bristoluniversitypress.co.uk

British Library Cataloguing in Publication Data
A catalogue record for this book is available from the British Library

ISBN 978-1-5292-2007-0 hardcover
ISBN 978-1-5292-2008-7 ePub
ISBN 978-1-5292-2009-4 ePdf

Cover design: Andrew Corbett
Front cover image: Alamy/Susan Vineyard
Bristol University Press use environmentally responsible print partners.
Printed in Great Britain by CPI Group (UK) Ltd, Croydon, CR0 4YY

Contents

List of Figures and Tables

Figures

Tables

Notes on Contributors

Emiliana Armano holds a PhD in economic sociology from the University of Milan. She is an independent researcher, collaborating in the study of digital capitalism, knowledge work, flexibility and precariousness, with a social inquiry and co-research approach. Her research focuses on the intertwining of work processes and the production of subjectivity. She has collaborated with Romano Alquati and Sergio Bologna, and has published several essays. She recently edited (with A. Bove and A. Murgia) *Mapping Precariousness, Labour Insecurity and Uncertain Livelihoods: Subjectivities and Resistance* (Routledge, 2017).

André Barata was born in Faro in 1972. He holds a PhD in contemporary philosophy and is Associate Professor at the University of Beira Interior in Portugal, where he directs the Faculty of Arts and Letters. His academic interests range from social and political philosophy to existential and phenomenological thought.

Jean-Claude Barbier is Emeritus Professor of Sociology at Université Panthéon Sorbonne. He is a specialist in European integration and social policy. In 2021, he published (with M. Zemmour) *Le système français de protection sociale* (La Découverte, 3rd edition) and, in 2013, *The Road to Social Europe: A Contemporary Approach to Political Cultures and Diversity in Europe* (Routledge).

Francesc X. Belvis is a sociologist with a degree in statistics and a PhD in the history of science. Since 2010 he has been a full-time researcher for the Research Group on Health Inequalities, Environment – Employment Conditions Network (GREDS-EMCONET), in the Department of Political and Social Sciences of the Pompeu Fabra University (UPF). His lines of interest include social determinants of health, inequalities, and working and employment conditions.

Mireia Bolíbar is Serra Hunter Assistant Professor (professora lectora) at the University of Barcelona. She held a Juan de la Cierva Formación postdoctoral fellowship at GREDS-EMCONET, in the Department of Political and Social Science, UPF.

Renato Miguel Carmo is Associate Professor in the Department of Sociology at the University Institute of Lisbon (ISCTE) and Research Fellow at the Centre for Research and Studies in Sociology (CIES). He is Director of the Inequality Observatory and Scientific Coordinator of the Collaborative Laboratory for Labour, Employment and Social Protection (CoLABOR), Portugal.

Joseph Choonara is Lecturer in the School of Business at the University of Leicester, where he is also Chair of the University and College Union branch. He co-convenes the Centre for Sustainable Work and Employment Futures. He is Editor of the journal *International Socialism* and his books include *Insecurity, Precarious Work and Labour Markets: Challenging the Orthodoxy* (Palgrave Macmillan, 2019).

Patrick Cingolani is Professor of Sociology at the University of Paris. His theoretical and empirical research focuses on social figures of precariousness as well as the micro-politics of emancipation. He has published a series of books, in particular, *Révolutions précaires* (La Découverte, 2014), *La précarité* (Presses Universitaires de France, 2017) and *La Colonisation du quotidien* (Éditions Amsterdam, 2021).

Klaus Dörre is Chair of Sociology of Work, and Economic and Industrial Sociology at Friedrich Schiller University Jena (FSU Jena). He was one of the Directors of the DFG-Research Group on Post-Growth Societies from 2011 to 2021; he is responsible for the Zentrum Digitale Transformation Thüringen (ZeTT), together with Professor Kraußlach; and he is Co-editor of the *Berliner Journal für Soziologie* and *Global Dialogue*. His research focuses on the theory of capitalism/financial market capitalism, precarious employment, strategic unionism, digitalization and right-wing populism.

Mariana Gutiérrez-Zamora is Predoctoral Researcher in the Department of Political and Social Sciences (UPF), for GREDS-EMCONET, and the Public Policy Centre, Johns Hopkins University (UPF-BSM). She has a degree in nutrition and a master's in public health. Her lines of interest include public health, public policy and the social determinants of health.

Jane Hardy was formerly Professor of Political Economy at the University of Hertfordshire. She is the author of *Nothing to Lose But Our Chains: Work and Resistance in 21st Century Britain* (Pluto, 2021) and *Poland's New*

Capitalism (Pluto, 2008). She is on the editorial board of the *International Socialism* journal.

Charlotta Hedberg is Associate Professor and Senior Lecturer in Human Geography, Umeå University. Her research focuses on spatial and social aspects of internal and international migration processes. Her current research concerns migrant workers in the Swedish wild berry industry, which is ethnographically analyzed from structural, transnational/translocal and individual perspectives.

Barbora Holubová is Researcher at the Central European Labour Studies Institute in Bratislava, Slovakia. Her professional background is in sociology. She has more than 15 years of experience working in applied social sciences, specifically looking at labour markets, social inequalities and inclusion, mainly analyzed from a gender perspective. Before assuming her current position, she worked in the European Institute for Gender Equality.

Marta Kahancová is Founder and Managing Director of the Central European Labour Studies Institute in Bratislava, Slovakia. Her research interests are in the sociology of organizations and work. In particular, she studies working conditions, industrial relations and atypical forms of work. She also serves as a labour market expert for the European Commission. Her publications have appeared in international peer-reviewed journals in industrial relations, sociology and human resource management.

Alice Mattoni is Associate Professor in the Department of Political and Social Sciences at the University of Bologna. Her research focuses on the intersections between media – digital and otherwise – and social movements. She has published extensively on this topic, focusing on precarious workers' movements, environmental civil society actors and anti-corruption grassroots initiatives.

Glenn Morgan is Honorary Professor at the School of Management, University of Bristol. He has published a range of articles on work and the political economy of capitalisms in journals and edited books. His current research focuses on the impact of the changing nature of work on political and social relations.

Cristina Morini is an independent researcher. Her research interests focus on gender, labour transformation processes, and the relationship between subjectivity and contemporary capitalism. She is a member of Effimera.org. Among her recent publications is 'Life is mine: feminism, self-determination and basic income', in *Radical Philosophy* (2020), and (with A. Fumagalli)

'Anthropomorphic capital and commonwealth value', in *Frontiers in Sociology* (2020).

Annalisa Murgia is Associate Professor at the Department of Social and Political Sciences, University of Milan. She is the PI of the ERC project 'SHARE – Seizing the Hybrid Areas of Work by Re-presenting Self-Employment' (GA 715950). Her research interests focus on precariousness, emerging forms of organizing and gender differences in organizations. Recent books include *Gender and Precarious Research Careers: A Comparative Analysis* (Routledge, 2019, with B. Poggio) and *Mapping Precariousness, Labour Insecurity and Uncertain Livelihoods: Subjectivities and Resistance* (Routledge, 2017, with E. Armano and A. Bove).

Agnieszka Piasna is Senior Researcher at the European Trade Union Institute (ETUI) in Brussels. Her research interests include job quality, working time and digital labour. She coordinates research activities in the framework of the ETUI Internet and Platform Work Survey. She has a PhD in sociology from the University of Cambridge.

Valeria Pulignano is Professor of Sociology of Work and Industrial Relations at KU Leuven. Her research interests include inequality, labour markets, employment relations, precarious work, job quality and workers' voice. She is principal coordinator of RN17 ESA; co-researcher at CRIMT; and principal investigator of ResPecTMe (ERC AdG). Recent books include *Shifting Solidarities* (Palgrave, 2020) and *Reconstructing Solidarity* (OUP, 2018).

Charles Umney is Associate Professor in the Work and Employment Relations Department at the University of Leeds. He has researched working conditions and industrial change in various contexts including cultural, social and healthcare work. He is the author of *Class Matters* (Pluto, 2018) and *Marketization* (with Ian Greer, forthcoming).

Introduction: Critical Perspectives on Precarity and Precariousness

Joseph Choonara, Annalisa Murgia and Renato Miguel Carmo

The rise of precarity and precariousness

The term *precarity* has, in recent years, emerged as a prominent category in discussions of contemporary work and employment, class, the transformation of social conditions and the subjectivities present in contemporary societies. Today, the word is widely used in academic research and, at times and in particular contexts, burrows through into wider public discourse or bursts on to the scene through protests and social movements. Google Scholar lists 15,700 publications containing the term in 2020 – an increase from just 65 in 2000 and 569 in 2010. In response to its expanding use in Anglophone academic research, the term was added to the *Oxford English Dictionary* in 2018, though its equivalents in other European languages have a far longer history. The related term, *precariousness*, has a much older pedigree in the English language, and its rise is less precipitous though also clearly evident; Google Scholar charts its growth from 1,720 occurrences (2000) to 4,480 (2010), and then to 12,900 (2020).

However, and in spite of their burgeoning use, there is no consensus on the precise definitions of these terms; how, or even whether, they add to our understanding of society; or precisely how the tendencies and transformations associated with them manifest. There are today, in short, many precarities and much precariousness present within academic discourse.

In spite of – some would say, because of – these ambiguities, the concepts have achieved a wide resonance. The French sociologist Pierre Bourdieu (1963, 1997, 1998), whose own use of the term *précarité* dates back to his writings on Algerian workers during the 1960s, captured a still emerging zeitgeist with an intervention in the late 1990s. Bourdieu took the casualization of work as his starting point. The resulting pervasive uncertainty 'prevents all rational anticipation', but he also noted that precarity touches everyone, even those 'apparently spared' casualized work, forming a key component of a 'mode of domination' based on 'a generalised and permanent state of insecurity'. Typically for its time, this intervention, whose title and leitmotif was '*La précarité est aujourd'hui partout*', was translated into English as 'Job insecurity is everywhere now'; today, the term precarity would undoubtedly be preferred.

Bourdieu's intervention is just one among myriad sources that inform discussions of precarity and precariousness.[1] The issues at stake in these different approaches include, to name but a few, tensions over the geographical and historical scope of the concept, along with the social category to which it attaches itself (class, work, social conditions, subjectivity, human existence in general); whether it is a measurable phenomenon; and its capacity to act as a basis for mobilization. Authors writing in English also differ on which of the terms, precarity or precariousness, is more appropriate in a given context, whether we should instead speak of a process of precarization, and whether these terms should be qualified, for instance, *employment* precarity or precarious *work*.

However, within this complex landscape of concepts and meanings lie several prominent landmarks that appear to have weathered the squalls and storms of academic debate more effectively than others, informing discussions over a prolonged period of time and serving as reference points for contemporary authors. For instance, one long-standing conception is that associated with Judith Butler's (2009: 2–3) work focusing on existential and ontological aspects of contingency. This links what she calls the 'more or less existential conception of "precariousness"', the 'vulnerability, injurability, interdependency' that constitute the human condition, to a 'more specifically political notion of "precarity"' whereby 'social and political organizations … have developed historically in order to maximise precariousness for some and minimise precariousness for others'.

By contrast with this ambitious ontological approach, precariousness or precarity can be more narrowly identified with a decline of the so-called 'standard employment relation', in particular in advanced capitalist countries during the neoliberal period. Work by the US sociologist Arne Kalleberg (2009, 2011) that focused on 'bad jobs' and 'polarized and precarious employment systems in the US' is emblematic of this line of thought. More broadly, a mass of literature within the sociology of work details the use of temporary or zero-hour contracts, platform work and other novel forms of employment relationships under the heading of precarity (Alberti et al, 2018).

A related approach, which also tends to draw on the notion of a decline of a Fordist social compromise, with its related systems of employment, posits not simply the deterioration of working conditions but the emergence of a novel social identity or social class. This potentially offers a new basis for mobilizations and struggles, distinct from those traditionally associated with the unionized workers of the Fordist period. In the case of Guy Standing's (2011) much criticized but also widely cited work, these groups form a 'precariat' – a 'class-in-the-making' – that can be distinguished from the 'old working class', and other groups he dubs the 'salariat' and 'proficians', by its members' lack of access to secure jobs and traditional systems of welfare. The neologism, precariat, which has been used within social movements since the early 2000s (Exposito, 2004; The Frassanito Network, 2006), was also given the stamp of approval by the British Broadcasting Corporation in its 'Great British Class Survey', overseen by the prominent sociologist Mike Savage (Savage et al, 2013).

For Standing (2011: 132–82), the precariat must be offered a progressive politics based on security and redistributive measures such as a universal basic income, lest it fall prey to the siren voice of populism, leading to a 'politics of inferno'. However, Standing has been criticized from more radical perspectives as one of those who has turned precarity 'into a synonym for insecurity or a sociological category', stripping 'precarity of its real social and political transformative potentials' (Papadopoulos, 2017: 138, 144). Such accounts stress that 'analyses and political struggles around precarity', of the kind envisaged by Standing, 'are often in danger of reasserting the politics of Fordism' as a result of their 'affective attachments to conservative agendas' (Mitropoulos, 2011).[2] What many of these critics have in mind is a view of precarity, at least potentially, as a new historic form for the 'refusal of work' that played a central strategic role in the arsenal of movements such as *operaismo* ('workerism') in Italy in the 1970s, which later flowed into the autonomist tradition associated with figures such as Mario Tronti, Antonio Negri, Sergio Bologna or Franco 'Bifo' Berardi (Wright, 2002; Mitropoulos, 2006; Bologna, 2014). Such approaches pose the question of whether precarity is simply a hardship to be endured or resisted, or potentially a condition to be radicalized, evoking a desire for an exodus from the capital–labour relation and a denial of the identity between work and life (Bove et al, 2017: 3).

Between the far-reaching ontological claims of Butler and a narrower conception of precarity founded in the sphere of work and employment are approaches to precariousness that view it as an emergent form of subjectivity, founded on the transfer of risk and responsibility to the individual, through which individuals become 'entrepreneurs of their own "social capital"' (Armano and Murgia, 2013). Such an approach can draw on a long-standing sociological literature on the 'risk society', 'liquid modernity' and the 'new capitalism' (Beck, 1992; Bauman, 2000; Sennett, 2006), or works such as Luc Boltanski and Eve Chiapello's (2005: 57–101) ambitious evocation of a 'new spirit of capitalism'. According to the latter, the incorporation of subjects into the system rests on the projection of an ideology of non-hierarchical, networked, flexible and responsive organizations, with the self-development of the individual the prerequisite for effective participation. Such transformations are, in this view, not limited to temporary or short-tenured work or the deterioration of working conditions but form an experiential state pervading the entire lives of individuals (Armano and Murgia, 2017: 48), deepening atomization and individualization, and reflected in a set of symptoms that affect the social and emotional wellbeing of individuals (Carmo and Matias, 2020: 29).

A critical intervention

As even this far from comprehensive typology suggests,[3] a number of unresolved conceptual tensions remain in the literature. The present volume does not advocate for a particular perspective. Instead, the distinctive aim of this work is to showcase, in a single collection, authors representing a range of critical perspectives on precarity and precariousness. The chapters respond to the unresolved conceptual issues, outline possible theoretical approaches and demonstrate how these contested concepts can be applied to contemporary society, considering also the new and unprecedented processes of precarization during the COVID-19 pandemic.

There is no pretence to a singular definition of precarity or precariousness among the contributors – or even among the editors – but rather an acknowledgement of the need for productive dialogue on these issues. While the authors of the various chapters are each interested in contemporary subjectivities or aspects of contemporary employment, or both, they are from different disciplines and traditions, within and beyond academia, different generations and different geographical locations within Europe.[4]

What the authors contributing to this collection have in common is their criticality. They are critical in two senses. First, they each aim to penetrate beyond common sense notions of precarity and precariousness, to identify the deeper causes and more pressing consequences of the social transformations that have brought these concepts to the fore. Second, they share a broadly critical stance towards contemporary social conditions. Beyond this shared critical perspective, there is no attempt to impose a common theoretical framework on the various chapters, but rather this work aims to offer the reader an opportunity to familiarize themselves with a broad field of enquiry in all its complexity.

The thematic structure of the book

The chapters of the work are tentatively presented in three parts. *Tentatively* because many contributions in actuality straddle more than one of the headings into which the editors have corralled them – but also because, given the range of voices involved in this project, any categorization will lack precision and run the risk of appearing arbitrary. Nonetheless, we feel that some thematic organization may help the reader navigate through the volume as a whole while better identifying common motifs.

The first part of the book deals with 'Conceptualizations, Subjectivities and Etymologies'. Here, Jean-Claude Barbier helps to set the scene by surveying 40 years of transnational research on precarity, precariousness and their equivalents in other languages. His chapter opens with a consideration of the growth of the use of the term *précarité* in French social theory from the 1970s, and then in other Latin countries in the 1980s, in parallel with the growing empirical interest in precarious employment within the Anglophone countries. From here, he shows how terms emerged in English and German seeking to capture and convey the various meanings of *précarité*, as evident in debates within the Latin countries. However, Barbier argues, pioneering studies in the 1970s and 1980s never achieved a universally recognized definition, and this led to the current landscape in which these terms acquire different meanings in different linguistic and conceptual contexts.

This is followed by two chapters that offer striking conceptualizations focused on the subjective experience of precariousness. The first, by Emiliana Armano, Cristina Morini and Annalisa Murgia, defends a conceptual distinction between precarity, manifest in the erosion of the Fordist employment regime, and precariousness, a subjective experience so extensive that it permeates the entire life of individuals. Focusing on the latter perspective, the authors argue that the precarious subject acquires sole responsibility for their destiny and is compelled to invest fully in the production of their subjectivity. Based on this approach, they offer an account of the acceleration of the digitization process under the conditions created by the COVID-19 pandemic, and ask what is required to leave behind the logic of individualization and enterprise. The authors call for individuals to recognize themselves as subjects with agency through practices of reappropriation and collective subjectification. A second conceptualization, offered by André Barata and Renato Miguel Carmo, places 'social time' at its centre. In the contemporary world, people tend increasingly to experience time as both 'fragmented', devoid of meaning, and 'accelerated', condemning people merely to experience its passage. The authors argue that these are two inherently interrelated aspects of the experience of time, ultimately resulting in precariousness as a 'temporary experience of vulnerability'. They chart the historical development of this situation through its various phases, beginning with the emergence of abstract time in the Middle Ages, through to the present day.

The second part of the book turns to accounts focused on the nature of 'Class, Work and Employment', themes that have often provided the terrain on which discussions of precarity have occurred.

Klaus Dörre's chapter draws on his empirical studies of precarity in the context of the German economy. Dörre argues for a class analytical approach in which categories such as precariousness and precarization, rather than perfectly capturing workers' experience, act as 'displaced class experiences' that fail to find adequate expression in the political system. The resulting gap between lived experience and a fictitious, staged social reality generates frustration, anger and rebellion. Dörre takes to task authors such as Standing who see a precariat as an emergent class. Instead, the boundaries between areas of inclusion and exclusion run predominantly within classes, denoting a line of conflict that presents challenges if consciously acting class movements are to form. Dörre's chapter is followed by a second preoccupied with class, this one by Charles Umney. Umney argues that the term precarity can be used in ways that are overly static when describing the experiences and situations of workers. He argues instead for an approach located in the Marxist concept of the labour–capital relationship, in which categories and institutions are remoulded and destabilized, and the social world often rendered incoherent or contradictory. Umney concludes that, rather than engaging in the rigid classification of people, a more effective theorization would adopt an aleatory Marxism, focused on the different conjunctures that arise, and the role of human agency in intervening to shape these conjunctures.

Two chapters then follow that, in different ways, consider the nature of labour markets. Joseph Choonara, like Umney, offers a sceptical take on the concept of precarity, preferring to focus on a parsimonious definition of 'precarious employment', defined as the degree to which work has become more contingent. He offers a survey of job tenure, the proliferation of temporary work and changes in the regulation of employment across the UK, Italy, France, Germany and the US. Choonara argues that explaining the diverse trends in employment outcomes – which combine precariousness with what he dubs 'stagnation', in which employment remains stable even if it deteriorates in quality – necessitates a theorization of concrete labour markets, rooted in Marxist political economy. Such an approach can integrate the different structural, institutional and contingent elements shaping employment relations. The following chapter, by Valeria Pulignano and Glenn Morgan, also considers the way that labour markets are shaped and reshaped in the context of neoliberalism. They emphasize approaches derived from critical labour studies and feminist analyses of the reproduction of capitalism, integrating the role of domestic labour. The growth of precarious work and the decline of welfare have, they argue, shifted the burdens of reproduction and the risks entailed in employment back on to the individual. This transmits precarity into the household itself, as the resources therein are made more flexible in order to meet these demands.

This part of the book concludes with two chapters exploring the growth of the platform economy as a mediator of employment relations, which has become a key topic in discussions of precarious work. In her chapter, Agnieszka Piasna analyzes the ways in which online labour platforms transform work, leading to unpredictable hours, casualization, shifts from salaried work to piecework, and from local to remote working. Piasna offers a wide-ranging assessment of the scale and social consequences of the proliferation of forms of platform work. Patrick Cingolani also considers the impact of phenomena such as the platform economy, exploring the way in which the COVID-19 pandemic has marked a turning point in the digitization of work and social life. Cingolani draws on two decades of prior research on precarious work, precarious subjectivities and 'precariousness', in the sense in which it appeared in French sociology, to denote a range of inequalities and insecurities. In his account, digital technology operates to weaken structures of employment and workers' rights – but it also creates the terrain on which new subjectivities and, along with this, new protests and new potential forms of solidarity, can emerge.

The third part of the book, covering 'Experiences, Concretizations and Struggles', offers a series of studies focused on how the various theorizations can explain and explore particular contemporary phenomena.

A chapter by Mireia Bolíbar, Francesc X. Belvis and Mariana Gutiérrez-Zamora looks at the impact of precarious work on the physical and mental health of younger workers in Catalonia, drawing on the 2017 Catalan Youth Survey. The authors use a mixed methods approach, first applying quantitative analysis to identify different clusters of pathways through the labour market – 'permanent', 'temporary' and 'discontinuous'. This then forms the basis for the second, qualitative, phase, in which a smaller number of participants, reflecting these different pathways, are interviewed, helping to identify the mechanisms at work in driving the health consequences of precarity.

The role of migrant labour has long featured in discussions of precarity, and the notion of precarity also increasingly informs the work of scholars of migration. Charlotta Hedberg here offers a chapter exploring the interplay of structure and agency, aspiration and exploitation, in the experiences of Thai wild berry pickers in Sweden. Her work draws on years of fieldwork in both Thailand and Sweden, and also considers the impact of COVID-19 during the 2020 and 2021 berry-picking seasons.

There is also a focus on the impact of the pandemic in the contribution by Barbora Holubová and Marta Kahancová. This chapter takes as its starting point a multidimensional concept of precarity, covering deteriorations in job security, livelihood, economic and social rights, and career opportunities. The authors chart the way in which COVID-19 has shone a spotlight on concerns related to health and safety at work, gender disparities and the growth of teleworking, adding to the dimensions of precarity.

Many of the authors in this collection insist on the potential agency of precarious workers, and this theme comes to the fore in the closing chapters.

Alice Mattoni draws on social movement scholarship to highlight how, in a fragmented workforce, those who feel under-represented by traditional trade unions have sought to organize. Mattoni considers the collective identities forged by precarious workers, their organizational patterns and how they diverge from those of other workers, and their distinctive repertoire of protest. Jane Hardy's chapter also concerns itself with labour struggles. She contests the notion that precarious workers cannot be organized due to their fragmented working relations or marginal statuses. In spite of a low level of labour struggle in the UK in recent years, there are examples of precarious workers in the country winning victories, both through small independent unions and large established ones. Hardy draws on case studies of low-paid women care workers; outsourced cleaners, often of Latinx origin; and warehouse agency workers from central and eastern Europe.

The volume as a whole concludes with an afterword by the editors, offering some avenues through which critical dialogue and debate about precarity and precariousness can be continued, deepened and developed, and noting the impact of COVID-19 on the ongoing discussions of these themes.

Notes

[1] The typology presented here draws principally on Bove et al (2017) and Choonara (2019).

[2] Also noteworthy in this regard is the work of Neilson and Rossiter (2008), which seeks to reassert precarity as a *political* concept, reflecting a set of experiences which are diverse, fluid and unstable, mediated through attempts to 'translate', rather than a *sociological* concept that can be grounded in empirical data.

[3] Not least because the term precarity, in particular, has now penetrated an extraordinary range of academic fields, including those such as anthropology, geography, cultural studies and area studies, where it has acquired yet more connotations.

[4] Limiting the scope to European scholarship was a conscious choice, and one that acknowledges the need for a distinctive 'view from the South' that has recently been articulated in discussions of precarity elsewhere (Lee and Kofman, 2012). For instance, outside the advanced capitalist states there are long-standing discussions of 'informality' and 'marginality', and a common understanding that work 'was always already precarious' (Munck et al, 2020).

References

Alberti, G., Bessa, I., Hardy, K., Trappmann, V. and Umney, C. (2018) 'In, against and beyond precarity: work in insecure times', *Work, Employment & Society*, 32(3): 447–57.

Armano, E. and Murgia, A. (2013) 'The precariousness of young knowledge workers: a subject-oriented approach', *Global Discourse: An Interdisciplinary Journal of Current Affairs and Applied Contemporary Thought*, 3(3–4): 486–501.

Armano, E. and Murgia, A. (2017) 'Hybrid areas of work in Italy: hypothesis to interpret the transformations of precariousness and subjectivity', in E. Armano, A. Bove and A. Murgia (eds) *Mapping Precariousness: Subjectivities and Resistance*, London: Routledge, pp 47–59.

Bauman, Z. (2000) *Liquid Modernity*, Oxford: Polity.

Beck, U. (1992) *The Risk Society: Towards a New Modernity*, London: Sage.

Bologna, S. (2014) 'Workerism: an inside view: from the mass-worker to self-employed labour', in M. Van der Linden and K. Heinz Roth (eds) *Beyond Marx: Theorising the Global Labour Relations of the Twenty-First Century*, Leiden and Boston: Brill, pp 121-44.

Boltanski, L. and Chiapello, E. (2005) *The New Spirit of Capitalism*, London: Verso.

Bourdieu, P. (1963) *Travail et Travailleurs en Algérie*, Paris: Mouton et Co.

Bourdieu, P. (1997) 'La précarité est aujourd'hui partout', Intervention at Lors des Rencontres européennes contre la précarité, Grenoble, 12–13 December 1997. Available from: https://www.ilo.org/wcmsp5/groups/public/@ed_dialogue/@actrav/documents/meetingdocument/wcms_161352.pdf [Accessed 8 June 2021].

Bourdieu, P. (1998) 'Job insecurity is everywhere now', in *Acts of Resistance: Against the New Myths of Our Time*, Cambridge: Polity, pp 81–7.

Bove, A., Murgia, A. and Armano, E. (2017) 'Mapping precariousness: subjectivities and resistance: an introduction', in *Mapping Precariousness: Subjectivities and Resistance*, London: Routledge, pp 1–12.

Butler, J. (2009) *Frames of War: When is Life Grievable?*, London: Verso.

Carmo, R.M. and Matias, A.R. (2020) 'Precarious futures: from non-standard jobs to an uncertain tomorrow', in R.M. Carmo and J.A.S. Simões (eds) *Protest, Youth and Precariousness: The Unfinished Fight against Austerity in Portugal*, New York and London: Berghahn Books, pp 13–32.

Choonara, J. (2019) *Insecurity, Precarious Work and Labour Markets: Challenging the Orthodoxy*, London: Palgrave Macmillan.

Exposito, M. (2004) 'L'Oceano Pacifico del precariato ribelle. Da Milano a Barcellona: la dimensione europea della MayDay Parade', *Posse*, 1.

The Frassanito Network (2006) 'Precarious, precarization, precariat? Impacts, traps and challenges of a complex term and its relationship to migration'. Available from: https://www.metamute.org/editorial/articles/precarious-precarisation-precariat [Accessed 22 December 2021].

Kalleberg, A.L. (2009) 'Precarious work, insecure workers: employment relations in transition', *American Sociological Review*, 74(1): 1–22.

Kalleberg, A.L. (2011) *Good Jobs, Bad Jobs: The Rise of Polarized and Precarious Employment Systems in the United States, 1970s to 2000s*, New York: Russell Sage Foundation.

Lee, C.K. and Kofman, Y. (2012) 'The politics of precarity: views beyond the United States', *Work and Occupations*, 39(4): 388–408.

Mitropoulos, A. (2006) 'Precari-us?', *Mute*, 1(29). Available from: https://transversal.at/transversal/0704/mitropoulos/en [Accessed 10 June 2021].

Mitropoulos, A. (2011) 'From precariousness to risk management and beyond', European Institute for Progressive Cultural Policies. Available from: https://transversal.at/transversal/0811/mitropoulos/en [Accessed 10 June 2021].

Munck, R., Pradella, L. and Wilson, T.D. (2020) 'Introduction: special issue on precarious and informal work', *Review of Radical Political Economics*, 52(3): 361–70.

Neilson, B. and Rossiter, N. (2008) 'Precarity as political concept, or, Fordism as exception', *Theory, Culture & Society*, 25(7–8): 51–72.

Papadopoulos, D. (2017) 'Two endings of the precarious movement', in E. Armano, A. Bove and A. Murgia (eds) *Mapping Precariousness: Subjectivities and Resistance*, London: Routledge, pp 137–48.

Savage, M., Devine, F., Cunningham, N., Taylor, M., Li, Y., Hjellbrekke, J., Roux, B.L., Friedman, S. and Miles, A. (2013) 'A new model of social class? Findings from the BBC's Great British Class Survey experiment', *Sociology*, 47(2): 219–50.

Sennett, R. (2006) *The Culture of the New Capitalism*, New Haven: Yale University Press.

Standing, G. (2011) *The Precariat: The New Dangerous Class*, London: Bloomsbury Academic.

Wright, S. (2002) *Storming Heaven: Class Composition and Struggle in Italian Autonomist Marxism*, London: Pluto Press.

PART I

Conceptualizations, Subjectivities and Etymologies

2

Précarité and Precarity: The Amazing Transnational Journey of Two Notions Unable to Form a Proper Concept in English

Jean-Claude Barbier

Introduction

By way of introduction, one should first recall the genesis of the French notion of *précarité* (precariousness). This very common French word acquired a new meaning from the late 1970s with regard to social policy. As the word originated from Latin (*prekor* = pray; *precarius* = obtained by praying), it was not surprising that its use spread rapidly in the 1980s in 'Latin'[1] countries (particularly Spain and Italy), with a meaning roughly similar to the French one.

At about the same time, the International Labour Organization (ILO) commissioned a path-breaking report (Rodgers and Rodgers, 1989). Its aim was to test the relevance of the term '*precariousness*' (a presumed English equivalent of *précarité*) as a concept, or at least as an analytical notion, in giving sense to the development of labour markets observed across the European Union (EU). The researchers involved in the project did not pay much attention as to whether English was able to provide a common notion; their goal was primarily pragmatic.[2] In parallel, as they worked together at the time, French and British sociologists coined a neologism for their own use, namely 'precarity' (Gallie and Paugam, 2000). This was a first testimony to the limitations of the English language in this domain. From such private use, extended usage ensued and the notion began to be circulated in cross-national forums of the European Union (both scientific and political). When a second important cross-national research project was funded by the European Union in the early 2000s (the European Study on Precarious Employment, ESOPE),[3] economic practices leading to changes in work and employment relationships were much more widespread and observable than 15 years before. Sticking to their 'employment precariousness' framework, the ESOPE research group was deeply divided over the interpretation of their findings and so two differing synthesis reports were published (Laparra et al, 2004). This did not facilitate the dissemination of these findings, which were often to be misquoted.[4]

However, in a later section we will see that, notably as an outcome of the ESOPE project, a fair identification and mapping of the state of 'employment precariousness' across the EU was achieved in the mid-2010s, despite enduring controversies. Sharp differences remained however, notably between analyses of national situations (embedded into the national institutions of labour markets) and the overall cross-national analysis. Despite retaining their own categories of analysis, countries which had not earlier analyzed their domestic situation in terms of precariousness became much more comparable (this was the case with the UK and Germany). Nevertheless, basic uncertainty about the concepts remained, as well as about the proper way to measure 'precariousness'.

In a later part of this chapter it will be shown that, as illustrated by Kalleberg's (2009) article, such fuzziness was here to stay. By the same token, no concept has emerged over the past 40 years that could be adopted to implement common measures of the distinct synthetic phenomenon now named 'precarity' (Barbier, 2011). Various researchers continue to make diverse choices, as for instance Choonara (2022) does in the present book.[5] Moreover, the neologism 'precarity' has now been so widely used that it has made a secure entry into English-language dictionaries.[6] The meaning of 'precarity' became ever more impossible to grasp and define, as it was now adopted by well-known authors like Judith Butler. The fact is that 'precarity' now belongs to an international English-type idiom that floats across the world. This idiom is available as a 'web of meanings' able to capture almost *any* meaning.

Out of a notion in French culture, a renewed view of labour markets in Europe's 'Latin' countries

When researchers limit their inquiry to drawing from the common vocabulary of the English Internet and international conferences, they are bound to miss what is essential to understand the genesis and substance of social policy and labour market notions (Béland and Pedersen, 2014). As will be seen in the conclusion to this chapter, a good example of such an absurd lopsided strategy is found in the work of the sociologist Arne Kalleberg (2000, 2009), who ignores the origins of 'precarity'. This is not at all strange in a transnational context where international English (English as the vernacular language) prevails everywhere in social science (Sartori, 1991) and has been the sole legitimate tongue for many years (Barbier, 2018). Nevertheless, precariousness, under its French form, *précarité*, was the locus where usage originally appeared and from where it was later disseminated to other 'Latin' languages (Barbier, 2005, 2002).

A key symbolic element of 1970s French political culture

From the start, the use of the term *précarité*, and later *précarité de l'emploi* (employment precariousness), held a rather controversial new meaning in French. While the controversial aspect has persisted over 40 years of usage, the word and the notion are very much now part of the French political culture (Barbier, 2013). Indeed, *précarité* belongs to the standard lexicon in French, and it rests on a long-standing presence in literature and philosophy. Malraux (1977), for instance, asserted that modern civilization has produced man as a precarious creature (*L'homme précaire*), whereas Christendom had produced man as a Christian. Philosophical or metaphysical, vaguely linked to religious interrogations, this connotation of the word was present when the term was first used within the context of social policy, and has been ever since. This is why, in passing, the capture of the word 'precariousness' and its transformation into the 21st-century English neologism *precarity* (see next paragraph) should not come as a surprise. The gradual but dogged extension of the meaning of *précarité* in French from the late 1970s was not a surprise for linguists either. And, immensely more successful than his numerous followers, Bourdieu (1998: 95–101) captured the gist of its symbolic value when he stated: '*la précarité est aujourd'hui partout*' ('today precariousness is everywhere').

As a specific notion used in the definition of social problems, '*précarité*' first appeared in France in the late 1970s. It was then applied to the life of families (Pitrou, 1978) and was closely connected to a discourse on 'new poverty' ('*nouvelle pauvreté*') (see Nicole-Drancourt, 1992; Paugam, 1993). For Pitrou, a sociologist, *précarité* was, from the beginning, used *absolutely* (with no qualifications), very much akin to a word like *pauvreté* (poverty). This was so true that French social scientists forged the notion of *pauvreté-précarité*, joining both words together.[7] Hence, *précarité* in French was, at first, a social condition, a situation, of families/households, and also a process potentially leading to poverty. Crucially, though, this first sociological use implied no reference to any precise distinctive social '*statut*' (social status)[8] and certainly not to precarious employment either. This link emerged only later on because, in a Fordist context, employment was identified as a key factor for such '*précarité*', here close to a sort of 'vulnerability' with many facets. The term was used in the wider context of emerging new employment forms ('atypical jobs'). From the late 1970s, and in particular, in statistical surveys, these forms were gradually categorized as *formes particulières d'emploi* (special forms of employment) (Michon and Germe, 1979), in contrast to full-time *contrats à durée indéterminée* (typical open-ended contracts). From the early 1980s *précarité* was not only used in political discourse but had turned into a category commonly used in legislation and social administration. As a 'state' category it was also later used in the *Code du travail* (Labour Code), referring precisely to precarious employment contracts. Because the word was now used more loosely, it tended to apply to society in general,[9] and for many observers, French society was now in the grip of '*précarisation*' (precarization), a process that provided a social background that was present everywhere in society. It took the form of overwhelming 'domination', in Bourdieusian terms.[10] Note that notions close to *précarité* used in social policy were also 'vulnerability' and 'fragility' (Paugam, 1993).

In 2021, *précarité* (as an absolute term) has retained the same legitimate currency in French society. In addition, whereas a sharp increase in de-standardized forms of employment (Koch and Fritz, 2013) was registered in European statistics after 1980, and especially in the 1990s, the superficial forecast according to which 'short-term' contracts were to gradually become the norm never materialized. For instance, up until the first year of the COVID-19 pandemic in France, the proportion of open-ended contracts (in stocks) on the labour market remained practically unchanged over the prior 20 years.[11] As the proportion of self-employed also remained roughly constant over the same period, in statistical terms at least, the Bourdieusian '*précarité partout*' spectre never materialized. In this respect, the sociologist Caillé (1994: 11) offered an extreme case of exaggeration in the early 1990s. For him, 'growth [would] not yield sufficient employment anymore and all the new jobs [were] marked by their precariousness'. France was experiencing 'the "collapsing" of the world we had known up to now'. For Regulation School analysts such as Castel, the process also involved an *erosion of the wage-earner condition* ('*effritement de la condition salariale*') (Castel, 1995: 385).

Latin countries versus Germany, the UK and Denmark – the 1980s to the early 2000s

There was, of course, no reason why such a transformation of labour markets should only affect France. However, again, specific cultural-political ways through which countries adjusted their institutions were documented. For instance, English-language analysis dealing with the 'flexibilization' of labour markets never mentioned any trace of 'precariousness' at this time, as is obvious from the books by Richard Sennett (1999) and Robert Reich (2001). Nevertheless, because of both the transformation of the international monetary regime (Barbier and Nadel, 2000; Koch and Fritz, 2013) and of the Fordist 'regulation' regime, the awareness of ensuing changes to labour markets spread. This clearly motivated the ILO's commissioning of the Rodgers and Rodgers (1989) report. Its researchers organized their research along four dimensions: the security and stability of jobs; the conditions of work in organizations/firms; remuneration; and, finally, the social protection attached to jobs. For ESOPE, the same framework was kept, and it is therefore interesting to note that similar conclusions were drawn by both groups of researchers. However, while ESOPE's team wished to overcome the limits of the 1989 ILO research, it failed on two grounds. First, it was unable to produce a small set of quantitative indicators in order to measure levels of 'employment precariousness' cross-nationally; second, they had to admit the impossibility of crafting a single concept of employment precariousness. In passing, one can note that, notwithstanding these limitations, article after article is published about a presumed increase of 'employment precariousness'. For instance, one can consider the Gutiérrez-Barbarrusa (2016) survey. Failing to define employment precariousness, this author tries to approach it by proxy, as the ILO and the ESOPE teams had before him, along with many others, repeating the same 'muddling through' techniques and choices of inadequate indicators: part-time work; share of open-ended contracts (and vaguely defined so-called 'temporary contracts'); share of self-employed jobs in the total workforce; and share of low-wage work. None of these indicators can really identify anything strictly 'precarious' in forms of employment and their aggregation does not change the problem.

Fortunately, despite their disappointing findings, ESOPE researchers (Laparra et al, 2004: 15–17)[12] were able to document that, in many countries, similar qualitative characteristics of jobs were experienced and observable. Focusing on the period from the 1980s to the early 2000s, a clear contrast existed between the group of Latin countries, on the one hand, and Germany and the UK on the other. The Scandinavian countries stood out on their own: they had not really heard about any 'precariousness of employment'; instead, they were preoccupied by *marginalizering* ('marginalization' in Danish), a situation that countries such as France and Spain had also experienced but in the 1960s. Yet it was impossible to ground such a cross-country assessment on homogenous indicators, for indicators varied immensely in their definitions and meanings across countries. To take but one example, the divide between 'open-ended' contracts[13] and so-called 'temporary contracts' never provided a common yardstick. It still does not today, although it is still used by international statisticians.

While ESOPE failed on both these quantitative and conceptual counts, it helped map the situation in many countries. ESOPE researchers stated that 'forms of employment precariousness' were always specific to a particular 'societal coherence' or political culture. These forms were crucially dependent on social protection systems (Barbier et al, 2021), meaning that 'employment precariousness' (if one dared to use such a term universally) had remained extremely marginal in Denmark and the Scandinavian countries. Except for these latter countries, though, comparable phenomena existed in all countries but, in the 1980s and 1990s, were framed and thought about in terms of 'precariousness' only in Latin countries. Here, the similarity of Latin languages played a determining role but also their similarly built system of social protection. Two societies, Germany and the UK, seemed to be collectively unaware of the growing importance of labour market instability. Moreover, when surveys were made in both countries, it was extremely difficult for researchers to find equivalent notions for comparison.

If France was alone in using *précarité* in an extensive manner, in Italian, *precarietà*, and in Spanish, *precaridad*, at the time of the research, were used only in the context of jobs and employment, and not in the context of any wholesale 'precarization' of society. For cross-national comparison with the UK or the US, French notions remained entirely inadequate; they were also inadequate for Germany and the Netherlands.[14] In the 1980s through to the 2000s, only in Italy and Spain did 'employment precariousness' evoke rigorously similar meanings (Laparra, 2006). Did this mean that the social phenomena that indirectly gave birth to the Latin notion had no equivalents outside the Latin world? Obviously not, but no clear statistical measure of employment precariousness could be reached. In France at the time, the standard employment relationship applied to about 90 per cent of the workforce. In Spain, *empleo precario*, *precaridad laboral* and *temporalidad* were the terms most widely used in the public debate and by social partners. If measured by the proportion of '*temporalidad*', it was above 25 per cent of the workforce. At the time of the research, the 1980 *Estatudo de los Trabajadores* was the basic law, which, although amended over the years, presumed an open-ended, full-time contract. Despite renewed efforts by the Zapatero government, *temporalidad* nevertheless still accounted for as much as 30 per cent of contracts in 2009. In Italy, *precarietà del lavoro*, *del impiego*, *del posto di lavoro* and *impiego precario* were the expressions commonly used.[15] What was considered as the standard employment relationship was, as in France, an open-ended contract with statutory protection against dismissal under article 18 of the 1970 *Statuto dei Lavoratori*.[16] Recourse to part-time contracts in Italy came only in 1997, much later than in other countries. The *parasubordinati* were employed as precarious employees. In the early 2000s, they amounted to about 10 per cent of all workers.

Thus, in three Latin countries,[17] as demonstrated during recurring social protests, a more or less explicit consensus prevailed about the fact that a standard job was expected to be open-ended and that all others were more or less exposed to 'employment precariousness' of some sort, including involuntary part-time jobs. In 2002 this was not the case in the UK, and, at that time, neither had Germany experienced such a situation. It was nevertheless possible to draw a comparable chart of qualitative elements (see Table 2.1, summing up the ESOPE comparison). It shows that in the three Latin countries analyzed, a similar institutional definition, under various names, was, in a legal sense, contrasted with de-standardized forms of employment, which were generally perceived as open-ended. This was also true in Germany, a country that did not use 'precariousness' at the time. The UK, like the Scandinavian countries, had a general preference for forms of employment relationships with very limited legal protection.

Awareness of employment precariousness spreads cross-nationally from 2005: Germany and the UK

Ways of defining and naming the main manifestations of social and economic institutions are in a constant state of re-creation, alongside the adoption of apparently universal forms such as the market. In the second half of the 2000s the mainstream representation of labour market situations was entirely overhauled in Germany (Castel and Dörre, 2009). A parallel but much less profound evolution affected the UK, whose structural reforms had happened much earlier.

Prekarität formally enters the German Öffentlichkeit (public space)

In Germany, the prevalent social norm for employment had certainly been the *Normalarbeitsverhältnis* (normal employment relationship), a notion even more deeply entrenched in society than in the Latin countries. Basic regulations applying to employment contracts in Germany date back to the 1950s, including the principle of full-time, open-ended contracts, and the associated social contributions and rights. However, public discussion of precariousness in Germany was to take more time to emerge than in the Latin countries. True, 'atypical jobs' were relatively numerous and went by the name of *geringfügige Beschäftigung* (small, marginal employment). These jobs, constituting 5–6 per cent of the workforce in the late 1990s (according to ESOPE), were later expanded into 'mini-jobs' and 'midi-jobs'. By the late 1990s attention was only just starting to be paid to certain types of non-standard employment relationship, notably quasi-self-employment (*Scheinselbstständigkeit*). In the lead-up to the Hartz reforms of the early 2000s, a crucial and bitter debate engulfed the whole country about the consequences of flexibilization for the quality of working conditions, especially for older workers. Marginal jobs, quasi-self-employment and new special jobs for assistance recipients could by then be seen as functional equivalents of 'employment precariousness'. Combined with the brutal

Table 2.1: Comparing 'employment precariousness' across five countries (before 2003)

Notions	France	Italy	Spain	Germany	UK
Use of 'employment precariousness'	Yes	Yes	Yes	No	No
Key relevant notion	*Précarité*	*Precarità del posto di lavoro*	*Precaridad laboral (temporalidad)*	*Unsichereit des Arbeits-verhältnisses*	None specified
Normal employment relationship	Permanent contract *(contrat à durée indéterminée, [CDI])*	Permanent contract *(tempo indeterminato)*	Permanent contract *(contrato indefinido)*	Permanent contract *(Normalarbeits-verhältnis [NAV] unbefristeter Arbeitsvertrag)*	Regular work
Mainstream legal reference	*Code du travail*	*Statuto dei lavoratori*	*Estatuto de los trabajadores*	Various *Gesetze* and collective agreements	None
Key job category seen as cross-national 'functional equivalent'	*Formes particulières d'emploi (FPE)*	*Parasubordinati: collaborazione coordinata continuativa; lavoro occasionale; associazione in partecipazione*	*Trabajo temporal Temporalidad*	*Geringfügige Beschäftigung Schein-selbstständigkeit Ein Euro-Jobs (from 2005)*	Bad/poor jobs

Source: Barbier (2005).

reform of unemployment insurance (Knuth, 2009), this led to the adoption of a new word with a collective meaning introduced in the German *Öffentlichkeit*, namely '*Prekariat*'. The relative stability of employment forms was finally challenged, although not as fundamentally as in the Latin countries. When compared, differences are certainly apparent between the Latin viewpoint and what the German public and labour market experts viewed as pertaining to an emerging 'Prekariat'. The German meaning seemed to be strictly focused on atypical and bad work, and its consequences. Roughly in the years 2007–10, the stress in German debates was more often than not placed on poor working conditions, especially at the level of the firm.[18] Later on, and especially with links to the Sozialdemokratische Partei Deutschlands programme in subsequent elections, the discussion over precariousness also included the theme of 'social injustice'.

Vulnerable workers in the UK draw increasing attention

The focus in Britain during the 2000s was on the 'vulnerability'[19] of workers and 'vulnerable workers' (Pollert and Charlwood, 2009). In the UK, researchers were well aware of occurrences of low paid and poor quality, insecure jobs, with limited or no career prospects, similar to those in Latin countries (Laparra et al, 2004). Yet, the social perception of the phenomenon, linked to a different normative system, appeared to be fundamentally different. Despite the existence of a broad conception of what was meant by a regular employment relationship, still common today, the UK had no legal equivalent for what existed in the four other countries (see Table 2.1). Moreover, the notion of atypical jobs was comparatively irrelevant: part-time jobs, which would pass as atypical in other countries (except the Netherlands), were typical. Employment relationships, whatever their duration, could pass as regular work. This was compatible with the existence in the UK of zero-hour contracts and casual workers,[20] as well as jobs that were certainly equivalents for 'precarious' jobs elsewhere, such as 'dead-end' jobs, jobs that yielded insufficient pay, had poor career prospects and so on. Yet overall, the dominant angle adopted in 2005 emphasized the situations of 'vulnerable workers'.

During the Labour government of 2007–10, under the leadership of Gordon Brown, the notion that there was a growing prevalence of 'bad jobs' in some sectors emerged as an increasingly influential qualification to the prevailing story, according to which the British labour market, because of its weak regulation, was a success. This change was partly due to the influence of 'Europe'. New developments came both from changes in the choices made by the EU and modified perceptions of the labour market. This brings empirical confirmation of the cross-national influence of social norms present in particular societies: here it concerns collective conceptions of 'precarious' work, in the sense of work (or employment) considered unacceptable or 'unfair'. A single English word was always insufficient to grasp such comparative diversity.

Transnational multidisciplinary new meanings emerge from an initial mistranslation

As for the neologism 'precarity', it was introduced into the international English vocabulary in two stages. The first stage is generally unknown, but a larger dissemination in activist milieus took place from the mid-2000s. It is rare for this stage of use to be clearly distinguished from the widespread use in various disciplines after 2010, which will be reviewed in the concluding section.

Franco-English 'precarity': almost a private joke

In the first stage, during the late 1990s, instead of using *precariousness*, the standard English word, researchers working closely with French sociologists[21] or writing papers for the European Trade Union Congress (ETUC) or the European Commission[22] used the term 'precarity'. At that time, it passed as a Gallicism. However, it was consciously adopted by many because of the meaning that the French ascribed to their *précarité*. With far-reaching and vague meanings in French, *précarité* without any qualifications but with many connotations was thus favoured by a small group of English-speaking actors – researchers, unionists and some officials who were familiar with the French concept. This use was to prove very different from the later use of 'precarity'.

'Precarity' favoured by activists across the world

In a second stage, the notion became much more widespread and durable. The term was captured by groups of activists and radicals in Europe and in the US, becoming a central concern of specialized networks and websites hostile to capitalism and neoliberalism. The term was used by activists such as the groups that organized the EuroMayday demonstrations in many cities in Europe in the second half of the 2000s (Doerr, 2010). These groups seemed to have in common an intention to give 'precarity' a mobilizing political content, using the term to encapsulate all the supposed detrimental impact on human life of current developments of capitalism. In addition, some academics started to try to set out an analytical distinction between 'precarity' and 'precariousness'. This endeavour is still ongoing. The first scholars to test the distinction were Neilson and Rossiter (2005). What they saw initially as an 'inelegant neologism' (Neilson and Rossiter, 2005: 1) had now acquired an autonomous life and had provided a 'rallying call and connecting device for struggles surrounding citizenships, labour rights, the social wage, and migration. And importantly, these struggles are imagined to require new methods of creative-social organisation that do not make recourse to social state models, trade union solidarities, or Fordist economic structures'.

The objective of providing a new form of contestation in the world of work was also present among many actors combining a political commitment and some form of activist consultancy. This is the case with Brody, among many others, who, in North America, apparently disregarding the rich production of French and English sociology, instead ascribed 'precarity' the widest possible meaning: 'I use the name precarity first of all to adopt the term that has been offered by social movements ...; social movements have begun to argue ... that the rise of precarity also offers a new opportunity for collective organizing' (Brody, 2006: 3). Interestingly, this line of thought tends not to restrict the analysis of employment precariousness to aspects detrimental for workers or employees but also to include potential positive aspects. In this sense, 'precarity' could also link to positive dimensions of the growing flexibility of work (Boyer, 1986; Barbier and Nadel, 2000). This perspective has also been pursued by other sociologists; witness, for instance, Cingolani's (2014) 'emancipatory' interpretation of '*précarité*'. All in all, in the second half of the 2000s, the domain in which 'precarity', along with precariousness and of course *précarité*, applied was mainly the area of labour markets and conditions of work. Yet, in the last leg of our travel, from the 2010s, this was to change entirely.

Precarity today: polysemy and the fuzziness of international English

There is perhaps no better way to illustrate the complete alteration of the usage of *precariousness* and *precarity* in social science and political forums from the mid-2000s[23] than to place in opposition two typical writings. On the one hand, we take Kalleberg's (2009) article: 'Precarious work, insecure workers', in the *American Sociological Review*; on the other, we refer to the lecture Judith Butler (2009) gave in Madrid at the time of the publication of her *Frames of War: When is Life Grievable?* The first text is a typical example of 'international' knowledge about the insecurity and instability of employment in the late 2000s. In it, Kalleberg seems not to be conscious of the fact that he is writing in English; as he refers to both Durkheim and Marx, it is as if the phenomenon he is naming 'precarity' was somehow eternal and universal, which it never was. When the article was published, one would have expected that, given his institutional position, Kalleberg's contribution would, in the future, pass as classic and that his way of defining 'precarity' would be the conceptual reference for sociologists across the world. In reality, this did not happen. Divergences about how to define and measure 'employment precariousness' and 'precarity' have persisted (Tasset, 2017), as Choonara (2019) convincingly argues. Even the term 'precarity' has failed to become prevalent within mainstream orthodox sociology in the English language.[24]

On the other hand, Butler chose, amid the powerful emotional echoes of the 9/11 events in the US, to seize on the theme of 'precarious life' in her book, *Precarious Life: The Powers of Mourning and Violence* (2004). She did not quote Malraux's 1977 *L'homme précaire* but she could have because her work is very much conceived in the environment of French philosophy and social science. This is presumably why she soon caught on to the distinction between *precariousness* and 'precarity' as a 'politically-made' part of the human condition − if I interpret correctly the distinction she makes between the notions. There was no Malraux reference in her 'precarity' because Malraux could not perform such a play of words, which is only available between the French and English languages. I confess I am no specialist of philosophy, but the dominant connotations of Butler's text very much remind me of the classic French meaning of *précarité* that I offer in the first part of this chapter. Contrasting it with the expected 'precariousness' of all life, she writes that 'precarity' 'designates that politically induced condition in which certain populations suffer from failing social and economic networks of support and become differentially exposed to injury, violence, and death' (Butler, 2009: ii).

Putting together these two instances of 'precarity' shows how polysemous the term has now become in an international English context. In the area of labour market and social policy, this undeniably brings renewed confusion to an already complex discussion. In my view, 'employment precariousness' would probably be more palatable for labour market experts than 'precarity', but no one is able to alter its spontaneous process of proliferation through English language forums.[25] We are bound to live with such limitations once we are forced to consider English as the only legitimate scientific language, which is of course preposterous. On the 15 April 2019 'precarity' entered Dr Goodword's online alphadictionary with the following meaning: 'A precarious existence, lacking in stability, job security, material or psychological welfare.' Long live precarity! But also, long live plurilingualism in the social sciences (Barbier, 2018).

Notes

[1] 'Latin' languages are variants derived from Latin and transformed from 'vernacular languages' into 'national' languages (Portuguese, Spanish, Italian, Romansh and so on).

[2] As Jill Rubery wrote in her chapter about the UK: 'as there is no statistical category "precarious work", the only way in which we can investigate precarious work is to look at employment forms which are expected to be in some sense precarious' (Rodgers and Rodgers, 1989: 49). A remarkable tautology indeed.

[3] 'Precarious employment in Europe: a comparative study of labour market related risks in flexible economies'.

[4] See, for instance, Gutierrez-Barbarrussa (2016).

[5] See the distinction between 'employment precarity' and 'insecurity' (subjective perceptions with respect to 'job tenure' and 'job status') in Choonara, 2019. This distinction is, of course, not shared by all.

[6] The Oxford Dictionary of English (online version), in 2015, included: ['precariat' (noun, origin 1990s)].

[7] 'Precarious families' of the 1970s were not standard clients of social assistance, and constituted a significant part of the lower classes, but certainly not an 'underclass' in the US sense (or an *Unterschicht*, in the sense of the post-2005 German debate).

[8] *Statut* in this current usage combines aspects of the sociological notion of 'status' and the legal meaning (see Schnapper, 1989).

[9] For instance, in his final meeting in the presidential election campaign in 2002, when he was fighting against a far-right candidate in exceptional circumstances, candidate Jacques Chirac pronounced a solemn call to resist both *précarité* and xenophobia. He won the election by a landslide.

[10] In this view, precariousness also affected those who might seem to be spared from its influence. It appeared as one of the aspects of a dominated condition in society, close to unemployment and exclusion, and these situations were explained as effects of a new 'mode of domination', which was underpinned by a generalized state of insecurity.

[11] A similar observation was made by Choonara (2019) with regard to the UK.

[12] The coordinators were: Economix (München) (Kurt Vogler-Ludwig and Nicola Düll); ICAS Barcelona (Carlos Frade); Universidad Navarra (Miguel Laparra Navarro); Warwick University (Robert Lindley); Centre d'études de l'emploi Paris (Jean-Claude Barbier); and CRES Roma (Luigi Frey).

[13] The *contrat à durée indéterminée*, so dear to a majority of French employees, or the *Normalarbeitsverhältnis*, similarly cherished by a majority of German employees (see Table 2.1).

[14] *Flexibele arbeid* was not precarious work.

[15] A mock '*San Precario*' was invented and fêted in demonstrations.

[16] Only a part of the workforce was covered by this article, mostly in firms with fewer than 16 employees.

[17] The Portuguese case shows features that are also comparable, but I have not studied it in detail.

[18] Take the example of a German list of features of what was seen as *prekäre Arbeit*, in 2008, by the union, Europäischer Metallgewerkschaftbund: '*Arbeit ist auf jeden Fall immer dann prekär, wenn einer der folgenden Punkte zutrifft: wenig oder fehlende Schutzmaßnahmen; Zahlung von niedrigen und unsicheren Löhnen; keine Sozialversicherung (in Bezug auf Renten, Krankenversicherung, Arbeitslosengeld); fehlender Kündigungsschutz; fehlende Berufsausbildung; wenig oder fehlender Schutz für Gesundheit und Sicherheit am Arbeitsplatz; keine Vertretung durch Gewerkschaften.*'

[19] Duncan Gallie (2008) notes, rightly, that 'vulnerability' has psychological undertones.

[20] A typically scandalous event happened in February 2004, with the drowning of 21 cockle pickers in Morecambe Bay.

[21] Duncan Gallie, working with Serge Paugam at that time, is a case in point. I spoke with both of them to understand why they first used the term 'precarity' and I hope I accurately report what they told me. Paugam and Russell wrote a chapter in Gallie and Paugam's collection, *Welfare Regimes and the Experience of Unemployment in Europe* (2000), the title of which was 'The effects of employment "precarity" and unemployment on social isolation'.

[22] The Dublin foundation and ETUC used the term for a time in the early 2000s, especially in their 'Benchmarking Social Europe' publications. For a short period, DG Employment and Social Affairs also used the term 'precarity' in the early 2000s (see, for instance, Gallie and Paugam, 2002).

[23] And, of course, supposedly equivalent notions in other languages – German, Spanish, Polish and so on.

[24] The uncertain conceptual foundation of Kalleberg's analysis probably explains the tiny dissemination of 'precarity' in the columns of the *American Sociological Review* (13 quotes from 2000 onwards in the journal's corpus).

[25] Undeniably, this is '*un procès sans sujet*' ('a process without a subject') in Althusserian terms.

References

Barbier, J.-C. (2002) 'A survey of the use of the term *précarité* in French economics and sociology', Documents de travail CEE, no.19, Noisy-le-Grand. Available from: https://ceet.cnam.fr/medias/fichier/19-precarite-france_1508414679138-pdf?ID_FICHE=1050492&INLINE=FALSE [Accessed 1 April 2022].

Barbier, J.-C. (2005a) 'Dealing anew with cross-national comparison: when words matter', in J.-C. Barbier and M.-T. Letablier (eds) *Politiques sociales: Enjeux méthodologiques et épistémologiques des comparaisons internationals* [*Social Policies: Epistemological and Methodological Issues in Cross National Comparison*], Brussels: PIE Pieter Lang, pp 45–68.

Barbier, J.-C. (2005b) 'La précarité, une catégorie française à l'épreuve de la comparaison internationale', *Revue Française de Sociologie*, 46: 351–71.

Barbier, J.-C. (2011) 'Employment precariousness in a European cross-national perspective. A sociological review of thirty years of research', CES Working Papers/Documents de Travail, no.2011.78, Paris, CES Université Paris 1 – Panthéon Sorbonne CNRS. Available from: https://ideas.repec.org/p/mse/cesdoc/11078.html [Accessed 12 July 2021].

Barbier, J.-C. (2013) *The Road to Social Europe: A Contemporary Approach to Political Cultures and Diversity in Europe*, Abingdon: Routledge.

Barbier, J.-C. (2018) 'The myth of English as a common language in the European Union (EU), and some of its political consequences', in M. Gazzola, T. Templin and B.-A. Wickström (eds) *Language Policy and Linguistic Justice: Economics, Philosophical and Sociolinguistics Approaches*, Berlin: Springer, pp 209–29.

Barbier, J.-C. and Nadel, H. (2000) *La flexibilité du travail et de l'emploi*, Paris: Flammarion.

Barbier, J.-C., Zemmour, M. and Théret, B. (2021) *Le système Français de protection sociale*, 3rd edition, Paris: La Découverte, Repères.

Béland, D. and Pedersen, K. (eds) (2014) *Analysing Social Policy Concepts and Language: Comparative and Transnational Perspectives*, Bristol: Policy Press.

Bourdieu, P. (1998) *Contrefeux*, Paris: Liber Raisons d'agir.

Boyer, R. (1986) *La flexibilité du travail en Europe*, Paris: La Découverte.

Brody, E. (2006) 'System error: labour precarity and collective organizing at Microsoft', *Canadian Journal of Communication*, 31(3): 1–17.

Butler, J. (2004) *Precarious Life: The Powers of Mourning and Violence*, London: Verso.

Butler, J. (2009) 'Performativity, precarity and sexual politics', *AIBR. Revista de Antropología Iberoamericana*, 4(3): i–xiii.

Caillé, A. (1994) *Temps choisi et revenu de citoyenneté, au delà du salariat universel*, Caen: Démosthène/Mauss.

Castel, R. (1995) *Les métamorphoses de la question sociale, une chronique du salariat*, Paris: Fayard.

Castel, R. and Dörre, K. (2009) *Prekarität, Abstieg, Ausgrenzung: Die Soziale Frage am Beginn des 21st Jahrunderts*, Frankfurt: Campus.

Choonara, J. (2019) *Insecurity, Precarious Work and Labour Markets: Challenging the Orthodoxy*, Basingstoke: Palgrave Macmillan.

Choonara, J. (2022) 'The problem with precarity: precarious employment and labour markets', in J. Choonara, A. Murgia and R.M. Carmo (eds), *Faces of Precarity: Critical Perspectives on Work, Subjectivities and Struggles*, Bristol: Bristol University Press.

Cingolani, P. (2014) *Révolutions précaires – essai sur l'avenir de l'émancipation*, Paris: La Découverte.

Doerr, N. (2010) 'Politicizing precarity, producing visual dialogues on migration: transnational public spaces in the EuroMayDay protests', paper presented at the Council for European Studies Conference in Montreal, April.

Gallie, D. (2008) (ed) *Employment Regimes and the Quality of Work*, Oxford: Oxford University Press.

Gallie, D. and Paugam, S. (eds) (2000) *Welfare Regimes and the Experience of Unemployment in Europe*, Oxford: Oxford University Press.

Gallie, D. and Paugam, S. (eds) (2002) 'Social Precarity and Social Integration', Brussels: European Commission, Eurobarometer 56.1.

Gutiérrez-Barbarrusa, T. (2016) 'The growth of precarious employment in Europe: concepts, indicators and the effects of the global economic crisis', *International Labour Review*, 155(4): 477–518.

Kalleberg, A.L. (2000) 'Non-standard employment relations: part-time, temporary or contract work', *Annual Review of Sociology*, 26(1): 341–65.

Kalleberg, A.L. (2009) 'Precarious work, insecure workers: employment relations in transition', *American Sociological Review*, 74: 1–22.

Knuth, M. (2009) 'Path shifting and path dependence: labour market policy reforms under German federalism', *International Journal of Public Administration*, 32(12): 1048–69.

Koch, M. and Fritz, M. (eds) (2013) *Non-standard Employment in Europe: Paradigms, Prevalence and Policy Responsiveness*, Basingstoke: Palgrave Macmillan.

Laparra, M. (2006) *La construction del empleo precario, dimensiones, causas y tendencias de la precariedad laboral*, Madrid: Caritas Española Editores.

Laparra, M., Barbier, J.-C., Darmon, I., Düll, N., Frade, C., Frey, L., Lindley, R. and Vogler-Ludwig, K. (eds) (2004) 'Managing labour market related risks in Europe: policy implications', final policy report, funded by the European Commission, V Framework Programme.

Malraux, A. (1977) *L'homme précaire et la littérature*, Paris: Gallimard.

Michon, F. and Germe, J.F. (1979) 'Stratégies des entreprises et formes particulières d'emploi', report for the Commissariat général du Plan, 2 volumes, Université de Paris I.

Neilson, B. and Rossiter, N. (2005) 'From precarity to precariousness and back again: labour, life and unstable networks', *Fibreculture Journal*, 5.

Nicole-Drancourt, C. (1992) 'L'idée de précarité revisitée', *Travail et emploi*, 52: 57–70.

Paugam, S. (1993) *La société française et ses pauvres*, Paris: PUF.

Paugam, S. and Russell, H. (2000) 'The effects of employment "precarity" and unemployment on social isolation', in D. Gallie and S. Paugam (eds) *Welfare Regimes and the Experience of Unemployment in Europe*, Oxford: Oxford University Press.

Pitrou A. (1978) *La vie précaire: des familles face à leurs difficultés*, Études CAF no. 21, Paris: Caisse nationale des allocations familiales.

Pollert, A. and Charlwood, A. (2009) 'The vulnerable worker in Britain and problems at work', *Work, Employment & Society*, 23(2): 343–62.

Reich, R. (2001) *The Future of Success*, London: Heineman.

Rodgers, G. and Rodgers, J. (eds) (1989) *Precarious Jobs in Labour Market Regulation: The Growth of Atypical Employment in Western Europe*, Free University of Brussels, Brussels: ILO.

Sartori, G. (1991) 'Comparazione e metodo comparato', in G. Sartori and L. Morlino (eds) *La comparazione nelle scienze sociali*, Bologna: Il Mulino.

Schnapper, D. (1989) 'Rapport à l'emploi, protection sociale et statuts sociaux', *Revue française de sociologie*, 30(1): 3–29.

Sennett, R. (1999) *The Corrosion of Character: The Personal Consequences of Work in the New Capitalism*, New York: WW Norton.

Tasset, C. (2017) 'La mesure des précaires: revisiter la genèse de l'idée de précarité à la lumière des rapports à la quantification', *Sociologie et Sociétés*, 49(1): 215–37.

3

Conceptualizing Precariousness: A Subject-oriented Approach

Emiliana Armano, Cristina Morini and Annalisa Murgia

Introduction

Recent decades have been characterized by the emergence of a vast body of literature on precarization processes (see Millar, 2017). More specifically, two main lines of inquiry have informed the sociological approaches towards precarious work. The first – here defined as studies on 'precarity' – has been developed primarily in the field of economic sociology and 'has sought to identify the structural forces that have converged to erode the Fordist employment regime for a growing proportion of the workforce' (Kalleberg and Vallas, 2018: 5). This first approach to precarious work invites us to consider the objective conditions of contingent employment and their consequences in terms of income and social protection (see Choonara, 2019). The second line of inquiry – what is termed here as studies on 'precariousness' – is instead more interested in a subjective experience that denotes a condition so extensive that it becomes an 'existential precariousness' (Fumagalli, 2007), which 'permeates individuals' entire lives' (Armano and Murgia, 2013: 488). Therefore, the focus here is on the effects that precarization has not only on labour but also on life and subjectivity (Armano, 2010; Morini and Fumagalli, 2010; Murgia, 2010; Armano et al, 2017).

This chapter pays attention to the topic of precariousness while observing its dynamics at the junction between three different levels: the subjectivity level, in which the social actors define the representation of reality that forms the backdrop to their action; the context level, that is, the social and cultural models available to the actors; and the level of meaningful actions, where the actors operate between representations, intentions and resources. What is meant by precariousness in terms of social representation, in particular in the time of the pandemic? How is it characterized and what are the dominant discourses in which it is embedded? How are uncertain identities managed and the possibilities of individual and collective actions perceived? Indeed, precariousness is not a characteristic of the context in question, nor does it pertain to the individual or social dimension alone. Rather, it is distinguished as situated social representation, which is built in the relations between the different dimensions that make up the subjects' lives, and it can be included in the framework of the complex dynamic between formation of the *subject*, *subjectivity* and *subjectivization* (Rebughini, 2014).

With the purpose of understanding how precarization processes impact on forms of subjectivity, the experiences and representations of precariousness are considered in the frame of the *génération precaire* (Bourdieu, 1998). This term concerns the forms of precarious subjectivization connected to the weakening of the social bonds. Indeed, it becomes difficult for subjects to rebuild the sense of their existence within the dominant economic and political dynamics, in the same way as it is difficult to regain a balance between the subjective and collective dimensions (Giannini, 2016). In this view, precarious subjectivity does not only refer to the condition of temporary or discontinuous employment but, above all, to being subjectively placed in a situation in which one has to self-activate resources (Ross, 2009) and take sole responsibility for one's choices and social protection.

Using the results of a series of research projects, carried out mainly in Italy, on this topic as a starting point (Armano, 2010; Armano and Murgia, 2013; Armano et al., 2015; Morini, 2010, 2014, 2016, 2022; Morini et al, 2014; Murgia, 2010; Murgia et al, 2020[1]), this chapter focuses its attention on how precariousness is represented, including in light of the COVID-19 pandemic. In particular, the chapter is set out as follows: the first part introduces the concepts of 'precarity' and 'precariousness', going on to concentrate on the latter and explore it in terms of the production of subjectivity. In our reading, the precarious subject appears as a 'precarious–enterprise worker', impelled to become the sole person responsible for their destiny and invest totally in the production of their subjectivity. The chapter continues with a reflection on the digitalization processes during the pandemic and their effects on the production of subjectivity. Finally, the last part asks about the possibilities of individual and collective action while discussing how, in the proposed perspective, potential forms of resistance to precariousness can be drawn up through the reappropriation of the corporeal and sensible dimensions, and the construction of social relations based on affective and corporeal encounters with others.

Precariousness as the production of subjectivity

The hypothesis that directs the analysis herein is that the diffusion of precarization processes is one of the fundamental traits of the current forms of subjectivization. In order to understand and interpret people's experiences in relation to work as well as other spheres of life, we therefore considered it useful to distinguish the concept of 'precarity' – which has been widely used in the European context to identify the erosion of standard employment relationships, namely, the condition of increasingly contingent employment – from that of 'precariousness', which instead refers to the transformation of social relations in the direction of uncertainty, both in terms of everyday experience and perception of the future (Bourdieu, 1998). From this point of view, it is worth dwelling on the difference between *condition* and *experience*. Precariousness cannot only be interpreted as the expression of a uniform and homogeneous working condition. Indeed, it is strongly characterized by the transformation of work, which on one hand, in the encounter with people's desire for autonomy, comes unstuck from Fordist enterprise and its unbending organizational discipline, and on the other is loaded with new investments, passing from the 'ethic of obligation' to that of 'self-realisation' (Meda, 2016). In this process, the boundaries of work are surpassed to reach a more immediately social and existential level (Murgia, 2010). So, to speak of *condition* does not pay justice to the various levels that draw the cognitive-emotional, multi-layered map of precarious subjectivity and its transformations, since it neither evokes nor represents the zones of transit – the passages and the crossings that are implicit in the *experience* of precarious lives – which change with the passing of time in relation to the different positions in work but also in space, the phases of life and relationships. Furthermore, while condition is, to a large extent, determined from above, experience acts directly and leads us to ask questions and try to break away from this same condition. All of this is more meaningful than ever if we focus our attention on the relationship between precarious experience and the bodies of precarious workers, as this chapter will try to do.

In terms of reconstructing experience, for those going through the passage from one job to another; from education to employment; from employment to non-employment; and those in the temporariness of work contracts, the greatest suffering seems to be linked to the difficulty in giving shape to an oriented narrative – in defining a story, in making out a 'plot' in the activities and identifying a recognizable objective to reach (Sennett, 1998). Having no long-term objectives can make us extremely vulnerable to the urgency of the moment. Significantly, on one hand, people continue to seek to draw up strategies to build future horizons, but on the other they tend to represent their future as the result of discontinuities beyond their individual control (Carmo et al, 2014). Uncertainty about one's individual future, but also about the contextual future, is thus accompanied by a strategic tendency to try to avoid stable bonds (Beck, 2000b). Hence, the difficult task of planning the future acts on the construction of the present and the capacity to act within it. Insecurity and the sense of isolation expand, inside a system where what stands out most is the weakness of the social bonds. This very weakness may well be the basis for the representation and experience of precariousness: the real perceived as changing, inviting the adoption of action strategies which are changing too. The upshot is that bonds and modes of belonging always appear reversible and partial, and medium-term strategies best adapt to the lives of individuals struggling to connect the level of values or long-term goals to the level of everyday action. In this view, precariousness can therefore be read as a weakening and breaking down of the social bond, accompanied by an increase in the sense of dependency on a changing context to which we have to be able to adapt as quickly as possible. These processes form one of the fundamental roots that characterize the experience and discursive repertoires of precarious subjectivity. In the symbolic order of their everyday life the social actors place themselves in a position of subalternity, and this devaluation forms the first step towards interiorizing the sense of powerlessness, lack of value and dependency. As a result, it also becomes complex and difficult to mutually coordinate individual pathways within society, and hence possible strategies of shared action.

Having adopted a subjective acceptation of precariousness (Armano and Murgia, 2013; Morini and Vignola, 2015), lastly, it is worth briefly recalling the notion of subjectivity used in this analysis. Subjectivity in the social sciences is a synonym for intentionality and, therefore, capability to identify ends and build meaningful courses of action, both with reference to a subject and other social actors. This requires the distinction of two categories implicit in the action of any intentional subject: the motivation to act and subjective meaning. Within the wide debate on subjectivity, our position dialogues with that of feminist thought (see Henriques et al, 1984; Butler, 1990), which has, first of all, always considered subjectivity to be situated and incorporated in power relations and dominant discourses, and consequently, secondly, felt the need to rethink subjectivity in terms that would allow for agency and political action.

The precarious subject as a self-entrepreneurial subject

In the picture described thus far, it is interesting to focus attention on how subjects are called upon to make their own destiny and be 'entrepreneurs of themselves' (Foucault, 2008), in a process that aims to transform citizens into entrepreneurs of their own human capital and therefore give rise to forms of subjectivization and self-construction based on individualization and business logic (Bröckling, 2016). In this connection, the experience of the 'precarious-enterprise worker' does not only or principally concern the forms of contingent work defined by a contractual condition of either subordinate or freelance employment but, more generally, the *hybrid* set of situations which push the single person to take on risk and invest totally in the production of their subjectivity. In neoliberalism, businesses and institutions tend to promote management and rhetorical discourses centred on autonomy, freedom and cooperation, using these elements as a lever to motivate participation in working life. Therefore, social and public life also seem to fit perfectly into this horizon of thought centred on the self-activation of one's own resources, risk-taking and the sense of guilt and inadequacy.

At the beginning of the century, André Gorz (2001) was already analyzing what worth the individual could hold for capitalism. In this logic, the precarious subject has to actively take part in the process of self-exploitation. Hence, these individuals are not exploited but are instead willing to self-invent, take risks, put themselves at stake and even get into debt for their own self-realization. Boltanski and Chiapello (1999) highlighted how, in the new, non-disciplinary spirit of capitalism (that is, not based on obedience or control), the neoliberal ideology manages to subsume the anti-authoritarian claims of participation and self-determination, the needs for creative and imaginative expression, and the criticism against the repetitiveness and alienation of work levelled since the social movements of the 1960s and 70s. In particular, the desire for a job that is a meaningful activity and can offer self-recognition exposes subjects to peculiar processes of subjectivization, owing to that same search to realize their own creativity. In a certain sense, subjects are captured in what could be called a 'passion trap' (Murgia et al, 2012). On one hand, they seek activities that are a source of passion and pleasure, but on the other hand, in this search, they experience passion in the most literal sense of the word: the pain, the suffering and the fatigue caused by the experience of precariousness. Therefore, we witness a phenomenon of 'capture', being entrapped by passions, emotions and human relations that go beyond work relations. And it is precisely individuals' capacity to put themselves in their work that becomes functional to the current production model (Morini, 2010).

While the neoliberal discourse welcomes the desire to be able to start from oneself and one's feelings, and from the subject under formation's claims of possible power, at the same time it is bent in the direction of realizing individual performances for the market. In this connection, Bologna (2018) underlined that independence and creativity are an attractive characteristic and, at the same time, a basic requirement of neoliberal subjectivity. It combines the urge to flee salaried work, the strong individualizing and libertarian drive to be able to decide and 'do-it-yourself' and the involvement of the whole person in the work performance. This means that, at times, the forms of exploitation at work become more intense than in the past precisely because they are based on the single person's assumption of responsibility, on the conviction that we alone are the maker and cause of our success or failure, and above all, on our incapability to read the system constraints. Mark Fisher (2009) expressed this concept in an interesting way.

In his view, one of the most successful tactics of managerial classes was to make the single individual 'responsible' and convince us to believe that our poverty, lack of opportunities or unemployment is our own fault alone. What he defined as 'magical voluntarism' – namely the conviction that we all have the power to become what we want to be – is today the dominant ideology and non-official religion of contemporary capitalistic society. It is thanks to this mechanism that the risk has been shifted from the system to the individual's capabilities, and individuals have been pushed to self-blame rather than blame the social structures, seeing themselves as the sole persons responsible for their success or defeat (Beck, 2000a).

In this framework, our interest lies in observing how the new *production of subjectivity* enacted by the neoliberal model takes shape and how it is pressed to change. If, in industrial capitalism, the condition behind accumulation was control of machines which tended to incorporate technical know-how, in neoliberal capitalism accumulation is also based on control of people's knowledge, and the knowledge of women in particular, who are asked to sustain capitalism in increasingly intimate and personal ways (Gill and Kanai, 2018). Therefore, the *enterprise* of which capitalism needs to come into possession is the human being, our social self and our being in relation (with each other).

Precarious subjectivity and digitalization in the time of a pandemic

Reflection on the economic contexts, the structure of the labour market and the paradigms of production/reproduction implies a reflection on the *precarious ontology* of the contemporary subject, whose existential dimensions (time of life and relations with the surrounding world) are eroded by mechanisms concerning the new technological processes and the *appropriative* capacities of capitalism. With our chapter, we aim to engage in the debate on the colonization of everyday life (Cingolani, 2021). Indeed, our reflection does not focus on a particular type of digital platform but concerns the production of precariousness in relation to the broader processes of digitalization, which have been significantly accelerated during the recent pandemic.

One of the main characteristics of contemporary capitalism, further highlighted by the global pandemic, concerns the widespread diffusion of digitalization, which has *re-medi(at)ed* the whole corpus of social relations (Bolter and Grusin, 1999). It was during the pandemic that the great leap was seen in the permanent integration of technology in every aspect of our lives, with the acceleration of the diffusion of digitalization. Homes are no longer exclusively personal spaces but also, thanks to high-speed digital connectivity, places of remote work, entertainment, education and social life. For the first time, forms of remote working and education were experienced in the home at mass level and on a global scale. More generally, while connectivity was a fundamental resource in the period of the pandemic crisis, at the same time these working and life activities became more proceduralized and replicable, and invariably more scarce in terms of informal empathetic interaction. This experience, which heightened the process of uprooting social relations from the local contexts of interaction, has reshaped the perception of trust as well as the dimension of risk and the concepts of security or danger. As Lupton and Willis (2021) recently wrote, with the COVID-19 pandemic, the concept of Beckian risk was brought to the forefront once more and, as a result, rethought. In digital-mediated human interaction, in particular through digital platforms, people are asked to place their trust in impersonal systems and principles, algorithmic procedures and anonymous people. Here, to experience precariousness is to feel part of a universe of events outside our control, which we do not fully understand. Therefore, it comes into contrast with the widespread expectation of neoliberalism that we can avail a world of unlimited and unbounded possibilities.

In this framework, digitalization acted on the processes producing precarious subjectivity in an ambivalent manner: on one hand, it offered the potential to free the cognitive and relational capacity by promising and allowing the physical limits set by rules of confinement to be overcome; on the other, it encouraged pre-set individual answers of a tendentially reactive kind in a process in which the *structuring of the inner self and human identity* underwent an *other-directed reorganization* with new upshots and profound effects on our existences (Möhring et al, 2021). The response routes set out by digital mediation do not permit broad spaces and times for deep reflection, and usually point towards reactive and immediate answers as they are built in such a way as to produce a series of impromptu experiences. The philosopher Han Byung-Chul (2015, 2017) wrote visionary and prophetic words about this digital presentism hinging on performance, performativity and competition (see also Chicchi and Simone, 2017; Gancitano and Colamedici, 2018). Specifically, his analyses highlighted how the obsession for hyperactivity and the increasingly great tendency towards reactive multitasking end up producing depressive and neurotic disorders. These expressions of malaise are interpreted as the consequence of the subject's incapacity to deal with the rhythms of post-capitalistic hyperproduction.

A further novelty that accompanies the production of precarious subjectivity in a context of the progressive diffusion of digitalization consists of the fact that the intermediate space of *connectivity*, where work relationships and learning as well as our entire social lives are built, becomes increasingly significant. In particular, time appears to be introjected and released from external formal control while at the same time impossibly extended, indefinite and dilatable. So, the ambivalence of connectivity, which can be understood as the result of the tension between (infra)structural elements and subjective practices, is clear, and even more so in a pandemic situation. In this context, in which relations are defined in terms of *user interactions*, social bonds necessarily become weaker, and subjectivity tends to become fragile. Indeed, they are relations that are configured following the logic of connection/disconnection, as they are more similar to *connections* and contacts in the working environment rather than solid relationships structured in time. Connection is the creation of a *temporary bond* based on trust in an objective, a *hyper-light, immensely weak* bond that can be thrown off immediately by disconnecting when need be (Castells, 1996), when the 'trust contract' between the parties no longer holds or the goal simply changes. The pandemic caused by COVID-19 gave new space to this type of relation centred around digital connectivity and, at the same time, took away the space of face-to-face relations and places of shared physical proximity. It overturned the world as it was and left us with a bed of anxiety about the present and, above all, about an uncertain future. It is the brutality of sudden change: contemporary forms of life cannot be as they were before, but we do not yet know what they will become.

Reclaiming bodies and social relations to resist precariousness

In the unfolding of the dual pandemic and economic crisis, we tend to enter further and further into the logic of unease, solitude and sadness, that is, frustration of the instincts connected to pleasure. So, in governing our lives we are given less and less room for those blandishments whose former purpose was to enchant people, through the belief in a false autonomy and an imagined freedom, while acting on pleasurable ideals, and desirous and outward-looking instincts. Goods, consumption, success: Paolo Godani was right when he wrote, 'if it didn't sound immediately ridiculous, one could say that, in its commanding enjoyment and consumption, post-Fordist capitalism merrily takes up pagan traditions'. Today, vice versa, 'it can be seen in several places how the current transformation of capitalism is bringing about a new overturning of the morality of austerity' (Godani, 2019: 15). Now we are dealing more crudely with forms of introversion, sacrifice, unease and unhappiness, moved by fear. But this paradigm of affliction and fear, this apotheosis of the absence of pleasure, this void of vision, lacking even the evocation and 'frantic harnessing of desire', which continuously opens the way to a 'constitutionally unsatisfied pleasure' (Godani, 2019: 23), plays in our favour. How? By once again calling upon our bodies and politicizing that which our body is able to say to us.

The inspiration notably comes from Donna Haraway's *situated knowledges* (1988), and the resulting assertion that knowledge is always partial because it is unavoidably imperfect, since every point of view is always 'situated' in its own time and space, and it cannot take in everything within its grasp. And it is also partial in the sense that knowledge is never passive, nor are the human beings who use it and move towards it and are spurred by interests and desires, and in the same way by prejudices. This perspective allows us to investigate the relationship between power and the norms at the heart of the processes to produce subjects (and objects). It is again Haraway (1997: 39) who suggests: 'The point is to learn to remember that we might have been otherwise, and might yet be, as a matter of embodied fact.' If feminism made the body immediately 'political', bringing the person, sexuality, affections and relationships directly back into history, culture, claims and political agendas, challenging those devices striving to determine a precise and blinkered order based on dichotomies (Haraway, 1995), then the practice of starting from ourselves also comes to our aid in trying to investigate the subalternity to which the 'precarious-enterprise worker' seems to be condemned.

Immersion in existential and generalized precariousness causes the *body to emerge*: that is, the most intimate, most fragile, most exposed part emerges, linked to the different phases of life, to reproduction and to keeping existence alive. The most fragile moments, those which the Keynesian social state was concerned with protecting (childhood, illness, old age, motherhood), appear exposed, owing to the increasing weakness of the collective frame. The precarious experience, so closely connected to existence and its advancement, highlights the contradictions – the eternal tension between 'private' and 'public': work absorbs life, the passions and desires, and then unloads imbalance and conflict onto that same life. To draw an existential balance, the social and affective dimension assumes new force and centrality, in the very moment the welfare systems are beginning to crumble: the *social* is becoming the *private*. This is why reference to the concept of precariousness seems to be effective and particularly pertinent. Judith Butler refers to precariousness as the political modality of the body, conceived of as a 'human animal', outside all working *conditions*, and capable of feelings such as empathy, which 'open onto the body of another, or a set of others'. Butler uses a beautiful image and writes, 'bodies are not self-enclosed kinds of entities. They are always in some sense outside themselves, exploring or navigating their environment, extended and even sometimes dispossessed' (Butler, 2015: 212). Following this inspiration, we think that questioning the body and the emotions that are produced in the relationship with other bodies can represent a sort of overturning of the socio-affective order that conditions the existence of the precarious–enterprise worker, enslaved to the *obsequium of wages* that is 'the quite generic affective mechanisms of the amorous search for recognition plunged into the general structure of the employment relation and into local realisation as an *enterprise*' (Lordon, 2015: 95, own translation).

'The erasure of the body encourages us to think that we are listening to neutral, objective facts, facts that are not particular to who is sharing the information … information [that] does not emerge from bodies … [We] have been compelled to return to the body to speak about ourselves as subjects in history', writes bell hooks (1994: 139). The disruptive political practice of feminism came into being within a path of recognition based on the recovery of corporeality, sexuality and materiality. Work rhythms, the lives that we live, the lack of happiness and the construction of roles useful for power have a crucial effect on sexuality, desire, and bodily and mental health. The oppression starts by breaking off those essential impulses of the body and mind connected to *eros*, *philia* and love, prompted by *attention* towards the Other, to give some references to a variegated and diversified emotional and sentimental universe, which today – owing to the experience of the COVID-19 disease – is also repressed and blocked by fear of illness.

From this point of view, the precarious body becomes determining in defining *integrated* (employed) and *marginalized* (unemployed), and often victimized and stigmatized, roles (Harvey, 1998). Therefore, the goal is to make ourselves into single, solo enterprises to all effects, always obliged to seek the best output levels, the best quality–price ratio, while aiming to reduce the social security costs as far as possible, in an outlook that aims to expel the Other's body. In this context, the precarious-enterprise worker is pushed to exclude the Other, since attention towards the Other could represent an obstacle to the logic of perennial productivism. Furthermore, the Other could be a dangerous antagonist – a more able, perhaps younger, more disciplined, compliant and optimistic competitor. In order to recognize these processes and to deconstruct the way in which power determines forms of subjection, it therefore becomes crucial to return to the state of being embodied, and hence to recognize subjectivity and the limits of the identity in order to put a stop to the objectivation required by the culture of domination. In looking back and forward at feminist thought, it is a matter of rereading and recognizing the knowledge embedded in the body in order to deconstruct the discourses of free choice, autonomy and entrepreneurship to which the precarious-enterprise worker is required to adhere.

Conclusion

This chapter has asked how precarious subjectivities have transformed in the times of neoliberalism and the pandemic, the presupposition for these reflections being that to understand the transformations underway, the phenomenon of precariousness cannot be seen as depending solely on the type of employment contract. The proposal is to read precarization processes by distinguishing the category of *precarity*, substantially linked to non-standard work, from that of *precariousness*, instead understood to be the *production of precarious subjectivity*. Taking a subject-oriented slant provides room to consider the *situated* and *open* dimension that is assumed by the whole contemporary working existence, and the plurality of possible conditions that can be gone through over time. This offers the opportunity to read precariousness through the gaze and intentional action of the subjects who live and describe it, starting from how they conceive time and the life phase they find themselves in. So, work becomes an imaginary, in a universe of possible *fragile and uncertain relations*, around which subjectivity is structured. This framework results in a rethinking of the very notion of precariousness: it is not something objective that depends exclusively on the lack of some typical forms of protection provided by wage employment, but the resulting *polysemy* of changing experiences and representations that take shape in relation to the drive towards self-entrepreneurship, to capturing the desires embedded in it, and to the experience of separation between body and mind, further exacerbated by the digital remoteness that was experienced during the pandemic. Hence, the concept of precariousness is redefined in relation to the perception of the relationship with the body, dispossessed of feeling and pushed to express itself in imaginary models and unreal masks of performativity and brilliance.

In light of the described processes, the acquisition of new spaces of speech and rights is (also) deemed to be a question of managing subjectivity and understanding how the neoliberal subject is produced. Indeed, contrasting precariousness does not only mean understanding how much, or how much more, subjects need to be paid or what contracts they should be hired on. It is also a matter of understanding how a social action can be constructed that leaves behind the logic of individualization and enterprise. By putting forward some interpretations of subjectivity, this chapter has sought to trace the different lines of the precarious, 'self-producing' subject in neoliberal culture. Therefore, a further goal of this exploration is to highlight some of the new challenges to which the precarious-enterprise worker is exposed: first of all, the need to acquire an *ethics* and *culture of care* in order to govern political relations (Tronto, 2015) and, second, to imagine a project for a society of care and bodies in order to *repair* the fundamental fabric of social relations (Cozza et al, 2021). In our view, *rediscovering bodies*, bodies brought to the uninterrupted attention expected by the current capitalist model, is already in itself a political act of breakage, in conflict with a (white, male and heterosexual) model of society based on the commodification of the living world. And this rediscovery should also restore the revolutionary possibilities of desire since 'the revolutionary opposition to capital is essentially an opposition of bodies' (Parinetto, 2015: 125, own translation), or, to use Judith Butler's (2015) powerful words, 'bodies in alliance'. Butler's reflections can be the key to turning around the precarious era by challenging us to grasp the insufficiency of identity ontologies and instead think of the problem of alliance between:

> the cross section of people at risk of losing employment and having their homes taken away by banks; the range of people who are differentially at risk for street harassment, criminalization, imprisonment, or pathologization; the specific racial and religious backgrounds of those people whose lives are targeted as dispensable by those who wage war. In my view, this perspective implies the need for a more generalized struggle against precarity, one that emerges from a felt sense of precarity. (Butler, 2015: 68–9)

Note

1 This chapter was partially developed within the SHARE project, which received funding from the European Research Council (ERC) under the European Union's Horizon 2020 research and innovation programme (Grant agreement No. 715950).

References

Armano E. (2010) *Precarietà e innovazione nel postfordismo. Una ricerca qualitativa sui lavoratori della conoscenza a Torino*, Bologna: Odoya.

Armano, E. and Murgia, A. (2013) 'The precariousnesses of young knowledge workers: a subject-oriented approach', *Global Discourse*, 3(3–4): 486–501.

Armano, E., Carls, K. and Morini, C. (2015) 'Autonomy, free labor and passions as devices of creative capitalism. Narratives from a co-research in journalism and the editing industry', in G. Cocco and B. Szaniecki (eds) *Creative Capitalism, Multitudinous Creativity: Radicalities and Alterities*, New York: Lexington, pp 201–26.

Armano E., Bove, A. and Murgia, A. (eds) (2017) *Mapping Precariousness, Labour Insecurity and Uncertain Livelihoods: Subjectivities and Resistance*, London: Routledge.

Beck, U. (2000a) *The Brave New World of Work*, Cambridge: Polity.

Beck, U. (2000b) *I rischi della libertà. L'individuo nell'epoca della globalizzazione*, Bologna: Il Mulino.

Bologna, S. (2018) *The Rise of the European Self-employed Workforce*, Milan: Mimesis.

Boltanski, L. and Chiapello, E. (1999) *Le nouvel esprit du capitalisme*, Paris: Gallimard.

Bolter, J.D. and Grusin, R. (1999) *Remediation: Understanding New Media*, Cambridge, MA: MIT Press.

Bourdieu, P. (1998) 'La précarité est aujourd'hui partout', in *Contre-feux*, Paris: Liber-Raison d'agir, pp 95–101.

Bröckling, U. (2016) *The Entrepreneurial Self: Fabricating a New Type of Subject*, Los Angeles: Sage.

Butler, J. (1990) *Gender Trouble: Feminism and the Subversion of Identity*, London: Routledge.

Butler, J. (2015) *Notes Toward a Performative Theory of Assembly*, Cambridge, MA: Harvard University Press.

Carmo, R., Cantante, F. and de Almeida Alves, N. (2014) 'Time projections: youth and precarious employment', *Time & Society*, 23(3): 337–57.

Castells, M. (1996) *The Rise of the Network Society*, Malden, MA: Blackwell.

Chicchi, F. and Simone, A. (2017) *La società della prestazione*, Rome: Ediesse.

Choonara, J. (2019) *Insecurity, Precarious Work and Labour Markets: Challenging the Orthodoxy*, London: Palgrave Macmillan.

Cingolani, P. (2021) *La colonisation du quotidien. Dans les laboratoires du capitalisme de plateforme*, Paris: Ed Amsterdam.

Cozza, M., Gherardi, S., Graziano, V., Johansson, J., Mondon-Navazo, M., Murgia, A. and Trogal, K. (2021) 'COVID-19 as a breakdown in the texture of social practices', *Gender, Work & Organization*, 28(51): 190–208.

Fisher, M. (2009) *Capitalist Realism – Is there no alternative?*, London: Hunt Publishing.

Foucault, M. (2008) *The Birth of Biopolitics: Lectures at the Collège de France 1978–1979*, Basingstoke and New York: Palgrave Macmillan.

Fumagalli, A. (2007) 'Precarietà', in Transform! Italia (ed.) *Parole di una nuova politica*, Rome: XL Edizioni, pp 27–34.

Gancitano, A. and Colamedici, M. (2018) *La società della performance*, Rome: Ed Tlon.

Giannini, M. (2016) 'Epistemologia della condizione precaria: oltre il declino del lavoro salariato', *Quaderni di teoria sociale*, 16(2): 97–124.

Gill, R. and Kanai, A. (2018) 'Mediating neoliberal capitalism: affect, subjectivity and inequality', *Journal of Communication*, 68(2): 318–26.

Godani, P. (2019) *Sul piacere che manca. Etica del desiderio e spirito del capitalismo*, Rome: DeriveApprodi.

Gorz, A. (2001) 'La personne devient une entreprise', *Revue du MAUSS*, 2: 61–6.

Han, B. (2015) *The Burnout Society*, Stanford: UP.

Han, B. (2017) *Psychopolitics: Neoliberalism and New Technologies of Power*, London and New York: Verso.

Haraway, J.D. (1988) 'Situated knowledge. The science question in feminism and the privilege of partial perspective', *Feminist Studies*, 14(3): 575–99.

Haraway, J.D. (1995) 'Manifesto for cyborgs: science, technology, and socialist feminism in the 1980s', *Socialist Review*, 80: 65–108.

Haraway, J.D. (1997) *Modest_Witness@Second_Millennium.FemaleMan©_Meets_OncoMouse™: Feminism and Technoscience*, New York: Routledge.

Harvey, D. (1998) 'The body as an accumulation strategy', *Environment and Planning D: Society and Space*, 16(4): 401–21.

Henriques, J., Hollway, W., Urwin, C., Venn, C. and Walkerdine, V. (eds) (1984) *Changing the Subject: Psychology, Social Regulations and Subjectivity*, London: Methuen.

hooks, b. (1994) *Teaching to Transgress. Education as the Practice of Freedom*, New York and Abingdon: Routledge.

Kalleberg, A.L. and Vallas, S.P. (2018) 'Probing precarious work: theory, research, and politics', *Research in the Sociology of Work*, 31(1): 1–30.

Lordon, F. (2015) *Imperium. Structures et affects des corps politiques*, Paris: La Fabrique.

Lupton, D. and Willis, K. (2021) (eds) *The COVID-19 Crisis: Social Perspectives*, London: Routledge.

Meda, D. (2016) 'The future of work: the meaning and value of work in Europe', ILO Research Paper 18.

Millar, K.M. (2017) 'Toward a critical politics of precarity', *Sociology Compass*, 11(6): e12483.

Möhring, K., Naumann, E., Reifenscheid, M., Wenz, A., Rettig, T., Krieger, U., Friedel, S., Finkel, M., Cornesse, C. and Blom, A.G. (2021) 'The COVID-19 pandemic and subjective well-being: longitudinal evidence on satisfaction with work and family', *European Societies*, 23: S601–S617.

Morini, C. (2010) *Per amore o per forza. Femminilizzazione del lavoro e biopolitiche dei corpi*, Verona: Ombre Corte.

Morini, C. (2014) 'Precarietà. Della cattura biocapitalista delle vite (e della loro potenza)', in F. Zappino, L. Coccoli and M. Trabacchini (eds), *Genealogie del presente. Lessico politico per tempi interessanti*, Milan: Mimesis, pp 179–94.

Morini, C. (2016) 'Femminismo e neoliberismo. Italian theory femminista e vite precarie', in F. Zappino (ed) *Il genere tra neoliberismo e neofondamentalismo*, Verona: Ombre Corte, pp 137–51.

Morini, C. (2022) *Vite lavorate. Corpi valore resistenze al disamore*, Rome: Manifestolibri.

Morini, C. and Fumagalli, A. (2010) 'Life put to work: towards a life theory of value', *Ephemera: Theory & Politics in Organization*, 10(3): 234–52.

Morini, C. and Vignola, P. (2015) *Piccola enciclopedia precaria. Dai Quaderni di San Precario*, Milan: Agenzia X Edizioni.

Morini, C., Carls, K. and Armano, E. (2014) 'Precarious passion or passionate precariousness? Narratives from co-research in journalism and editing', *Recherches sociologiques et anthropologiques*, 45(2): 61–83.

Murgia, A. (2010) *Dalla precarietà lavorativa alla precarietà sociale: biografie in transito tra lavoro e non lavoro*, Bologna: Odoya.

Murgia, A., Poggio, B. and Torchio, N. (2012) 'Italy: precariousness and skill mismatch', in M. Samek Lodovici and R. Semenza (eds.) *Precarious Work and Young Highly Skilled Workers in Europe. Risk Transitions and Missing Policies*, Milan: Angeli, pp 71–111.

Murgia, A., Bozzon, R., Digennaro, P., Mezihorak, P., Mondon-Navazo, M. and Borghi, P. (2020) 'Hybrid areas of work between employment and self-employment: Emerging challenges and future research directions', *Frontiers in Sociology*, 4(86), doi: 10.3389/fsoc.2019.00086.

Parinetto, L. (2015) *Corpo e rivoluzione in Marx. Morte, diavolo, analità*, Milan: Mimesis.

Rebughini, P. (2014) 'Subject, Subjectivity, Subjectivation', in Sociopedia. isa. Available from: https://sociopedia.isaportal.org/resources/resource/subject-subjectivity-subjectivation/download/ [Accessed 30 March 2022].

Ross, A. (2009) *Nice Work If You Can Get It: Life and Labor in Precarious Times*, New York: New York University Press.

Sennett, R. (1998) *The Corrosion of Character: The Personal Consequences of Work in the New Capitalism*, New York: WW Norton.

Tronto, J.C. (2015) *Who Cares? How to Reshape a Democratic Politics*, Ithaca: Cornell University Press.

4

The Experience of Precariousness as Vulnerable Time

André Barata and Renato Miguel Carmo

Introduction

Social time in late modernity is characterized either by a fragmented experience of time, in which it becomes a movement devoid of any orientation conferring meaning, or by an acceleration of the experience of time, which tends to condemn it to a mere experience of its passage.[1] The historical priority between these two perspectives has been debated, but they are conceptually significant both as a fragmentation of the experience of time caused by its acceleration and as an acceleration of the experience of time resulting from the attempt to compensate dissatisfaction with its social fragmentation. This chapter maintains that both perspectives, being contemporary, feed off one another and constitute a temporal context that expresses precariousness as an eminently temporal experience of vulnerability. This living of time could not be socially constituted without the emergence of an abstract concept of time: time as disentangled from events. Stemming from late medieval to early modern times, this understanding of time has since been consolidated by the progress of industrialized production and the transformation of the concept of labour into abstract labour. Time calculated in working hours became a social relation measured by clock time. In close articulation with these origins, the changes in social time that have occurred in the contemporary world operate across at least two aspects and have a profound social impact, experienced particularly through job insecurity. Firstly, humans tend to live their own relations with time less and less as subjects with their own autonomy and, secondly, more and more as objects of a transcendent and external time. In fact, the subject's own time is increasingly vulnerable and powerless, while the time that socially regulates their existence, for example, economically, is increasingly an imperturbable continuity outside of the order of events (Barata, 2018).

This chapter aims to understand to what extent these two temporal aspects constitute and are incorporated in contemporary forms of labour precarization. The chapter is organized in three parts. In the first, we elaborate on a historical and genealogical contextualization of the emergence of abstract time (Thompson, 1967; Postone, 1993) and how it has become increasingly dominant in societies. In the second part, we reflect on the relationship between acceleration and fragmentation of time to realize that these processes tend to be interdependent (Rosa, 2013 [2005]; Han, 2009). Lastly, we describe precariousness as a vulnerable condition resulting, in part, from the experience of fragmented and accelerating time that, paradoxically, induces a risk of the one-dimensionality of social and individual life (Marcuse, 1991 [1964]). This last section is based on sociological research recently conducted on the labour market in Portugal.[2]

The historical advent of the abstract time

In *Technics and Civilization* (1934), the sociologist and philosopher of technique Lewis Mumford notes the historical conditions that enabled the concept of time that was imposed throughout modernity to prevail. According to Mumford, two historical facts stand out. On the one hand, it was the clock and not the steam engine that was the 'key machine' of the modern industrial age. Daniel Bell (1976) and Herbert Marcuse (1991 [1964]), years later, would insist on this privileged articulation between industrialization and a certain relationship with time. And now, in the present era, which is experiencing a regime of relations that Bernard Stiegler (2018 [2004]) has called hyper-industry, it is once again not the factory, which is less and less present, but time that industrializes all aspects of social life. On the other hand, according to Mumford, it was the mechanical clock that dissociated time 'from human events and helped create the belief in an independent world of mathematically measurable sequences' (Mumford, 1934: 15). The novelty brought by the monks of the lower Middle Ages, during the flourishing of the trade routes, was the separation they made between time and events. Made a reality independent from events, which transcends them and makes them possible, time becomes an unquestionable, impartial and absolutely reliable measure. Determined by mechanical clocks, this time, detached from events in order to better measure them, established the basis for the absolute conception of time that later, well into modernity, science and philosophy would embrace with Newton and Kant.

In Jacques Le Goff's (1960) famous essay 'Temps de l'Église et temps du marchand', the historian distinguishes two times and describes the transition from one to the other. The first belongs only to God, the time which is in itself an *event*, and the second, which *measures events*, should preferably stand apart from the events themselves, becoming only a measured quantity without qualities of its own.

The contrast made between *technological* and *natural environments*, described in terms of a contrast between measured time, predictable and continuous, on the one hand, and unpredictable time, which always begins again, expresses a profound modification of the social relationship with time. The new time does not need to start over, which turns it into a non-event, removing it from history and from the human domain that would freely lead it. In this change, there is a reversal in the relation of domination. If merchants think they can better dominate time by measuring it, so no longer being dominated by its unpredictability, the opposite happens instead, as measured time came, above all, to measure inexorably and imperturbably human work and activities.

In a sense very close to these considerations of Mumford (1934) and Le Goff (1960), Postone (1993) organizes these great transformations of the conception of time through the difference he establishes between two characterizations of time, one *concrete*, dependent on events, and therefore relational, and another *abstract*, absolutely independent of events. According to Postone, this abstract time is a European invention, enshrined by Newton but going back to the final centuries of the Middle Ages:

> Such an understanding, which is related to the idea of motion as a change of place functionally dependent on time, did not exist in the ancient Greece, the Islamic world, early medieval Europe, India, or China (although constant time units did exist in the latter). The division of time into commensurable, interchangeable segments would have been alien to the world of antiquity and the early Middle Ages. (Postone, 1993: 202)

Postone stresses that the creation of the abstract conception of time was not due to any technical advance outside the reach of other latitudes, for example in China, but to the social circumstance, which was imposing the commodity as a 'form of social relations'. In other words, it was not the mechanical clock that determined the change in the way time was conceived but, on the contrary, it was this change that made the technology of the mechanical clock necessary. Therefore, the lower Middle Ages already carry in the dynamics of their social life a new time – that of the merchants – which is measurable, predictable, separate from events and, therefore, abstract.

In contrast, the high Middle Ages were much more committed to a conception of time as an ordered reality, which can be measured, but which stands out not by its measure but by its flexible ordering, expressing a relational appropriation of time. Moreover, the flexible duration of the hour had been persistent since the ancient Egyptians, to whom the division of the day into 12 daytime hours and 12 night-time hours is attributed, which implied longer daytime hours in summer and longer night-time hours in winter. But both theoretically and technically, the conditions had long since been met for variable time to give way to constant time. This had been the case as early as the astronomer and geometrician Hipparchus, in the 2nd century BCE (two centuries before Ptolemy), who had proposed to subdivide the day into 24 hours with reference to the days of the equinox, thus ensuring constancy in the duration of time under all circumstances. Quite simply, this constancy was not something society needed; on the contrary, it was not in line with the way it related to time.

In short, it is quite clear that the first major modification of the concept of time and its social experience happens in Europe by the end of the Middle Ages. In a context of growing presence of the market as an organizing form of social relations, with its demands for rigorous measurement in market exchanges and absolute referents to ensure the objectivity of measurement. This explains the historical need to establish, in market societies, a concept of abstract, absolute time, independent of events, of which the mechanical clock was the instrument.

Nevertheless, after the demands for precision of time measurement in market exchanges, it was the formation of a conception of *abstract human labour*, detached from concrete labour, in the terms described by Marx (2015 [1867]) in the first volume of *Capital*, that confirmed the hegemony of the abstract conception of time, disembedded from concrete time. For Marx, what counts for the formation of value (and consequent surplus value extracted through exploitation) is the abstract human labour involved in production, defining it exclusively in terms of time – more exactly, the average labour time that society needs to produce a type of commodity. Such an abstract conception of human labour, dependent on a measure of time, would not be possible without an abstract conception of time itself, capable of being accumulated, bought and spent. As Thompson notes, in the context of industrial labour relations, time is no longer passed but spent:

> This measurement embodies a simple relationship. Those who are employed experience a distinction between their employer's time and their 'own' time. And the employer must use the time of his labour, and see it is not wasted: not the task but the value of time when reduced to money is dominant. Time is now currency: it is not passed but spent. (Thompson, 1967: 61)

This progressive centrality of the market and industrial labour relations in European societies induced the passage from a relational conception of social time to an absolute, abstract and non-relational conception of measured time. Yet time lived by subjects tended to become weaker. With the advance of modernity, subjects became less and less masters of their own time. Although apparently opposed, an excessively transcendent measured-time and an immanent-time lived in an increasingly vulnerable way both express the loss of relational value of social time.

The advent of powerless, accelerated and fragmentary temporality

Many authors, from different disciplinary backgrounds, have, in recent decades, noted an acceleration of social time, which in fact reflects a trend from the age of modernity. Hartmut Rosa supports this view, even in terms of making it an essential feature of modernity, in two books, *Social Acceleration: A New Theory of Modernity* (2013 [2005]) and *Alienation and Acceleration: Towards a Critical Theory of Late-Modern Temporality* (2010). Byung-Chul Han (2009) disagrees with Rosa, stressing instead another alteration – that time has lost narrative duration and therefore has become meaningless, without direction. Han does not disagree that there is an acceleration of time in modernity, he simply does not agree that this fact should be given more value than that of a symptom. Therefore, it should not, except for simplicity, be considered structuring or constitutive of modernity itself. In his words:

> [T]he cause of shrinking present, or the disappearing of duration, is not acceleration, as many mistakenly believe. The relationship between the loss of duration and acceleration is far more complex than that. Time tumbles on [*stürst fort*], like an avalanche, precisely because it no longer contains anything to *hold on to* within itself. (Han, 2009: 12)

Despite presenting this as Rosa's simplified scheme, Han quotes Rosa several times, of which we reproduce two of these instances:

> [T]hat acceleration represents an intuitive solution to the problem of a limited lifetime or the divergence of the time of the world and the time of life in a secular culture. In this context, the maximal enjoyment of worldly opportunities and the optimal actualization of one's own abilities, and hence the ideal of the fulfilled life, has become the paradigm of a successful life. Whoever lives twice as fast can realise twice as many worldly possibilities and thus, as it were, live two lives in the span of one. (Rosa, 2013 [2005]: 310; Han, 2009: 16)

It seems that the dynamic forces of acceleration themselves produce the institutions and forms of practice they need in accordance with the respective requirements of their further unfolding and then annihilate them again upon reaching the speed limits those forms have made possible. From this perspective … it appears that is the increase of speed. … That is the real driving force of (modern) history. (Rosa, 2013 [2005]: 93; Han, 2009: 40)

Reading these passages, it is difficult to follow Han in attributing to Rosa the thesis that acceleration is the constitutive fact of the experience of time in modernity. Two caveats, from the quotations Han himself offers, add nuance to the point in question. First, Rosa presents acceleration not as an initial fact but as a response strategy ('an intuitive solution') to a modification of time that precedes it. The modification Rosa has in mind is that of a secular culture that has imposed a conception of quantifiable time and that tends to reduce the experience of time to that of its quantification. This is in line with the transition, exposed earlier, to an abstract conception of time. Second, this strategy of response, appearing, for Rosa, as the engine of modern history, says much less that acceleration is a constitutive fact than that history is, in fact, a reactive history.

On the other hand, Han's critique does not really dispute that there is an increase in speed, 'an avalanche', in his words. He disputes that this is the determining element. In fact, what Han recognizes in the effects Rosa identifies is a kind of symptomatology, which, alongside the rupture of duration, must find another, more fundamental, cause. For him, what is really at stake is an absence of meaning that holds time to time, binds it together, gives it a direction of being. What is missing in the understanding of time today is that it is a time without a foundation that attributes meaning to it. In other words, this is a time without temporality, a time without interiority, like having the syntax without the semantics. But this is an expected consequence of the transition from a conception of time as a reality intricately connected with the events, itself an event, to a conception of time as a reality outside the events, where these take place. The emergence of abstract time implied the suppression of *Kayrós* – or qualitative time – the other face of the ancient Greek understanding of time, which balanced with *Chronos* – the quantitative time – that is, between the time shown in clocks and the time of events, between the time of measured information and the time of meaning, between the time of causality and external explanation, and the time of understanding and interpretation. This consequence echoes others, which, outside the sphere of time consideration, echo the same movement: the progressive substitution of metaphor, of the figurative, the symbolic, the mythical, the relational, by the literal, transparent, objective, unambivalent.

Both readings can, therefore, be intertwined. The way we live time is accelerated because time as a place of meaning has been lost. Accelerated time is a time in flight, a flight forward, in anxiety to overcome the lack of meaning on which it has settled. It only had to speed up to compensate for its lack of robustness. But, parallel to this modification, the acceleration of the social, psychological and cultural experience of time also modifies the relationship with time in several ways. One is a more fragmented experience of time. Fragmentation may, in Han's light, be parallel to or even more profound than acceleration, but it is not wrong to say that the acceleration of the experience of time also promotes its fragmentation.

Before Rosa and Han, the sociologist Richard Sennett (1998) had already emphasized how the passage to a context of short-term capitalism contributed to the deterioration of an integral relationship with time, which involves all its dimensions in a meaningful way, thus undermining the construction of a person's character. It makes sense to associate the fragmentation of time with its acceleration, which is, in turn, a consequence of the value of the time variable in the productive logic, which is ultimately associated with the phenomenon of the commodification of time itself.

Often, rather than getting it wrong, as Han comments, for example, about Hannah Arendt,[3] the authors he comments on will only have overlooked an aspect on which he himself places greater emphasis, while nevertheless framing what these authors have defended in his justification of his commentary.

If Han is right in considering the acceleration of the social experience of time more as an aspect of symptomatology, we also think that the same judgement should be applied to Han's perspective: that fragmented time, without narrative unity, is equally of the order of symptomatology as well. In fact, it is because both perspectives are situated in the order of symptoms that it is difficult to establish which to prioritize. Fragmentation induces acceleration, as Han claims, and acceleration fragments, as we have just seen with Sennett, long before Rosa said the same. But what then are these partial perspectives, albeit true, symptoms of? Of the separation of the reality of time from the reality of events, making, of these two realities, the first an omnipotent and poised ghost that runs through the second.

What is pointed to today as the culmination of a process that results in the history of modernity (Rosa, 2013 [2005]) may in fact be pointed to as a process that, to a large extent, is the history of humanity itself. The Catalan philosopher Jorge Riechmann (2004) makes an apology for slowness from an ecological reading of the relationship with time. In this framework, an understanding on an ecological scale leads Riechmann to indicate three moments of what he calls 'brutal acceleration' carried out by great 'changes of pace': the passage from biological evolution to culture, the passage to sedentarization and to agricultural cultures with the Neolithic revolution and, finally, modernity with its world economy.

In the light of these observations, rather than an equivalence between modernity and acceleration, two hypotheses should be noted: first, that human history can be told as a tale of stages of acceleration and, second, that modernity is equivalent to one of these stages of acceleration. But if not all acceleration is modern, and if one wants to grasp a sense of modernity, it is important to shift attention from the pure fact of acceleration to what makes it possible in modernity, making it distinctive.

On this constituent plane of modernity itself, the most historically differentiating modification of the social experience of time was not its acceleration, which already came from the past, but neither was it the fragmentation of a time without narrative duration, as Han claims. Before the two perspectives, and capable of framing them, the relevant modification was the unprecedented configuration of social time as an abstract time, independent and detached from events. Arising in Europe at the end of the Middle Ages, it set the stage for the dawn of modernity (Barata, 2020), evolving and consolidating throughout modernity and the implantation of an industrial regime of social existence. This time, which is conceived and practiced in a non-relational way, is, however, a time with which social subjects must live. It is in this tension that we frame the contemporary social experience of precariousness as a mode of a relationship with time. Uncertainty in the face of time, lack of autonomy in its experience, in short, indicators of what can be characterized as a social situation of temporal vulnerability in late modernity.

Precariousness as temporal vulnerability
Precariousness and the extension of the present

The Latin word *precarius*, formed with the radical *prex*, which also means to pray, expresses the idea of something that is sustained only through a supplication addressed to another, or at least through their favour, on whose good will one is left to depend. The contemporary experience that the word 'precariousness' evokes takes on a broader meaning when considering the asymmetrical relationship signaled in the etymology. It highlights the same sense of a fragile condition, in which uncertainty, imbalance and a sense of imminent collapse are permanent. From a personal reality, which was expressed even in legal forms (*jus precarium*),[4] precariousness then came to mean a certain situation in time, a very particular way in which something subsists arduously in time, without meeting the conditions of its own subsistence.

Meanwhile, the social phenomenon of precariousness that has emerged in contemporary secularized societies, particularly the permanently unattached labour condition beyond the shortest term that has become prevalent, somewhat ironically resembles the Latin meaning of the word. It implies a social relationship of unequal dependence comparable to supplication before God. This semantic evolution gives to the word 'precariousness' the meaning of a phenomenon described as a situation in time but also in an intersubjective relationship. It is a vulnerability comparable to subsistence by supplication before the other, perpetuated over time and, therefore, by human responsibility. It is caused and maintained intersubjectively, in a socially disseminated relational structure of extreme inequality, at the limit comparable to the inequality between the human person and the divine.

According to this idea, we might consider that today's labour precariousness is, to a certain extent, the contemporary and secular mode of an older experience of existential precariousness, meaning that both are forms of temporal vulnerability. However, the former is embedded in the conception of time that has been imposed throughout modernity: abstract, accelerated and fragmented.

In this part of the chapter, we will characterize the phenomenon of labour precariousness as a social condition marked both by various socio-economic vulnerabilities and by the loss of control and sovereignty over lived time.[5] Analyzing the condition of immigrants living in precarious situations, Cwerner (2001) defines heteronomous time as when individuals lose control over their lived time and become subject to an uncontrollable increase of social uncertainty in their daily and personal lives. Although this concept was used by Cwerner to characterize extreme forms of social and labour vulnerability arising from migration experiences, it makes sense to use it with a broader scope, which addresses, as well, the experience of labour precariousness (Carmo and d'Avelar, 2021).

In this regard, the generalization of modalities of precarious work has contributed decisively to the forms of temporal reconfiguration alluded to previously, incorporating the characteristic dimensions of heteronomous time (Carmo et al, 2014; Carmo and d'Avelar, 2021). The precarious worker, contracted on a temporary or fixed-term basis (which may include a very diverse number of contractual possibilities, sometimes difficult to inventory and identify), lives in permanent uncertainty. The uncertainty is largely a result of their unstable contractual situation, from which it is difficult to discern the sequence and evolution of their future career path, as well as to have the guarantee of social protection that protects them from the risks of unemployment and/or substantial loss of income. The perception and social experience of uncertainty become almost inseparable and constitutive of the social and subjective condition of precariousness, and result in the expansion of a present that is rarely completed or finalized. In addition to contractual uncertainty, the daily uncertainty resulting from labour precariousness extends the present beyond its usual limits, in the sense that an activity, a task or a work contract is almost always in an unfinished, temporary state, which remains unresolved or unfinished.

The precarious worker seems to be facing a door that is permanently ajar, which keeps them waiting for a new contract or for the emergence of a new project. In fact, in most cases, working time and activity become part of daily life, both in the task still to be completed and in the persistent perception of uncertainty resulting from contractual instability (Reith, 2004). Uncertainty erodes daily working life and interferes with other dimensions of social and personal life (Sennett, 1998). In this way, it seems that there is no way out of a recursive and continuous present that drives the subject towards the same unfinished condition (still unfinished or unresolved) regardless of the work carried out or the nature of the project and the functions performed.

On the other hand, precariousness develops in a context of compression and acceleration of time, for example, in the shortening of temporary employment objectified in work contracts of increasingly shorter duration (counted in months, weeks or even days) and the consequent acceleration of the circulation and rotation of the worker, who moves from job to precarious job (ILO, 2018). A kind of contradiction is established between this impetus for movement (which in many cases is forced) and the perception that one does not leave the same place, in the sense that there is no opportunity or expectation of professional progress and of achieving an effective career (Carmo and Matias, 2019). This reinforces the idea of an endless present (Carmo and d'Avelar, 2021).

The experience of full acceleration amplifies the feeling that nothing substantial has changed compared to the initial precarious situation. The condition and the action of the subject tend to reduce progressively to a certain one-dimensionality (of tasks and procedures that are repeated, or of daily gestures that become routine), from which it is difficult to get out or to overcome. The contradiction between the vertiginous experience of change brought about by the consecutive changes in the professional situation and context, and the feeling that despite these changes everything remains basically the same (though one is almost always changing jobs or activities), is a telling symptom that living time in an accelerated mode does not necessarily mean one is experiencing effective and structural social changes. This dissonance has the potential to be generative of a deep malaise (with consequences on mental health), which is socially reproduced and runs through many of the workers in precarious employment (Wilkinson and Pickett, 2018). In a sense, excessive acceleration produces intense movement in everyday life but does not necessarily mean a structural change in professional status and labour condition.

A symptom of vertigo is the lack of differentiation between working and non-working times that is induced by economic and technological systems that encourage productivity (Han, 2019). This undifferentiation can be framed in the perspective of some contributions of so-called critical theory, particularly from authors such as Herbert Marcuse (1941, 1991 [1964]), who wrote about the risk of the one-dimensionality of social and individual life. For Marcuse, the generalization of the use of technology in the most diverse sectors of the economy and society has determined the constitution of an apparatus that tends to control and dominate daily life within the largest companies and modern institutions. The sociologist refers to the emergence of a technical rationality, which is taking over all sectors of professional and daily life, based on the principle of competitiveness and efficiency aimed at maximizing productivity and profit. It is a rationality of an instrumental nature, based on multiple bureaucratic and administrative procedures, that urges one to act in accordance with regulations, forms, goals, objectives to be achieved and so on. The author developed this idea of one-dimensionality, which deepens the notion that technical rationality spreads and irradiates through the various domains of social life, in the professional sphere, the private sphere and even the affective sphere (Marcuse, 1991 [1964]).

According to Marcuse, although it does not disappear completely, the notion of individuality becomes dependent on and strongly conditioned by standards of efficiency that are external to the subject himself and to their will, and which, we would add, characterize so-called abstract time. In fact, technical rationality imposes itself at the cost of the erosion of critical and irreverent rationality, guided by factors of individual autonomy and emancipation. That is, rational behaviour progressively submits to and, in a certain sense, moulds itself to the technological apparatus regulated and robotized by abstract and unidirectional time.

The aforementioned one-dimensionality identified by Marcuse is fundamental to understand the nature and the social consequences that arise from the heteronomous time. One of its most salient expressions is the generalization of a continuous time or an endless present, which partly results from the combination of acceleration and recursiveness of actions and situations experienced. The pressure for progressive productivity, which no longer is consistent with the rigid separation between working hours and non-working time, causes a notion of continuity in time that knows no interruptions or gaps, and is reflected in the common perception of always being at work or not being able to stop working. In short, abstract time, external to the individual, imposes a social and subjective one-dimensionality that absorbs and standardizes the diversity of events and situations. From Marcuse's perspective we can say that the singularity of the subject and his autonomy are diluted in the technological apparatus supported by the gears of abstract time. In line with this, Han refers to how the permanent coercion to be productive, induced by the current capitalist system, deprives things of their own specific durability (Han, 2019: 13). In this sense, precarity is a condition and the radicalized social expression of the abstract, external and standardized time that becomes dominant and unavoidable.

Frail future, vulnerable temporalities

The colonization of the future represents the construction of a temporal horizon, a possibility of action, from which one intends to reach a given goal. It is a previously outlined and planned path that is expected to be followed until the defined objective is effectively reached. However, the ability to colonize the future necessarily depends on a relative stabilization of material and existential security in the present time. Giddens (1991) refers to the importance of so-called *ontological security* as being a fundamental requirement of stability and trust for the social life of individuals. It presumes the existence and sharing of rules and resources capable of organizing social relations in a routinized way that guarantees the possibility of building a certain time horizon based on a strong probability of fulfilment. A greater stabilization of ontological security during present-day daily life ensures the ability to foresee and project a probable future.

The domain of uncertainty that jeopardizes stabilization of material and existential security in the present moment tends to compromise the possibility of projecting well-defined time horizons with a probability of objectivation. Faced with this framework of uncertainty, many individuals tend to project several time horizons simultaneously to engender more or less viable future alternatives. These horizons may even be contradictory in terms of the path they outline, thus generating a kind of collection of different weak possibilities for which the individual must expect their eventual realization (Carmo and Matias, 2019; Carmo and d'Avelar, 2020). The future becomes indecipherable because it is too open to a series of possibilities, whose objectives may compete. The consecutive updating and reconstruction of temporal scenarios of weak possibilities incorporates a strong social and emotional exhaustion in the sense that almost nothing is acquired and stabilized. Therefore, uncertainty becomes a constant factor and a condition experienced and perceived as permanent.

In this sense, the precariousness experienced in the present is projected in the consequent precariousness of the capacity or autonomy to build a predictable future horizon with a strong probability of happening. The horizons outlined are weak and with little margin to be fully realized. The precarious individual is deprived of the sovereignty of his own temporality, to the extent that they are subjected (subjugated) to an external gear over which they do not have the slightest control. This gearing is partly supported by the abstract time that tends to colonize everything and everyone. Turning to Habermas (1981), we can say that the subject is disconnected from the sphere of his or her life-world (from his or her relatively autonomous frameworks and contexts of everyday interaction) and repositioned in the robotic and one-dimensional devices that feed technological systems and liberalized markets. Thus, the experience of precariousness radicalizes the dominance of abstract time, which is increasingly absolute and without room for gaps or escapes. The individual becomes even more dependent on a relationship of strong inequality, where the experience of accelerated time means the expression of a system manufactured and oriented solely towards continuous and endless productivity. In a way, the fragmented temporality, marked by permanent uncertainty and loss of autonomy, experienced by the precarious is the other side of the mirror of abstract, continuous, impervious, and unbreakable time. It is this strong asymmetric dependency that reciprocally feeds and deepens in late modernity.

Conclusion

It is possible to conclude that the contemporary social phenomenon of precariousness, although emerging from the sphere of labour relations, expresses a broader social condition whose sources are linked to modernity's trend to configure the experience of time as an experience of vulnerability, but bearing roots that go back to the experience of supplication, whether in a legal or even religious sense. Social time reveals itself to be increasingly transcendent, in an unperturbed gapless continuum resulting from the compulsion to be productive, while the temporality experienced by the subject reveals itself to be increasingly fragmentary and clinging to a present that is extended without the unfolding of a relationship with the past and the future. The asymmetrical relationship between, on the one hand, an excessively powerful time of hyper-industrialized, economic, and technological systems (abstract time) and, on the other hand, subjects with a temporality that is woefully powerless (heteronomous time) is particularly notorious in the social condition of precariousness and its expression of unidimensionality. This asymmetry has profound consequences in the loss of self-determination and individual autonomy, and is therefore a determining element in deepening the experience of vulnerable time.

Notes

[1] This chapter was translated with the support of the research unit of Praxis – Centre of Philosophy, Politics and Culture (UIDB/05451/2020) and FCT, the Portuguese national funding agency for science, research and technology.

[2] Several research projects about precarious work and unemployment involving the author Renato Miguel Carmo have been developed over almost a decade. Most of these were focused on a qualitative approach, using intensive methodologies and content analysis of in-depth interviews conducted with several categories of workers (Carmo et al, 2014; Carmo and Matias, 2019; Carmo and d'Avelar, 2020, 2021).

[3] In *The Scent of Time*, Han categorically points out an error to Hannah Arendt where perhaps a more subtle interpretation would have been possible. When he says that 'it is erroneous to assume that the primacy of contemplation is responsible for the reduction of the *vita activa* to labour' (Han, 2009: 105), Han is right, but this is simply not Arendt's thinking, for whom the problem lies not in the *vita contemplativa* but in the way in which this was conceived as opposed to the *vita activa*.

[4] '*Jus Precarium* – In civil law, a right to a thing held for another, for which there was no remedy by legal action, but only by entreaty or request' (*Black's Law Dictionary* [2nd edition]: 680).

[5] This section of the chapter is based fundamentally on recent sociological research published in Portuguese, and deepens and reframes the theoretical analysis on job precariousness, subjectivities and the labour market in Portugal (Carmo and Matias, 2019; Carmo and d'Avelar, 2020).

References

Barata, A. (2018) *E se parássemos de sobreviver? Pequeno livro para agir e pensar contra a ditadura do tempo*, Lisbon: Documenta.

Barata, A. (2020) *O desligamento do mundo e a questão do humano*, Lisbon: Documenta.

Bell, D. (1976) 'The coming of the post-industrial society', *The Educational Forum*, 40(4): 574–9.

Carmo, R.M. and d'Avelar, M.M. (2020) *A Miséria do Tempo: Vidas Suspensas pelo Desemprego*, Lisbon: Tinta da China.

Carmo, R.M. and d'Avelar, M.M. (2021) 'The weight of time and the unemployment experience: daily life and future prospects', *Current Sociology*, https://doi.org/10.1177/0011392120986222

Carmo, R.M. and Matias, A.R. (2019) *Retratos da Precariedade: Quotidianos e Aspirações dos Trabalhadores Jovens*, Lisbon: Tinta da China.

Carmo, R.M., Cantante, F. and Alves, N. (2014) 'Time projections: youth and precarious employment', *Time & Society*, 23(3): 337–57.

Cwerner, S.B. (2001) 'The times of migration', *Journal of Ethnic and Migration Studies*, 27(1): 7–36.

Giddens, A. (1991) *Modernity and Self-Identity – Self and Society in the Late Modern Age*, Cambridge: Polity Press.

Habermas, J. (1981) *The Theory of Communicative Action*, Cambridge: Polity Press.

Han, B.-C. (2009) *The Scent of Time: A Philosophical Essay on the Art of Lingering*, Cambridge: Polity Press.

Han, B.-C. (2019) *O Desaparecimento dos Rituais*, Lisbon: Relógio D'Água.

ILO (2018) *Decent work in Portugal 2008–18: From Crisis to Recovery*, Geneva: International Labour Organization.

Le Goff, J. (1960) 'Temps de l'Église et temps du marchand', *Annales*, 15(3), 417–33.

Marcuse, H. (1941) 'Some social implications of modern technology', *Studies in Philosophy and Social Sciences*, 9(3): 414–39.

Marcuse, H. (1991 [1964]) *One-Dimensional Man*, London: Routledge & Kegan Paul.

Marx, K. (2015 [1867]) *Capital*, Moscow: Progress Publishers.

Mumford, L. (1934) *Technics and Civilization*, London: Routledge & Kegan Paul.

Postone, M. (1993) *Time, Labour and Social Domination. A Reinterpretation of Marx's Critical Theory*, Cambridge: Cambridge University Press.

Reith, G. (2004) 'Uncertain times: the notion of "risk" and the development of modernity', *Time & Society* 13(2/3): 383–402.

Riechmann, J. (2004) *Gente que no quiere viajar a Marte. Ensayos sobre ecología, ética y autolimitación*, Madrid: Catarata.

Rosa, H. (2010) *Alienation and Acceleration: Towards a Critical Theory of Late-Modern Temporality*, Malmö/Aarhus: NSU Press.

Rosa, H. (2013 [2005]) *Social Acceleration: A New Theory of Modernity*, New York and Chichester: Columbia University Press.

Sennett, R. (1998) *The Corrosion of Character: The Personal Consequences of Work in the New Capitalism*, New York: Norton.

Stiegler, B. (2018 [2004]) *Da Miséria Simbólica – I. A Era Hiperindustrial*, Lisbon: Orfeu Negro.

Thompson, E.P. (1967) 'Time, work-discipline, and industrial capitalism', *Past & Present*, 38: 56–97.

Wilkinson, R. and Pickett, K. (2018) *The Inner Level: How More Equal Societies Reduce Stress, Restore Sanity and Improve Everyone's Well-being*, London: Allen Lane.

PART II

Class, Work and Employment

5

Above-Below, Inside-
Outside: Precarity, Underclass and
Social Exclusion in Demobilized
Class Societies

Klaus Dörre

Introduction

For three decades, vertical, class-specific inequalities have been on the
rise once again in most countries worldwide.[1] While inequalities *between*
countries are decreasing – mainly as a result of rapid growth and catch-up
processes in large emerging economies – income and wealth inequality
within nation states is becoming more pronounced (Milanovic, 2011, 2016;
Therborn, 2012). The primary beneficiaries of globalization are the elites
who reside mainly in the affluent societies of the Global North. Some 44
per cent of the total increase in income between 1988 and 2008 went to
the wealthiest 5 per cent, and almost one fifth went to the richest 1 per cent
of the world's adult population. The rising middle classes in the emerging
economies of the South received only 2 to 4 per cent of total income
increases (Milanovic, 2011, 2016). Large groups of wage earners – production
workers and the growing service proletariat in particular – find themselves
on the losing side of globalization. They no longer benefit from what
Branko Milanovic describes as the 'citizenship rent' of wealth distribution
(2011: 120). The privilege of being born in a rich country has ceased to
serve as protection from downward social mobility. At the same time, new
divisions and inequalities are becoming more pronounced and making their
presence felt even *within* directly or indirectly wage-dependent classes. Even
in societies with a flourishing economy, precarious work and employment
relations have become the ' "normal" organisational form' of social life

(Castel, 2011: 136). At the same time, another form of exclusion is also taking place. At the very top of the social hierarchy, we find one group expanding, namely the – albeit still tiny – group of super-rich owners of wealth who largely live outside the rules that apply to the rest of the population. At the bottom of the social hierarchy, by contrast, large social groups are forming that fall outside the established social order in an entirely different way. These groups are excluded not only from regular gainful employment but also stripped of basic social and democratic rights; from the perspective of mainstream society, they simply appear 'superfluous'. These underclasses comprise between 10 and 15 per cent of the total population in almost all of the early industrialized countries (Mann, 2013: 91f.).

But how can this structural heterogeneity of social dislocations and disparities be conceptualized in a scientifically accurate and helpful way? Answers to this question differ substantially. It is obvious from countless debates that sociology and the social sciences currently lack adequate theoretical concepts and analytical tools to capture the confusing melange of social divisions, social polarization, widespread precarity and exclusion. The persistent blind spots in sociological research on inequality cannot be corrected overnight. However, at least a step in this direction would be to consider the key concepts of 'exclusion' and 'precarity' in a way that carves out both their differences from and intersections with the concept of class. This will be attempted in what remains of this chapter. To start off, we clarify the basic concepts of exclusion and precarity. From there, we consider the political construction of the new underclasses and the emergence of a precarious full-employment society in Germany. To conclude, we address what would be required for a critical theory of social exclusion and precarity.

The fundamental concepts of exclusion and precarity

From the mid-1980s, German sociology was dominated by a discourse that construed inequalities primarily in terms of individualization. In a pointed summary of the sociological debates of that decade, Ulrich Beck proclaimed an irreversible process of dissolution of industrial class society: the logic of class-specific wealth distribution was increasingly being replaced by the logic of ecological risks, which were not specific to class. A renewed surge of individualization, Beck contended, had divested the social forms of industrial modernity (above all, class, status and gender) of their cohesive force: 'The individual himself or herself becomes the reproductive unit for the social in the lifeworld' (Beck, 1992: 130).

In retrospect, there can be little doubt that Ulrich Beck and the authors who built on his analysis address an important dimension of socio-structural change by pointing to the liberation of the individual from traditional social milieus, predetermined gender roles and religious ties. Yet the emphasis of the individualization thesis on a 'capitalism without classes' (Beck, 1992: 88) has proven highly problematic, not least in light of the dramatic increase in vertical inequalities that the early industrialized societies have witnessed in recent decades.

The germ of truth in the individualization thesis is that there are problems with existing theories of class that need to be addressed. Regardless of their general heterogeneity, these theories have tended to assign individuals and collectives a more or less fixed position in the social structure of modern societies: even subaltern classes, for all the oppression they experience, have been seen as members of society. The challenge to such theories comes when subaltern groups are no longer integrated into society but instead 'decoupled' or 'disaffiliated' (Castel, 2002), where they are systematically excluded from social sub-systems (Luhmann, 1995a) and even become wholly 'expendable' (Kronauer, 2002).

Blind spots of theories of class

Theories of social exclusion thus highlight a blind spot of numerous class analyses. Such analyses often focus on organized social actors, for example unions and workers' parties, who tend to pursue the class struggle in a way that seeks the social integration of both conflict parties. Though such conflicts are often fiercely fought out, they are conducted on the grounds of guaranteed economic and social rights of wage earners. The erstwhile 'wild' class struggle becomes a dispute between collective bargaining parties; it is institutionalized, regulated and pacified. And yet, the less friction the systemic integration of the democratic class struggle causes, the more apparent the social divisions that erupt outside the regulated sector. These divisions have a disintegrating effect on society, without having any system-transcending impact. In other words, class theories' focus on exploitation often overlooks the large social groups who are excluded from even the limited rights associated with wage labour.

In Marx's class theory, such groups feature as the industrial reserve army or are discussed in terms of an exclusively negatively connoted *Lumpenproletariat*. To Marx, the industrial reserve army, in its various manifestations, constitutes an unemployed segment of the proletariat, and overcoming the divisions between active and passive workers is therefore a matter of 'planned co-operation between the employed and the unemployed' (Marx, 1976 [1867]: 793), and thus of political and trade unionist class unity. Even orphans and pauper children are regarded as 'candidates for the industrial reserve army' (Marx, 1976 [1867]: 797), who are 'enrolled in the army of active workers both speedily and in large numbers' in times of economic prosperity (Marx, 1976 [1867]: 797). In contrast, Marx considers vagabonds and criminals, the incapacitated, the mutilated and the sickly to be the 'pauperized sections' [in the original: '*Lazarus layer*'] (Marx, 1976 [1867]: 798), unable to be integrated into the working class, and which will tend, time and again, to rally to forces of political reaction. In the *Communist Manifesto*, Marx and Engels refer to the *Lumpenproletariat* as that 'passively rotting mass thrown off by the lowest layers of old society' (Marx and Engels, 1976 [1848]: 494) who, as a result of their entire way of life, are predestined for the part as a 'bribed tool of reactionary intrigue' (Marx and Engels, 1976 [1848]).

This rather resentful view ascribes to the social outsiders all those negative characteristics which supposedly do not apply to the potentially revolutionary proletariat (Bescherer, 2013). Needless to say, such classifications are untenable historically. Irish immigration, for example, which Engels commented on with a mix of dismissal and contempt – since it 'degraded' (Engels, 1975 [1845]: 393) the English working class due to the competition and uncivilized behaviour it imported – actually became one of the first focal points of organized labour movements as a result of its numerous struggles (Thompson, 1991).

When applied to the lowest levels of the social pyramid, Max Weber's conceptual framework has little to offer in the way of alternatives to Marx's class theory. That said, in Weber we do find, alongside some vague hints at deprivileged classes and strata, the social figure of the 'Pariah' and the category of the 'Pariah people' (Weber, 1978 [1921]: 492ff.), which, as Weber explains with the example of Jewish people (Weber, 1978 [1921]: 492ff.), correspond to specific forms of intentionally precipitated social exclusion.

In more recent class analyses that build upon Marx and Weber, the analysis of underclasses forming 'below' the level of the working population also remains peculiarly weak. Everything that is located below the middle classes, so to speak, is classified as being 'at the bottom'. Such ascriptions can even be found in Pierre Bourdieu's magnum opus *Distinction* (1984). From today's perspective, Bourdieu's description of a pragmatic 'taste of necessity' (Bourdieu, 1984: 6) typifying the lower classes appears to correspond more to the blue- and white-collar workers of 1960s France than to today's world. As we will see, however, Bourdieu's work contains, on closer inspection, ideas that an analysis of exclusion, precarity and the underclasses could take as a starting point.

Social exclusion

The debate surrounding social exclusion addresses what neither Marx nor Weber anticipated in their conceptions of class: the formation of social groups that are considered worthless in terms of economic valorization and useless for mainstream society, and are, as such, expendable. These 'superfluous' (Kronauer, 2002: 116; Bude and Willisch, 2008: 31–49) groups are not even part of the industrial reserve army, as they are simply not needed (any longer) for the creation of value. The fact that 'superfluous' groups in society exist in the first place also represents a challenge for those social theories that assume, at least implicitly, a progressive inclusion of social sub-systems. When surveying the Brazilian favelas, Niklas Luhmann encountered people who were 'without function' for highly differentiated social sub-systems and thus posed a theoretical problem (Luhmann, 1995a, 1995b). The concept of exclusion thus allows a particular variant of the social question to intrude into the theory of the functional differentiation of society. Since Luhmann's time, the question of exactly who is excluded, and how, has become the object of fierce controversies. One group of theorists, among them Armin Nassehi, even vehemently rejects the use of the term 'exclusion' (Nassehi, 2008: 122f.). An intermediary position has been formulated by Martin Kronauer. For him, persons and groups may be included in modern societies in certain respects but excluded in others: 'In the continuing custody of welfare state assistance, the excluded find themselves in the paradoxical situation of an institutionalized simultaneity of inside and outside' (Kronauer, 2002: 204, translation amended).

Precarity

Martin Kronauer's dynamic, multidimensional concept of exclusion places him, both theoretically and analytically, close to a discourse on precarity that was originally influenced by French sociology, and especially by Pierre Bourdieu (1998) and Robert Castel (2002, 2008, 2011). Robert Castel traces his use of the word back to the Latin *precarium*, which meant a loan (of an object, of land or rights), the right to use of which could be revoked by the donor at any time. Precarity thus describes an insecure, unstable and revokable relationship – a relationship of extreme dependence. The opposite would be a stable, secure relationship, characterized by equal rights. Of course, this would make precarity anything but new. The history of widespread precarious working can be traced back to at least the 14th century AD (Schultheis and Herold, 2010). In the feudal order, beggars and vagabonds were subjected to the disciplining violence of the guilds and the police. The liberation from the hierarchical order that occurred during the transition to the industrial capitalist mode of production furthered precarity in the form of forced pauperization. In the crumbling feudal order, state power was used against potential wage workers; what emerged was the phenomenon of 'undignified' wage labour (Castel, 2011: 63). According to Bourdieu and Castel, the retrenchment of welfare-state social security systems today has led to the return of this phenomenon – albeit at an entirely different level of social wealth and security. Precarious wage earners are thus the new 'vagabonds' of the 21st century, entering the stage in the wake of the deregulation of work and employment (Castel, 2011: 68) and who, as a result of their partial disenfranchisement, become 'denizens' excluded from social and democratic rights (Standing, 2011).

Contemporary usages of the term precarity tend to fall into two categories. As a *socio-analytical concept*, sometimes narrowly conceived, it is often seen as a special form of atypical employment (Keller and Seifert 2007); as a social position between poverty and normality (Kraemer 2009); as externalization on the labour market (Bartelheimer, 2011; Krause and Köhler, 2012); or as the growth of informal migrant service work in 'global care chains' (Aulenbacher, 2009; Hochschild, 2001). As a *historical-diagnostic* concept, by contrast, precarity addresses wider changes at the interface of gainful employment, the welfare state and democracy. The term points to 'a general convulsion of society' (Ehrenberg, 2011: 366; Barbier, 2013), to the increasing fragility of social reproduction, and to a form of social vulnerability that originates at the heart of work-centred society and must be distinguished from phenomena such as poverty, unemployment or exclusion (Vogel, 2009). In this latter usage, the term precarity can be refined in a way that highlights its strengths, for instance by construing it not so much as a social condition but as a regime of power, control and discipline that influences and changes the 'work-centred society' (*Arbeitsgesellschaft*) as a whole (Dörre, 2009).

Both forms of usage of the term precarity have been influenced by the works of Robert Castel. According to Castel, the post-Fordist work-centred societies of the affluent North are divided into distinct 'zones' of differing levels of (social) security (Castel, 2002: 304f.). Although a majority of wage earners in the advanced capitalisms are still situated within a zone of integration, with protected full-time employment and more or less intact social safety nets, below that level a *zone of precarity* is expanding, marked by both uncertain employment and eroding social security. Lower still down the hierarchy, a *zone of decoupling or detachment* is taking shape, comprising groups who have no real chance at integration into the still protected segments of the labour market and its social safety nets. Castel's zonal model has served as a heuristic template for numerous authors to conduct their own empirical research. Today, the applicability of this analytical model to Germany and other European societies has been sufficiently demonstrated (see, for example, Schultheis and Schulz, 2005; Brinkmann et al, 2006; Castel and Dörre, 2009; Pelizzari, 2009; Sander, 2012; Allmendinger et al, 2018).

On the political construction of new underclasses

When comparing Castel's concept of precarity to a differential concept of exclusion, such as Kronauer's, the common aspects are immediately obvious. Kronauer's multidimensional concept refers primarily to groups located close to the status of welfare recipient. To Castel, and those whose analyses build on his work (Dörre, 2005; Dörre et al, 2013), the 'decoupled' or 'disaffiliated' (*désaffilé*) mark, so to speak, the lowest reference point of precarity. They constitute the counterpart to the underclass in the United States, albeit less socio-structurally entrenched and, in political terms, by no means entirely excluded. The formation of underclasses is also the point at which the link with theories of class mentioned at the beginning of this chapter surfaces. Here we see that, contra Guy Standing's assertion, the precariat is not a class, nor even 'a class-in-the-making' (Standing, 2011: 7, 2014) that could replace the organized industrial proletariat as a collective actor in social conflicts. Indeed, if we substitute precariat with underclass, the chances of an accurate analysis improve. In particular, vulnerability as a result of proximity to the status of welfare recipient represents a social positioning that unites members of the underclass despite otherwise highly varied backgrounds.

At the threshold of social respectability

Pierre Bourdieu and the research group surrounding him described this social positioning quite accurately when studying the French *banlieues*. In *The Weight of the World*, the category of the 'outcasts on the inside' (Bourdieu et al, 1999: 421–506) is introduced. This group includes, among others, second-generation immigrants. Their experience is of intransigent barriers to upward social mobility, even despite successful educational achievement. To Bourdieu, however, the internal outcasts of the *banlieues* represent only one manifestation of the tendency towards precarization. Already in his study of Kabyle society in his book *Algeria 1960* (1979), Bourdieu had pointed to two other markers of social security: 'permanent employment and regular income, together with the whole set of assurances about the future which they guarantee, bring people on to what we may call the *security plateau*' (Bourdieu, 1979: 54, emphasis added). Below this plateau we find unstable forms of work and life. Above it, a '*threshold of calculability* (or enterprise)' can be reached by those fortunate enough to have 'incomes sufficient to overcome the concern with simple subsistence' (Bourdieu, 1979: 54, emphasis added).

Intriguingly, Bourdieu makes implicit reference to a third threshold. This marks the outer limit of social respectability and appreciation by others. It is indicated by an institutionalized welfare status. Below this threshold of respectability, autonomous social reproduction becomes impossible without the assistance of the community or society. That is to say, the welfare recipient status epitomizes society's zone of exclusion. Anyone situated in proximity to it inevitably becomes the target of negative (including sexist or racist) classifications. Wherever social conditions solidify that are located around or below this threshold of respectability, we may speak of the emergence of socially devalued underclasses.

The formation of underclasses through devaluation

The formation of new underclasses in the capitalist metropoles does not follow a natural law. Their emergence and consolidation are based on the formation of political blocs, through which social elites, in alliance with segments of the 'performing' middle and working classes, revoke their solidarity with and protection of the allegedly 'unproductive', 'superfluous' members of the new underclasses. The same process is additionally and substantially advanced by government policies of demarcation, which – be it openly or implicitly – amount to the collective depreciation of the most vulnerable groups in society.

Underclasses emerge in regulated welfare state capitalisms when entire population segments are permanently forced below the threshold of social respectability as a result of carefully designed scarcity and symbolic devaluation. Depending on the varying policies and welfare state regimes, class formation through demarcation and symbolic devaluation can, however, manifest itself in very different ways.

In France, the social rift can be situated spatially; the demarcation vis-à-vis the underclasses takes place in the form of *socio-spatial isolation and separation*. Whoever lives in the *banlieues* moves below the threshold of respectability and stands little chance of entering the circle of respected citizens, even with a good education. Those affected include, above all, but not only, immigrants who originally came from the French colonies, as well as their children and grandchildren.

In the United States we find the mechanism of *demarcation through criminalization*. Over the course of 40 years, the number of prison inmates has grown fivefold, most of them poor people of colour. One in nine young African-American men are incarcerated; about 60 per cent of those who never graduate from high school have been to prison by their mid-30s (Goffman, 2014: xiii). In such a scenario, contact between the state and members of the underclasses can easily turn into armed confrontation. Time and again, police use the slightest excuse (if any) to inflict deadly force on unarmed people of colour, as they identify the latter – precisely because of their complexion – as members of threatening, dangerous classes.

The formation of underclasses may also take place in a more subtle way, however, for example as a result of a gradual *proliferation of 'undignified' labour*, that is, of badly paid, barely appreciated work. A glance behind the façade of the so-called German 'job miracle' illustrates what this means. Over the course of a decade, a precarious full-employment society has emerged, where a decreasing volume of paid working hours is asymmetrically distributed to a record number of economically active people. For large groups in German society today, integration into the labour market occurs via non-standardized, precarious, underpaid labour with few to no participatory rights (Allmendinger et al, 2018; Dörre et al, 2018).

The spread of 'undignified' labour occurs in accordance with the logic of *the 'activating' labour market regime*, where welfare benefits are set at levels designed to make even precarious work more attractive than unemployment. Despite the fact that the vast majority of benefit recipients proactively expend great efforts to exit their welfare status, most fail to make the step into regular employment. What we see instead is a kind of *circular mobility*: although the number of long-term unemployed persons in Germany declined by about 40 per cent between 2006 and 2011, and has remained at that level ever since, there is a solid core of about one million people who have been unable to move off welfare in a decade. As their welfare status is prolonged, they are forced to come to terms with a situation of material scarcity, a lack of social recognition and strict bureaucratic surveillance of their everyday life. If they actually manage to come to terms with all this, their way of life becomes an even better target for collective devaluation by mainstream society.

Social exclusion: class-theoretical perspectives

The mechanisms of exclusion inevitably differ in different countries. But what each has in common is that they show the formation of underclasses in affluent societies by means of precarization. A question remains, though, as to how these new underclasses relate to traditional classes.

Competing classes

In advanced capitalisms, classes, including underclasses, are *competing classes*. They arise from rivalry and competition, as the product of political measures and symbolic demarcations. That is why they are not socially homogeneous. In Germany, the underclass is by no means identical with 'the long-term unemployed'. Only about 53 per cent of working-age benefit recipients are unemployed, while 25 per cent supplement their income with 'Hartz IV' benefits (the so-called '*Aufstocker*'). At least 50.8 per cent of benefit recipients have completed vocational training or even obtained a master craftsman's certificate, and 7.2 per cent even have a polytechnic degree (IAB, 2014). Yet this does nothing to change their position at (or below) the threshold of social respectability. The activating labour market regime, so to speak, 'forcibly homogenizes' all benefit recipients – who otherwise differ markedly in terms of social background.

This politically constructed levelling leads to *tensions and strategies of distinction*. In the struggles surrounding distinction, which often target the 'lazy unemployed', the 'labour immigrant' or the 'social freeloader' (though there is no evidence of widespread benefit fraud in Germany (IAB, 2014)), the aim is to at least symbolically shift the threshold of respectability. In the immediate social vicinity of welfare benefits or the '*Aufstocker*', struggles for distinction are fought out particularly fiercely. At the top end of the threshold of respectability there are overlaps with precarious workers and a service proletariat whose occupations provide – despite uncertainty and low income – opportunities for positive identification, particularly in the social and care sectors. Below the level of 'Hartz IV' benefits we find the illegal immigrants, the informally employed, the homeless and beggars, to whom even the stigma of welfare represents the promise of some minimal status.

Such strategies of devaluation illustrate that underclasses only ever exist *as part of a process and in (inter-)relation to other classes.* Precisely because of their – real or assumed – willingness to actively adapt to the most adverse conditions, underclasses increasingly become a perceived security problem for the still relatively secure groups of wage earners. Whoever comes close to the status of benefit recipient, or even acquiesces to benefit dependence, is surrendering themselves, in the eyes of unionized blue- and white-collar workers, to a situation of extreme alienation. In fact, there are trade union activists who react to such forms of adjustment with downright disgust. The unionized worker typically demarcates him- or herself not only from 'capital', 'the employer' or 'the board', but also from the 'other' or 'those at the bottom' (Dörre et al, 2018). Such symbolic demarcations reveal a fear that the world of the precarious and 'outcasts' is never far away. If not at one's own workplace, the reality that one would rather not face is looming at the plant down the road, or even in one's neighbourhood.

One fundamental problem those subjected to negative classification face is that class positions which arise from these negative classifications are *unsuitable as the foundation of a positive collective identity.* In our empirical studies we found a considerable proportion of respondents had difficulties when asked to position themselves socially. The unemployed and precariously employed complain about discrimination, but most of them do not describe themselves as poor, nor do they agree to being grouped with the lower levels of society. When asked, some ostentatiously place themselves 'in the middle'. The fact that members of the underclass refuse to use terms such as poverty, lower strata and so on to describe their position can likely be explained by the negative connotations of these labels. Our respondents' fear seemed to be that it might place even more strain on their already difficult situation if it is referred to with 'contaminated' language. An important upshot of our empirical studies is that neither underclass nor precarity currently seem to provide an associative framework of interpretation from which a positive collective identity may arise.

Precarious full-employment society

Facilitated by the mechanisms outlined earlier, a precarious full-employment society has emerged in Germany (Dörre et al, 2013). That is to say, mass unemployment has been made to 'disappear' through an expansion of uncertain, badly paid and poorly recognized employment (Castel, 2011). This trend has been ongoing since 2005 (Reusch et al, 2019). The official unemployment rate, which had reached its peak at 11.7 per cent in 2005, receded to below 5 per cent on average by 2018. Simultaneously, the number of economically active people reached a new record high of about 45 million in 2018. Between 1991 and 2017, the number of wage earners rose from 35.227 million to about 40 million, but the volume of paid working hours actually fell (50.930 million hours in 2017 compared with 52.098 million in 1991). During this same period, the number of full-time positions declined from about 29 million to roughly 24 million (low point: 2010, 22.825 million), while the share of part-time positions sharply increased (1991: 17.1 per cent; 2017: 39.1 per cent). The German 'job miracle' thus largely rests on a strongly asymmetrical distribution of an – at best – stagnating volume of paid working hours relative to a markedly increased number of economically active people (Reusch et al. 2019).

The coronavirus, which first struck in 2020, has, similarly to other plagues in the past, served to amplify inequality and to further drive precarization. As if under a spotlight, the disease reveals all those social uncertainties and inequalities that modern capitalist societies have been (re)producing for a long time. Previous inequalities included the socially unequal distribution of health risks – this becomes all the more apparent in the case of COVID-19 infections. As the German health body, the Robert Koch Institute, has noted, the risk of infection is particularly high wherever material hardship and crowded living conditions make social distancing almost impossible. If we 'trace the infection chains', we come upon precarious working conditions, overcrowded living quarters and neighbourhoods with high proportions of people living off welfare benefits. The 'zone of precarity', which, despite the alleged German 'job miracle' comprises at least one fifth of the economically active population, is a coronavirus hotspot.

Requirements for a critical theory of precariat and underclass formation

In order to assess the possibility and likelihood of the emergence of collective (class) action in the 'zone of precarity' we require a critical theory of the precariat and of the formation of social underclasses. An understanding of class formation through exclusion and precarizsation would have to be at the heart of such a theory, breaking with an objectified, ideologically distorted view that 'naturally' burdens members of the underclass with negative classifications. Instead – fully in the spirit of Marxian class theory, and yet going beyond it – such a theory would have to critically consider the socio-economic and political causes of exclusion. The aim of such a theory would be to strengthen the confidence of the underclasses, enabling them to not only cope with but change their own lives – based on solidarity. In my view, any theoretical approach that could offer as much would have to address a number of specific facets, as will now be discussed.

Firstly, the fact that members of the new underclasses have not been identical with the classic '*Lumpenproletariat*' for a long time. Today, we are mostly talking about people who are fully capable of working but who are being deprived of the basic means of reproduction (Castel, 2008).

Secondly, this can only change if the alleged uselessness of the seemingly 'superfluous' is challenged both symbolically and politically. This entails conceiving of work not merely as gainful employment, and of exploitation not merely as taking advantage of wage earners, but instead construing both more broadly. Social groups located in proximity to the welfare status are usually anything but 'lazy' or 'passive'. In fact, they often have to work harder than most to manage their situation. What their specific activities are, however, is determined, to a considerable extent, by state authorities. Part-time employment (so-called 'mini-jobs') and obligatory work placements can easily add up to a 48-hour week at times. On top of this, there are the demands of family life and child-rearing. There is a powerful motive behind all these activities. To the respondents in our interviews, it appeared as if they could realistically reach the next level up in the social hierarchy, promising a modicum of social normality, on their own steam. Yet along with the already slim chances of upward social mobility, the state-orchestrated competitive benefit system stifles their initiative. The same applies to care activities, which may well reward those performing them with a sense of fulfilment, but, again, rarely brings them closer to a position of economic 'normality'.

Thirdly, this tendency of wage labour to hide unpaid forms of work, especially care work, can only be remedied once that work is publicly exposed and the devalued workers or integrated outcasts who perform it are appreciated both symbolically and in real terms. Members of the underclasses could achieve a potentially politicizing self-confidence from such a 'proof of performance', based not just on paid (wage) labour but on a much wider range of work activities, that is, on the recognition of socially valuable work in the broadest sense. Such a self-confidence would, fourthly, find the support of a critical social theory that makes the formation of a precariat and an underclass in the zone of exclusion its central object of study. Theories of capitalist *Landnahme*, which essentially rest on the assumption that the capitalist dynamic relies on the constant internalization of an external (non-capitalist) 'Other' (Dörre, 2015; Luxemburg, 2015 [1913]: 256–257; Harvey, 2018), may prove fruitful in this endeavour. In this context, one promising approach, as proposed by Silvia Federici (2004), may be to analyze two distinct modes of production, one of which is being increasingly subordinated to the other. The dominant capitalist mode of production, in which human labour power is used for the profit-oriented production of goods and services, is inextricably bound up with a mode of production that serves the (re)creation of labour power. Even in Germany, the dynamism of the export sector relies on a particularly pronounced form of collective devaluation of both paid and unpaid care work (Aulenbacher et al, 2014; Dörre et al, 2014).

From the perspective of a theory of continuous *Landnahmen*, the new underclasses constitute a politically generated but non-commodified (or at least not fully commodified) 'Other', which at the same time turns out to be instrumental in securing domination in capitalist societies. From this perspective, the new underclasses are no longer to be construed as a 'Lazarus layer', but as a social force that is doubtlessly capable of self-organizing and forging coalitions with working and middle classes. As Göran Therborn (2012) at least hints at in his remarkable call for a 'return of class', such a perspective may become significant beyond the capitalist centres: in the rich countries of the Global North, Therborn argues, a comprehensive process of deindustrialization has led to a decline in the labour force, its power resources and organizations. Yet the growing working classes in the emerging countries have the very real prospect of climbing up the social ladder and becoming part of the expanding middle classes. One consequence of this, according to Therborn, is that the focal point of the conflict dynamic shifts either towards the educated groups, who are nevertheless partially without professional opportunities or prospects, or towards those plebeian masses who dominate the social structure below the working class and its weakened organizations in both quantitative and qualitative terms.

The energy for new and powerful protest may also come from the supposedly apathetic, disorganized underclasses. Spontaneous riots, uprisings or revolts, such as the Black Lives Matter movement, can radiate far into other classes and inspire worldwide protest movements. These non-standardized conflicts, which are waged outside the framework of institutionalized procedures, have also become the common form of collective protest and rebellion in many countries of the Global South. They can, in fact, become an important catalyst for collective empowerment, precisely because they proceed, as in the case of Black Lives Matter, from a social context profoundly shaped by 'race, class, gender, sexuality, disability, and religion' (Davis, 2018: xii). To capture this analytically and to ensure that the excluded and 'semi-citizens' are given a public voice would be the task of precarization research conducted as public sociology.

Note

[1]   I would like to thank Adrian Wilding for the translation and editing of this chapter.

References

Allmendinger, J., Jahn, K., Promberger, M., Schels, B. and Stuth, S. (2018) 'Prekäre Beschäftigung und unsichere Haushaltslagen im Lebensverlauf: Gibt es in Deutschland ein verfestigtes Prekariat?', *WSI-Mitteilungen*, 71(4): 259–69.

Aulenbacher, B. (2009) 'Die soziale Frage neu gestellt: Gesellschaftsanalysen der Prekarisierungs-und Geschlechterforschung', in R. Castel and K. Dörre (eds) *Prekarität, Abstieg, Ausgrenzung: Die soziale Frage am Beginn des 21. Jahrhunderts*, Frankfurt am Main and New York: Campus, pp 65–80.

Aulenbacher, B., Riegraf, B. and Theobald, H. (eds) (2014) *Sorge: Arbeit, Verhältnisse, Regime [Care: Work, Relations, Regimes]*, Baden-Baden: Nomos.

Barbier, J.-C. (2013) 'A conceptual approach of the destandardization of employment in Europe since the 1970s', in M. Koch and M. Fritz (eds) *Non-standard Employment in Europe: Paradigms, Prevalence and Policy Responses*, Basingstoke: Palgrave Macmillan, pp 13–28.

Bartelheimer, P. (2011) 'Unsichere Erwerbsbeteiligung und Prekarität', *WSI-Mitteilungen*, 64(8): 286–393.

Beck, U. (1992) *Risk Society: Towards a New Modernity*, London: Sage.

Bescherer, P. (2013) *Vom Lumpenproletariat zur Unterschicht: Produktivistische Theorie und politische Praxis.* Frankfurt am Main: Campus (Labour Studies, 6).

Bourdieu, P. (1979) *Algeria 1960: The Disenchantment of the World*, Cambridge: Cambridge University Press.

Bourdieu, P. (1984) *Distinction: A Social Critique of the Judgement of Taste*, Cambridge, MA: Harvard University Press.

Bourdieu, P. (1998) *Acts of Resistance: Against the New Myths of our Time*, Cambridge and Oxford: Polity.

Bourdieu, P. et al (1999) *The Weight of the World: Social Suffering in Contemporary Society*, California: Stanford University Press.

Brinkmann, U., Dörre, K., Röbenack, S., Kraemer, K. and Speidel, F. (2006) *Prekäre Arbeit: Ursachen, Ausmaß, soziale Folgen und subjektive Verarbeitungsformen unsicherer Beschäftigungsverhältnisse*, Bonn: Friedrich-Ebert-Stiftung.

Bude, H. and Willisch, A. (eds) (2008) *Exklusion: Die Debatte über die 'Überflüssigen'*, Frankfurt am Main: Suhrkamp.

Castel, R. (2002) *From Manual Workers to Wage Labourers*, New Brunswick: Transaction.

Castel, R. (2008) 'Die Fallstricke des Exklusionsbegriffs', in H. Bude and A. Willisch (eds) *Exklusion: Die Debatte über die 'Überflüssigen'*, Frankfurt am Main: Suhrkamp, pp 69–87.

Castel, R. (2011) *Die Krise der Arbeit: Neue Unsicherheiten und die Zukunft des Individuums*, Hamburg: Hamburger Edition.

Castel, R. and Dörre, K. (2009) (eds) *Prekarität, Abstieg, Ausgrenzung: Die soziale Frage am Beginn des 21. Jahrhunderts*, Frankfurst am Main and New York: Campus.

Davis, A. (2018) 'Foreword', in P. Khan-Cullors and A. Bandele, *When They Call You a Terrorist: A Black Lives Matter Memoir*, Edinburgh: Canongate, pp xi–xiv.

Dörre, K. (2005) 'Prekarität: eine arbeitspolitische Herausforderung', *WSI-Mitteilungen*, 58(5): 250–8.

Dörre, K. (2009) 'Prekarität im Finanzmarkt-Kapitalismus', in R. Castel and K. Dörre (eds) *Prekarität, Abstieg, Ausgrenzung: Die soziale Frage am Beginn des 21. Jahrhunderts*, Frankfurt am Main and New York: Campus, pp 35–64.

Dörre, K. (2015) 'The new Landnahme: dynamics and limits of financial market capitalism', in K. Dörre, H. Rosa and S. Lessenich (eds), *Sociology, Capitalism, Critique*, London and New York: Verso, pp 11–66.

Dörre, K., Happ, A. and Matuschek, I. (eds) (2013) *Das Gesellschaftsbild der LohnarbeiterInnen: Soziologische Untersuchungen in ost- und westdeutschen Industriegebieten*, Hamburg: VSA.

Dörre, K., Ehrlich, M. and Haubner, T. (2014) 'Landnahmen im Feld der Sorgearbeit', in B. Aulenbacher, B. Riegraf and H. Theobald (eds), *Sorge: Arbeit, Verhältnisse, Regime [Care: Work, Relations, Regimes]*, Baden-Baden: Nomos, pp 107–24.

Dörre, K., Bose, S., Lütten, J. and Köster, J. (2018) 'Arbeiterbewegung von rechts? Motive und Grenzen einer imaginären Revolte', *Berliner Journal für Soziologie*, 28(1), 55–89.

Ehrenberg, A. (2011) *Das Unbehagen in der Gesellschaft*, Berlin: Suhrkamp.

Engels, F. (1975 [1845]) 'The condition of the working class in England', in *Marx and Engels Collected Works (MECW)*, Volume 4, New York: International Publishers.

Federici, S. (2004) *Caliban and The Witch: Women, The Body, and Primitive Accumulation*, New York: Autonomedia.

Goffman, A. (2014) *On the Run: Fugitive Life in an American City*, New York: Picador.

Harvey, D. (2018) *A Companion to Marx's Capital. The Complete Edition*, London and New York: Verso.

Hochschild, A.R. (2001) 'Global care chains and emotional surplus value', in W. Hutton and A. Giddens (eds) *On the Edge: Living with Global Capitalism*, London: Vintage and Jonathan Cape, pp 130–46.

IAB (2014) *Zuwanderungsmonitor Bulgarien und Rumänien. Jahresrückblick 2014. Arbeitnehmerfreizügigkeit bewirkt starkes Beschäftigungswachstum*, Nürnberg: Institut für Arbeitsmarkt- und Berufsforschung der Bundesagentur für Arbeit.

Keller, B. and Seifert, H. (eds) (2007) *Atypische Beschäftigung: Flexibilisierung und soziale Risiken*, Berlin: Edition Sigma.

Kraemer, K. (2009) 'Prekarisierung – jenseits von Stand und Klasse?', in R. Castel and K. Dörre (eds) *Prekarität, Abstieg, Ausgrenzung: Die soziale Frage am Beginn des 21. Jahrhunderts*, Frankfurt am Main and New York: Campus, pp 241–52.

Krause, A. and Köhler, C. (2012) *Arbeit als Ware: Zur Theorie flexibler Arbeitsmärkte*, Bielefeld: Transcript (Gesellschaft der Unterschiede, 6).

Kronauer, M. (2002) *Exklusion: Die Gefährdung des Sozialen im hoch entwickelten Kapitalismus*, Frankfurt am Main and New York: Campus.

Luhmann, N. (ed) (1995a) *Soziologische Aufklärung 6: Die Soziologie und der Mensch*, Opladen: Westdeutscher Verlag.

Luhmann, N. (1995b) 'Inklusion und exklusion', in Niklas Luhmann (ed) *Soziologische Aufklärung 6: Die Soziologie und der Mensch*, Opladen: Westdeutscher Verlag, pp 247–64.

Luxemburg, R. (2015 [1913]) 'The accumulation of capital', in *The Complete Works of Rosa Luxemburg: Volume II, Economic Writings 2*, London and New York: Verso, pp 7–344.

Mann, M. (2013) 'The end may be nigh, but for whom?', in I. Wallerstein, R. Collins, M. Mann, G. Derluguian and C. Calhoun, *Does Capitalism have a Future?*, Oxford: Oxford University Press, pp 71–98.

Marx, K. (1976 [1867]): *Capital: A Critique of Political Economy*, Volume I, New York: Penguin.

Marx, K. and Engels, F. (1976 [1848]): 'Manifesto of the Communist Party', in *Marx and Engels Collected Works (MECW)*, Volume 6, New York: International Publishers.

Milanovic, B. (2011) *The Haves and the Have-Nots: A Brief and Idiosyncratic History of Global Inequality*, New York: Basic Books.

Milanovic, B. (2016) *Global Inequality: A New Approach for the Age of Globalization*, Cambridge, MA: Harvard University Press.

Nassehi, A. (2008) 'Exklusion als soziologischer oder sozialpolitischer Begriff?', in H. Bude and A. Willisch (eds) *Exklusion: Die Debatte über die "Überflüssigen"*, Frankfurt am Main: Suhrkamp, pp 121–31.

Pelizzari, A. (2009) *Dynamiken der Prekarisierung: Atypische Erwerbsverhältnisse und milieuspezifische Unsicherheitsbewältigung*, Konstanz: UVK.

Reusch, J. et al (2019) 'Basisdaten zu Arbeitsbedingungen und Arbeitsverhältnissen', in L. Schröder and H.-J. Urban (eds) *Gute Arbeit. Digitale Arbeitswelt – Trends und Anforderungen*, Köln: Bundverlag, pp 281 ff.

Sander, N. (2012) *Das akademische Prekariat: Leben zwischen Frist und Plan*, Konstanz: UVK.

Schultheis, F. and Herold, S. (2010) 'Précarité und Prekarität. Zur Thematisierung der sozialen Frage des 21. Jahrhunderts im deutsch-französischen Vergleich', in M. Busch, J. Jeskow and R. Stutz (eds) *Zwischen Prekarisierung und Protest: Die Lebenslagen und Generationsbilder von Jugendlichen in Ost und West*, Bielefeld: Transcript, pp 243–74.

Schultheis, F. and Schulz, K. (eds) (2005) *Gesellschaft mit begrenzter Haftung: Zumutungen und Leiden im deutschen Alltag*, Konstanz: UVK.

Standing, G. (2011) *The Precariat: The New Dangerous Class*, London and New York: Bloomsbury Academic.

Standing, G. (2014) *A Precariat Charter: From Denizens to Citizens*, London: Bloomsbury Academic.

Therborn, G. (2012) 'Class in the 21st century', *New Left Review*, 78: 5–29.

Thompson, E.P. (1991) *The Making of the English Working Class*, Toronto: Penguin.

Vogel, B. (2009) *Wohlstandskonflikte: Soziale Fragen, die aus der Mitte kommen*, Hamburg: HIS-Verlag.

Weber, M. (1978 [1921]) *Economy and Society: An Outline of Interpretive Sociology*, Berkeley: UCLA Press.

6

Class, Classification and Conjunctures: The Use of 'Precarity' in Social Research

Charles Umney

Introduction

Sociological research frequently involves classification.[1] Often, the contribution of a research article will be a novel way of sorting individuals or organizations into a new classificatory system; or else offering a new piece of terminology for describing a hitherto 'unidentified' section of the population. Classification systems can be used to list different kinds of actor or behaviour, as well as more intangible things, as in the classification of workers' 'power resources' (Joyce et al, 2020). To what end do we classify?

Classification in some form is a vital building block of social research. However, social analysis suffers when classification is conceived as an end in itself. It can become an exercise in arguing over which specific bits of vocabulary best describe social reality, and can present any revisions or additions to this vocabulary as understanding. But even the best conceived sociological category faces some immediate problems: the danger of understating the difference between cases assigned to the same category, and overstating the differences between cases inside and outside the category. And these immediate problems are contained within an overarching one: an over-emphasis on classification can lead to a misleadingly 'clean' analysis that jeopardizes our ability to understand social change, which is often tangled and unpredictable.

The concept of 'precarity' as applied in the sociology of work is a case in point. Some of the characteristics associated with precarity – including things as broad as employment-related 'unpredictability' – are too diffuse and widespread to constitute a category that individuals can be placed into or removed from (Choonara, 2020). Hence, attempts to group together 'precarious' workers into a distinct class (such as Standing's [2014] 'precariat' concept) end up amalgamating too many different actors to be coherent (Manolchev et al, 2018). Conversely, these kinds of groupings also elide the extent to which employment-related 'unpredictability' and insecurity are applicable much more broadly across labour markets (Alberti et al, 2018; Umney, 2018)

These practical difficulties reflect a deeper problem of research method. Classification systems provide a snapshot of social reality at a given moment. But social reality is subject to constant change pressures. This means that even the neatest classification systems are apt to be buffeted and disorganized by underlying processes and conflicts that change the wider context. Therefore, unless used with great care, classification risks becoming a 'static' attempt to freeze a particular image of society in place, to the detriment of a more 'dynamic' understanding of the factors driving societies to change (see Allen, 1975).

In this chapter, I will use these ideas to appraise 'precarity' as a concept. I will advocate a focus on *class relations* as a fundamental source of dynamism in capitalist societies, arguing that this focus encourages a healthy scepticism about the utility of classification as a methodological strategy. Class, of course, is itself frequently an object of classification. Researchers have often debated the most appropriate terminological apparatus for describing class systems in societies like the UK. Sometimes they explicitly build precarity (or the related term 'precariat') into these systems (Savage, 2015). But looking at class relations prompts a different methodological approach, which emphasizes the *conjuncture* – and with it the themes of contingency and unpredictability – rather than classification frameworks that purport to generate a stable conceptual toolbox.

Ultimately, the problems facing the concept of precarity are also the problems facing any attempt to develop classificatory systems. The word precarity seeks to define and label a particular state, but in its application the concept can become stretched. Often it has to be so in order not to exclude important actors and experiences that don't meet a strict definition of the term but where the same underlying dynamics are clearly also relevant. Not only this, it also obscures the underpinning processes and relationships that act on people and groups, which drive changes in situations but which cannot be encapsulated by classificatory labels. If we seek to try and define who within a population is and isn't 'in precarity', we miss the way situations – or conjunctures – are shaped by dynamics that transcend any classification imposed by the analyst. In short, we need less focus on 'static' (Allen, 1975) classification systems, which invoke notions of precarity to identify particular class groups, and more attention to class relations and how they drive change in society.

Precarity, classification and conjunctures

An emphasis on classification for classification's sake is encouraged by the way academia functions. To be published in a prestigious journal, a paper must have a defined 'contribution'. This contribution is supposed to be some kind of succinct conclusion or insight that is intended to act as a discrete steppingstone on the path to incrementally increasing knowledge. A paper is unlikely to be accepted if its contribution cannot be neatly defined in a paragraph. Moreover, for a contribution to be convincing, it is also necessary to 'intervene in debates', meaning positioning the work as an incremental improvement of a specific lexicon or set of concepts. Thus, the emphasis on concisely definable contributions as the currency of published academic research leads to a proliferation of new classifications and concepts presenting an expanded and increasingly complex vocabulary for describing social reality. But in doing so, the research risks losing sight of the unpredictability and changeability that characterizes many social situations. Concepts are neatly defined and our understanding of them is expanded in discrete instalments, imparting an illusory sense of expanding knowledge (and increasing 'nuance' in the pejorative sense excoriated by Healy [2017]). This may also involve the development of conceptual frameworks, which mesh together categories into a generally applicable system for generating predictions and explanations.

This approach contrasts with a more Marxian focus on the conjuncture, which is less amenable to producing neatly packaged contributions. Sometimes the word 'conjuncture' can be used quite vaguely, as a rough synonym for 'situation' or 'context'. However, it can also be used more specifically to imply a particular methodological approach to social analysis. It suggests an approach where empirical situations are analyzed as the (often unstable) products of the confluence of underpinning dynamics. These dynamics have their own causal effects and can be described in the abstract, but the actual causal mechanisms that can be identified in a given empirical situation are not reducible to them. Rather, they are shaped by the unique ways in which different underlying dynamics intersect. Different combinations of factors produce different types of causal relationships when they rub together in different conjunctures. In this chapter, I will argue that conjunctures can be viewed from an *aleatory* perspective (Read, 2002): while 'general tendencies' (such as sharpening class divisions and capitalist accumulation) are important in understanding how and why conjunctures are unstable and prone to change, the way this plays out in the empirical world is highly unpredictable, and the causal mechanisms at work in an empirical situation are often some degrees removed from these tendencies. This point is examined further in the next section.

Because empirical situations are the products of the intersection of different underlying dynamics in different contexts, they are inherently unstable.

This instability cannot be fully understood by classification systems and conceptual frameworks that capture a snapshot of reality, however pristine (Allen, 1975). By contrast, the approach to research that I am advancing here involves, firstly, unpicking what underpinning factors have tangled together to produce a given situation; secondly, identifying what kind of causal dynamics are being generated as these factors tangle together; and thirdly, considering how people might intervene to (re)shape these dynamics. This approach entails a view of social reality that is usually messier than can be encapsulated in a concise 'contribution'.

These considerations will be developed further in the next section, but for now, why is this methodological reflection relevant to precarity? Because the application of this concept risks falling foul of the problems facing classification generally. The word precarity is now very widespread, and used to define a particular state of heightened insecurity and unpredictability (often in loose relation to employment). If it defines a state, then we must be able to determine who falls into it and who doesn't. Often, however, this is not possible because its definition is so diffuse. Hence, when the term is adopted and operationalized, we find that, in practice, it is often used to describe a *situation* rather than a defined set of actors. This is evident from a brief look at the use of 'precarity' in the sociology of cultural and social service work. These two examples are chosen because later I will make reference to my own research (with collaborators) in these specific areas.

Baines et al's (2014) study of work in non-profit social service organizations illustrates this point. Discarding the notion of the 'precariat' as a categorization, Baines et al offer a much more diffuse concept of 'precarity' to indicate heightened unpredictability and insecurity in many areas of life, particularly employment. This operationalization is, of course, very wide-ranging, and potentially could lead us to argue that in some circumstances (such as during a global pandemic) the near entirety of human society is in a state of precarity. As such, in their study, Baines et al wisely choose not to delineate who is in precarity and who isn't. But what, then, is the point of the term? In their argument, it appears that what is precarious is the *situation* they are describing. They examine how funding arrangements have changed for the organizations they study, concluding that a shift towards intensified competition in funding awards and greater reliance on project-type organization has made the context in which they operate more unpredictable. This, in turn, has increased the perception of insecurity for all workers involved in the situation, including those on permanent contracts. 'Precarity' is thus used to describe a pervading insecurity across the wider ecosystem of social service organizations in the wake of marketizing reforms.

Likewise, in Samaluk's (2017) study of Slovenian social services, precarity once again describes a situation rather than a category. The project ecosystem she examines was rendered unpredictable by shifts towards austerity pressures and a 'workfare' agenda pushed from the European level, and this had wide-ranging consequences for the relationships between workers and employers in the sector. The aim, again, is not to define a distinct category of precarity that includes some and excludes others but to illustrate a deterioration in the stability of the system under discussion. This deteriorating stability is an objective characteristic of the conjuncture in question, even if individuals involved experience this in very different ways. Samaluk is a collaborator and I will discuss one of our joint research projects in due course. At this point, suffice to say that these studies apply the concept of precarity to describe a wider situation rather than a state that individuals can be sorted into or not (though clearly some experience the negative effects of this situation more deeply than others for a vast array of reasons). This is not always the explicit analytical strategy, but it becomes necessary in practice in order to fit the term with reality.

A similar point pertains to research on cultural work. Here, 'precarity' is defined equally broadly. For instance, in Murray and Gollmitzer's (2012) study of the creative and cultural sectors, it means 'existence without security'. It is often assumed that precarity is endemic in arts and cultural work. For instance, Chafe and Kaida (2020) take the widespread existence of precarity among musicians as a starting point, and proceed to explore how individuals cope with it. Some discussion thus refers to the 'artistic precariat' (Bain and McLean, 2013). But the danger here is of overstating the ubiquity of precarity and neglecting variegation among the 'precarious'. For Banks (2019), the 'precarity' of artistic work is conditioned by wider patterns of insecurity: some feel it much more intensely than others (see also Umney and Kretsos, 2015).

Murray and Gollmitzer (2012) use the metaphor of precarity as a 'trap' out of which arts and cultural workers must climb. Ostensibly, then, precarity here is presented as a category you can enter or leave. But once again, in its operationalization, precarity emerges as more of a situation. In their paper, there is (quite justifiably) little focus placed on defining how we can decide who is and isn't in the 'precarity trap', and more emphasis on showing how the extent and menace of this trap is shaped by the ongoing restructuring of creative industries. Note that in some cases, precarity as a wider aspect of the situation facing cultural workers is presented on a very broad scale indeed, gesturing towards a planetary flux as neoliberal insecurity pervades and Fordist labour politics break down (De Peuter, 2011).

From these brief comments we could consider some propositions. The concept of precarity has limited value as a means of classification. It is too difficult (and of questionable benefit) to formulate a definition of who is and isn't 'in precarity' with any precision. Even if we were to attempt this, we would overlook the extent to which groups outside the category also experience things like insecurity and unpredictability in employment, and the dynamics that cut across these distinctions. Consequently, in practice, authors have got more mileage out of the concept by using it to describe a wider situation. In some cases this is very broad and epochal in scope (for instance, De Peuter, 2011), whereas in other cases it refers to specific shifts in the way particular sectors are structured (Murray and Gollmitzer, 2012; Baines et al, 2014; Samaluk, 2021). This more dynamic way of looking at 'precarity' also resonates with recent contributions that emphasize a focus on 'precarization' as a 'process' (Alberti et al, 2018; Samaluk, 2021). The next step of my argument will be that a view centred on the situation brings us close to the Marxian idea of the conjuncture as the object of analysis. Some conjunctures are more precarious than others and it is useful to consider what factors make them so. But to fully draw this out, we need to focus more on underpinning class relations rather than classificatory systems.

Labour-capital relationships and the conjuncture

Marxist social analysis views *class relationships* as a vital dynamic influencing the structure of capitalist societies. To study class is not to draw up a list of categorizations for ordering populations at a given point in time. Rather, it is to study the ongoing interaction between those people who are forced to sell their labour power in order to survive, and those that profit from the value produced by that labour power. We do not sort individuals as 'labour' and 'capital' (to some extent we could, but it would be rather blunt and unhelpful). These words describe processes that people enter into. They are things people do rather than things people are. And in acting as labour or in acting as capitalists, individuals create lasting relationships with others. These ongoing relationships have their own conflict-laden dynamics, which lead to the constant possibility of change. From this perspective, more interesting than the question –

"what group can this individual be classified as part of?"

is –

"what are the ongoing processes and relationships that shape how this person's life, and the world around them, develops?"

The labour-capital relationship is dialectical. This means that the relationship between labour and capital is mutually constituting but also antagonistic. The process of investing capital, extracting profit, and then reinvesting it, creates a group of people who are required to sell their labour power in order to survive. Conversely, without the latter, capital cannot exist. However, despite being mutually constituting, the interests of the people involved in these processes on both sides are also fundamentally conflictual because profits come at the expense of those who act as labour. So, there is an ongoing 'contradiction', which in a capitalist society, is never actually resolved. It is only mitigated or contained in specific ways for limited time periods. This constant bubbling tension renders society unstable and prone to change. The balances these relationships assume at a given moment contribute to different types of causal dynamics that are observed in the empirical world. Examining these relationships, and the balances they find, helps us comprehend the forces that shape and destabilize societies. They don't provide all the answers but they are likely to be important in many cases.

This approach prompts a methodological focus on the conjuncture. In its Althusserian definition, this means the particular 'crystallized' configuration of forces that shape a particular reality at a given time and place (Hardy, 2013). Clearly, this is not only about the labour–capital relationship. Various political, economic, social and ideological factors also collide and rub against each other to produce each conjuncture as unique. But the dialectical labour–capital relationship is a particularly important factor. Because it is based on both mutual dependence and antagonism it can never be fully 'resolved', and any given balance between labour and capital is transient (Gallas, 2017). So, this means that any conjuncture is likely to be destabilized as the imperatives of this relationship percolate.

In his *Social Analysis* (1975), Allen argues that this kind of dialectical perspective needs to avoid various established tactics of social research, which he argues are overly 'static'. For instance, he dismisses the notion of the conceptual framework. A conceptual framework is a stable 'model' that sets out a series of concepts and specifies the relationship between them. It can ostensibly be applied to help analyze, explain and make predictions about social reality. The purpose of such a framework is to be generalizable. It is supposed to act as a multi-use tool for understanding situations. If a conceptual framework only applies to one situation, then there's no point in it; it is like a screwdriver that only connects with one individual screw. Hence, conceptual frameworks are an important part of the toolbox of the 'problem-solving sociologist'. The latter was a figure criticized by Allen: a social researcher who, equipped with conceptual frameworks, can arrive at the scene of some kind of sociological emergency to effectively and authoritatively prescribe solutions for social problems encountered. Arguably, proliferating notions of 'impact' increasingly require all social researchers to present themselves thus.

The problem, of course, is that conceptual frameworks depend on a coherent and stable set of categories, with regular causal mechanisms existing between them that can be isolated and applied to many situations. But a focus on class relationships and conjunctures suggests this is not possible. The classification systems used to build these conceptual frameworks are often transient, meaning there are limits on their reliability as tools. This kind of framework can provide a snapshot of a given conjuncture (and insofar as it does this, it can be useful), but we should be sceptical about the possibility of generalization and prediction.

I want to emphasize themes of unpredictability and contingency in social analysis, even if this is unhelpful from the perspective of our 'pathways to impact'. In this sense, I will take some ideas from 'aleatory materialism'. This is the view that the combination of forces in a particular conjuncture collide in ways that are fundamentally unpredictable. A particular combination of forces can produce logics and causal principles that wouldn't pertain under different conditions. Conjunctures are therefore the product of 'chance encounters'. Our inquiry into the social world is like trying to capture a 'moving train', where it is impossible to discern the destination (Suchting, 2004): we can pick apart certain events and forces, but not all, and we can't predict what lies ahead on this basis (Hardy, 2013; Navarro, 2015).

This approach differs somewhat from more prevalent Marxist approaches to social analysis that make abstract tendencies, and their manifestation in the concrete, the focus of the analysis. For example, in classical Marxism, the developing labour-capital relationship generates an emerging working class. Various things may get in the way of this, but over time, there will be a general gravitation towards this outcome. This is one of the most important abstract tendencies. An aleatory perspective, however, argues that there is a consequent danger in presenting class as a kind of collectivized 'great man of history' with particular classes emerging as coherent categories to reshape society (Read, 2002) (arguably Standing's 'precariat' is a non-Marxist attempt to do the same). Instead, class formation should be seen as much more fragmented and unpredictable, prone to travel in many different directions.

Clearly, it is not possible nor desirable to jettison an understanding of these abstract tendencies, since they are likely needed to explain how and why conjunctures change. But in my account, the imperatives derived from these abstract tendencies (towards intensified class exploitation, expanded capitalist accumulation and so on) are like an irregular pulsation that reverberates across empirical conjunctures, shaking them around. These pulsations can lead to disorganization or shifts in direction, but the empirical ways in which they play out are 'aleatory' in that their effects are mediated by myriad other factors with their own causal mechanisms, and hence difficult to anticipate.

Where does this leave us with the concept of precarity? Precarity has limited utility as a means of describing specific aspects of a given conjuncture. It doesn't help us to distinguish specific components of that conjuncture from one another. We can't reliably identify individuals or groups who are defined by their state of precarity. Or rather, this can be done, but in practice it tends not to help much. We might, for instance, say that those on temporary contracts are in precarity. However, as noted in relation to the examples mentioned earlier, this may understate the 'insecurity and unpredictability' experienced by those with different contract types, as well as the often sizeable variation in the level of insecurity experienced by temporary workers themselves. This problem, it should be stressed, is not necessarily a specific one of precarity as a classification, but an inherent problem of treating classification as an end in itself.

As I have already suggested, it is conceivable that 'precarious' may be evocative as an adjective used in describing conjunctures themselves. Doing so risks being rather glib: sweeping declarations that the world and its population have entered a new era defined by 'precarity' have little benefit beyond the rhetorical. But applied in a more concrete way, thinking about precarity may help draw attention to specific situations where things are deteriorating into disorganization and flux.

This is where labour–capital relationships come into play. Evidently, from an 'aleatory' perspective, we should be careful about using the labour–capital relationship to pinpoint 'laws' (or tendencies) that play out similarly across different conjunctures. Rather, we need to be more circumspect: suffice to say, the labour–capital relationship, and the processes and imperatives it implies, is an important factor in shaping conjunctures in capitalist societies. The need to intensify and expand profit extraction and reinvestment, and the tendency of people who act as labour to combine in unforeseen ways to advance their own interests, thus presenting an obstacle to this cycle, are perpetual destabilizing forces. This ongoing dynamic interacts with other factors, which have their own trajectories, such as the way political systems are structured or the way ideological forces are configured, to produce new conjunctures with their own logics. The changes they precipitate reverberate in different and often unpredictable empirical ways. Hence, a useful role for social research is to try and unpick which factors, or combinations of factors, make certain conjunctures precarious, and how people can intervene to shape them.

Precarious conjunctures

In what remains, I will reflect on a couple of recent research projects that engaged with the concept of precarity. Both are taken from a wider research programme conducted with various colleagues looking at 'marketization' and its effects. Marketization, in this context, refers to situations where state and business agency seeks to intensify price competition as a means of organizing economic activity. The examples are drawn from social services and cultural work. The focus in these research projects was mainly on how marketization shaped working life for people in these sectors. In both cases, the conjunctures studied were characterized primarily by project-based work; in other words, work which is organized in terms of discrete and time-limited 'projects' associated with a particular task, for which workers and organizations typically have to compete (for instance, by submitting a bid to a public authority to deliver a specific public service contract, or by pitching to create a specific service for a corporate actor). On the face of things, project-based work might be seen as inherently precarious because, by its definition, it is short-term and unpredictable. But on closer inspection it becomes clear that notions like precarity are superficial and misleading when severed from a wider conjunctural focus.

The first example is a study of non-profit welfare-to-work services in France and Slovenia (Schulte et al, 2018; Greer et al, 2019). The study examined the use of European Social Fund (ESF) monies, and how they were distributed and used by small organizations providing frontline services. Our research showed how ESF funding conditionality had tightened, imposing new requirements on recipients. In particular, there was pressure to shift towards an 'activation' agenda in service delivery (in other words, a policy change whereby unemployed recipients of welfare payments are pushed more strongly into work). National states were acting as a kind of intermediary, interpreting and imposing these requirements on local authorities and providers, as they connected them with funds (Samaluk, 2017).

The 'headline' finding of the research was that, despite frontline workers in both French and Slovenian systems being dependent on temporary project funding (itself tied to changing requirements evolving at European Union [EU] level), French ones were significantly less 'precarious'. They had much greater certitude that the services they were providing would continue to be commissioned in future years. By contrast, in Slovenia, the turnover of projects was rapid and erratic, and the deterioration of the project landscape had also driven the disorganization of the profession: the availability of training and of secure work for non-profit social service workers had collapsed in both public and private social work.

A number of factors were present in both cases but combined in different ways and with different consequences. Activation is a transnational policy trend that reflects an increasingly disciplinarian turn by capitalist states as they seek to remould working populations to suit the requirements of highly mobile international capital (Umney et al, 2018). Hence the urgency of profit extraction and labour discipline (put most abstractly, the imperatives of the labour-capital relationship at a particular point in history) reshaping the macro-level political economic context. But then the diffusion of the activation agenda collided with political factors, specifically the dynamics of European integration and a growing emphasis on budget restraint among EU member states. Concurrently, across Europe, transnational enterprises were increasingly seeking to profit from involvement in welfare-to-work provision. These dynamics intersected differently, leading to different effects.

In Slovenia, exacerbated by austerity and the pressures of accession, the state had imposed the requirements of 'activation' with comparably little protest. This involved radically reconfiguring the requirements imposed on local organizations looking to access funding to deliver services. Long-established organizations suddenly found themselves having to defend and pitch their work in new ways, and against a chaotic array of for-profit competitors. Professional trajectories deteriorated and administrative burdens and 'target culture' increased. To find organizations that could meet the new requirements, local state actors had to change the criteria they were using, abandoning existing networks and casting around reaching for relevant providers, upon who few could be relied. Thus, state capacity to organize social service projects had declined due to the confluence of austerity, accession and funding conditionality. It was in this context that the situation facing social service project workers had become precarious (see Samaluk, 2017; Greer et al, 2019).

By contrast, in France, this had not happened. Local authorities had selectively integrated elements of the activation agenda, but this was manifested in incremental changes to existing agreements with long-established local providers. In terms of the length of contract awards for projects, there was little difference with Slovenia, but in France the local state tended to prioritize established local organizations, where necessary altering the brief they were given, but giving them a voice in the co-evolution of services. The organizations could therefore be relatively assured that their contracts would be renewed, albeit with possible changes. Moreover, because of this, the frontline participants in this ecosystem had managed to maintain and defend a more holistic vision of social service work that created a hostile environment for for-profit multinationals seeking to integrate themselves into these service networks (Schulte et al, 2018).

Hence, while standards of job security and quality had collapsed in Slovenia, they remained relatively stable in France. In the former case, there was a churn of organizations as the state sought to adapt to ESF strictures and the austerity context. Work was increasingly targetized, bureaucratized and deprofessionalized, and paths to secure jobs in social care dried up. In France, workers retained high degrees of professional autonomy and job security, and professional pathways remained stable. The capacity of local French state actors to organize services had held up much better, leading to radically different outcomes.

We need to ask what the analytical value of 'precarity' is in this context. To apply it to project work in general would be blunt and misleading. To say it applied to Slovenian project workers but not French ones would be somewhat more accurate, but would simply offer us a description. It would tell us nothing about the underpinning dynamics that influence both situations: class discipline; austerity; the need to extract profits; and the desire of frontline workers to shape the terms of service delivery. Both conjunctures were shaped by these forces, which are inexplicable without some notion of an ongoing dialectical labour-capital relationship, but they collided in different ways with different outcomes, owing to a complex mesh of factors that were only decipherable from the ground. It is more interesting and useful to untangle this interaction of factors than it is to parse who is and isn't in a state of precarity.

The next example is a study of cultural work in Hull during City of Culture 2017 (Umney and Symon, 2020). As noted, arts and cultural workers are often reflexively seen as almost synonymous with precarity. But the research among cultural workers in Hull, however, once again revealed the limits of this kind of label.

The experience of Hull's cultural workers during the city's tenure as City of Culture is the product of a number of colliding factors. There is the macro-level context of austerity, which has seen fierce downward pressure on the funding of arts ecosystems. There is also the wider process of post-industrial restructuring, where cities like Hull are required to compete against each other for inward investment in the absence of a coherent national industrial strategy. These factors imply the need for City of Culture to facilitate increasing the attractiveness of Hull as a site for visitors and investment. However, this logic coexisted with an influential discourse of expanded community participation in the arts, which has developed over decades in the UK and which also influenced the situation (Hewison, 2014). Then there is the existing arts and cultural network in Hull, which has developed as a tightly knit community over several years. These factors, and others, collided to produce the distinctive dynamics of Hull in 2017.

In Hull, an infrastructure had to be created very rapidly to absorb the spike in funds entailed in being awarded City of Culture state. The delivery organization created, reflecting the divergent factors identified previously, had to balance various priorities. There was a pot of funds for encouraging participation in the arts at grassroots level among Hull residents, especially those who previously had been little engaged. But there were also major commissions for established national organizations (and some landmark Hull ones, but relatively few) to deal with the pressure of creating a dense programme of events that could last a year and create a favourable impression on a national level. Between these objectives, research suggested that a more mid-range goal that was traditionally fulfilled by the Council had been relatively less prioritized: capacity-building support for 'jobbing' artists in areas of strategic weakness for the city. Austerity, in fact, meant the Council was, in practice, unable to do this, though it had been ear-marked this function in the planning for the event.

So, the situation had to be understood as reflecting the confluence of different economic, political and ideological factors, which combined in unique and, to some extent, unpredictable ways (certainly, they were unpredictable to me, as the researcher going into the situation, though it cannot be ruled out that others may have more predictive insight). It rapidly becomes apparent that 'precarity' as a concept adds little here, as there was so much variegation and nuance in the ways these factors played out in practice. To refer off-handedly to the 'precarity' of Hull arts workers would erase this complexity.

Hence the research project identified three movements that split the 'artistic precariat' in the city into fragments. First, people who had previously never been professionally involved in the arts and who had never received funding for a creative project (and who, in many cases, did not aspire to an arts career) were given the confidence and opportunity to apply for money to implement one-off projects (University of Hull, 2018). Second, a select group of arts workers who had previously been surviving as project workers were able, due to the exposure from the year, to gain larger and more stable audiences and funding streams to enable them to (in some cases) escape the cycle of short-term project funding altogether. Third, a group in the middle – of professional arts workers who did not secure major commissions during City of Culture – experienced intensified competitive pressure and therefore, in some respects, heightened insecurity. They had more competitors for funding, for venue space and for audiences (owing to the first development). And, new requirements from funders (such as the need to demonstrate a community engagement element to the work they did) imposed additional work, which often went unrewarded.

Referring simply to the precarity of arts workers obscures these dynamics. Hull City of Culture 2017 saw a confluence of different processes and logics that led to unpredictable patterns of fragmentation and differentiation. New patterns of risk and inequality were being generated as existing relationships and processes were rejigged in the wake of City of Culture. We could develop a typology to categorize the results of this fragmentation in as much detail as possible. This may serve a useful descriptive purpose. But the point is, such a typology would be transient, reflecting the aleatory collision of specific dynamics in a specific conjuncture, and thus could not provide a general analytical toolkit. We do not learn much from declaring some of these people to be more precarious than others. Rather, we can see that the *conjuncture* facing arts workers in Hull was precarious, and we should try to understand what made it so, and consider how the situation could best be reshaped. Sorting actors according to relative levels of precarity is not wrong, per se, but what does it add?

Conclusion

This chapter has juxtaposed a Marxian approach to social analysis focused on the conjuncture with more mainstream sociological tools such as classification. It has used this tension to examine the concept of precarity. Often, it appears precarity is being used as a category: it is a state, or a 'trap', that people can be in or out of, or else it is the hallmark of a distinct group like the precariat. However, when it is operationalized, we find it tends to be most evocatively applied to situations. A particular situation may be precarious, but it doesn't make sense to sort the people embroiled in it according to whether they are or not. This, however, is not a critique of the concept of precarity per se, so much as a critique of the broader sociological principle of classification when treated as an end in itself. Classifications tend to understate difference between people to whom a category is applied, and understate similarities between people within and outside the category. The same can be said of precarity. The point is not to jettison classification as a methodological tool, but to put it in its place: as a means of describing and comparing aspects of particular situations without getting at the underlying forces that shape them. And to recognize its fragility.

This idea of precarity describing situations rather than being a means of classification is often only implicit in the literature: it is simply how the concept needs to be applied in practice if it isn't to become incoherent or restrictive. I have sought to draw this aspect out by referring to 'aleatory' Marxist methodological thinking about conjunctures and the labour-capital relationship. Situations should be seen as the somewhat unpredictable and contingent products of unstable confluences of underpinning factors. Untangling these requires us to think – not only, but particularly – about dialectical labour-capital relationships and how they pulsate across empirical situations. These conceptual tools help us to unpick what factors make certain conjunctures more precarious than others.

Not only this, but in unpicking situations in this way, we can prioritize figuring out how human agency can intervene to shape the forces that produce different conjunctures. Classification and conceptual frameworks do not lend themselves to this objective. This is not to say they necessarily preclude it, but mainstream social analysis has tended towards a highly ideological model of 'impact' focused around problem solving, and classificatory systems have accordingly become part of the problem-solving social scientist's toolbox. It is hardly surprising that mainstream academic research should discourage a more dynamic and holistic reading of social reality, but true 'impact' is to disentangle the forces that shape the world more deeply.

Note

[1] Many thanks to the editors of this volume and the anonymous reviews for comments. Thanks also to Ian Greer and Barbara Samaluk for thoughts on drafts of the chapter.

References

Alberti, G., Bessa, I., Hardy, K., Trappmann, V. and Umney, C. (2018) 'In, against and beyond precarity: work in insecure times', *Work, Employment and Society*, 32(3): 447–57.

Allen, V.L. (1975) *Social Analysis: A Marxist Critique and Alternative*, London and New York: Longman.

Bain, A. and McLean, H. (2013) 'The artistic precariat', *Cambridge Journal of Regions, Economy and Society*, 6(1): 93–111.

Baines, D., Cunningham, I., Campey, J. and Shields, J. (2014) 'Not profiting from precarity: the work of nonprofit service delivery and the creation of precasiousness', *Just Labour*, 22:74–93.

Banks, M. (2019) 'Precarity, biography, and event: work and time in the cultural industries', *Sociological Research Online*, 24(4): 541–56.

Chafe, D. and Kaida, L. (2020) 'Harmonic dissonance: coping with employment precarity among professional musicians in St John's, Canada', *Work, Employment and Society*, 34(3): 407–23.

Choonara, J. (2020) 'The precarious concept of precarity', *Review of Radical Political Economics*, 52(3): 427–46.

De Peuter, G. (2011) 'Creative economy and labor precarity: a contested convergence', *Journal of Communication Inquiry*, 35(4): 417–25.

Gallas, A. (2017) 'Revisiting conjunctural marxism: Althusser and Poulantzas on the state', *Rethinking Marxism*, 29(2): 256–80.

Greer, I., Samaluk, B. and Umney, C. (2019) 'Toward a precarious projectariat? Project dynamics in Slovenian and French social services', *Organization Studies*, 40(12): 1873–95.

Hardy, N. (2013) 'Theory from the conjuncture: Althusser's aleatory materialism and Machiavelli's dispositif', *Décalages*, 1(3): 5.

Healy, K. (2017) 'Fuck nuance', *Sociological Theory*, 35(2): 118–27.

Hewison, R. (2014) *Cultural Capital: The Rise and Fall of Creative Britain*, London: Verso.

Joyce, S., Neumann, D., Trappmann, V. and Umney, C. (2020) 'A global struggle: worker protest in the platform economy', *ETUI Research Paper – Policy Brief*, 2. Available from: https://www.etui.org/publications/policy-briefs/european-economic-employment-and-social-policy/a-global-struggle-worker-protest-in-the-platform-economy [Accessed 18 March 2022].

Manolchev, C., Saundry, R. and Lewis, D. (2018) 'Breaking up the "precariat": personalisation, differentiation and deindividuation in precarious work groups', *Economic and Industrial Democracy*, 42(3): 828–51.

Murray, C. and Gollmitzer, M. (2012) 'Escaping the precarity trap: a call for creative labour policy', *International Journal of Cultural Policy*, 18(4): 419–38.

Navarro, F. (2015) 'Celebrating Althusser's legacy', *Crisis & Critique*, 2(2): 46–61.

Read, J. (2002) 'Primitive accumulation: the aleatory foundation of capitalism', *Rethinking Marxism*, 14(2): 24–49.

Samaluk, B. (2017) 'Austerity stabilised through European funds: the impact on Slovenian welfare administration and provision', *Industrial Relations Journal*, 48(1): 56–71.

Samaluk, B. (2021) 'Precarious education-to-work transitions: entering welfare professions under a workfarist regime', *Work, Employment and Society*, 35(1): 137–56.

Savage, M. (2015) *Social Class in the 21st Century*, London: Penguin.

Schulte, L., Greer, I., Umney, C., Symon, G. and Iankova, K. (2018) 'Insertion as an alternative to workfare: active labour-market schemes in the Parisian suburbs', *Journal of European Social Policy*, 28(4): 326–41.

Standing, G. (2014) 'The Precariat: the new dangerous class', *Amalgam*, 6(6–7): 115–19.

Suchting, W. (2004) 'Althusser's late thinking about materialism', *Historical materialism*, 12(1): 3–70.

Umney, C. (2018) *Class Matters: Inequality and Exploitation in 21st Century Britain*, London: Pluto.

Umney, C. and Kretsos, L. (2015) '"That's the experience": passion, work precarity, and life transitions among London jazz musicians', *Work and Occupations*, 42(3), 313–34.

Umney, C. and Symon, G. (2020), 'Creative placemaking and the cultural projectariat: artistic work in the wake of Hull City of Culture 2017', *Capital & Class*, 44(4): 595–615.

Umney, C., Greer, I., Onaran, Ö. and Symon, G. (2018) 'The state and class discipline: European labour market policy after the financial crisis', *Capital & Class*, 42(2): 333–51.

University of Hull (2018) 'Cultural transformations: the impact of Hull UK City of Culture 2017', Culture, Place and Policy Institute, University of Hull.

7

The Problem with Precarity: Precarious Employment and Labour Markets

Joseph Choonara

The rise of precarity

Precarity has suffered terribly from its modishness. Academic use of the term has risen precipitously since the 2000s (Figure 7.1). In this time, it has become not so much evacuated of meaning as subjected to so many meanings, in such diverse fields (Figure 7.2), as to be almost unintelligible. The story of how it entered the English lexicon is a complex, cross-border story, told elsewhere (Choonara, 2020a; Chapter 2, this volume). My concern here is with the responsibility of scholars who use the word, which has been present in Anglophone academic discourse for two decades.

One credible reason to use a term is that it offers clear scientific purchase on a problem. With precarity, this is questionable. Browsing the most cited of 142 academic outputs from 2019 containing the term in their title, we find the following: 'Precarity ... is characterised be [sic] a lack of security and predictability ... which manifests as material and psycho-social deprivation'; 'precarity has come to designate growing existential and structural uncertainties in an era of neoliberal capitalism'; 'precarity as an ontological experience relates to precarious conditions in one or more domains of an individual's life'; 'precarity precedes affect, and induces embodiments, such as anxiety and fear'; 'the "body" is the surface where precarity and its politics are made and unmade'; and 'the notion of precarity evokes an intrinsic sense of uncertainty resulting from coping with cumulative pressures while trying to preserve a sense of independence' (Ivancheva et al, 2019; Joronen and Griffiths, 2019; Lain

Figure 7.1: 'Precarity' in English-language academic outputs (titles or abstracts)

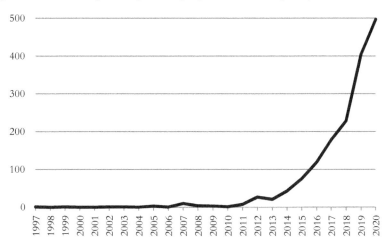

Source: *Web of Science*

et al, 2019; Lancione, 2019; Portacolone et al, 2019; Robinson et al, 2019). This process could easily be extended without any consensus emerging. Sources for the term in just these six works include Guy Standing's (2011) book about contemporary work; Judith Butler's (2016) meditation on the precariousness of life in the wake of 9/11; and Paulo Virno's (2004) *A Grammar of the Multitude*, which is in this case commended for its use of Heidegger's distinction between fear and anguish. This is a choir of discordant voices. Subject matter ranges from home demolitions in occupied Palestine to university working conditions. These topics are certainly connected, but the concept of precarity is being asked to do altogether too much work in joining the dots.

A second credible reason to use the term precarity would be if it had acquired a commonly accepted meaning in society at large. That is not the case. Precarity is used almost exclusively in English *within* academia or adjacent fields, such as the more rarefied corners of art and activism. Terms such as 'precarious employment' *are*, by contrast, widely used and understood. It is on this concept that I will focus in the current chapter.

The rest of this chapter proceeds as follows. First, a parsimonious definition of 'precarious employment' is set out, one which seeks to give a clear meaning to what is often termed 'precarity' in literature on work and employment. Then, data for five member countries of the Organisation for Economic Co-operation and Development (OECD) are set out, showing that precarious employment develops along different trajectories rather than being a straightforward reflex of neoliberalism. Finally, it is argued that

Figure 7.2: Area of publication: English-language academic outputs with 'precarity' in the title or abstract, 2020 (areas with at least 10 outputs)

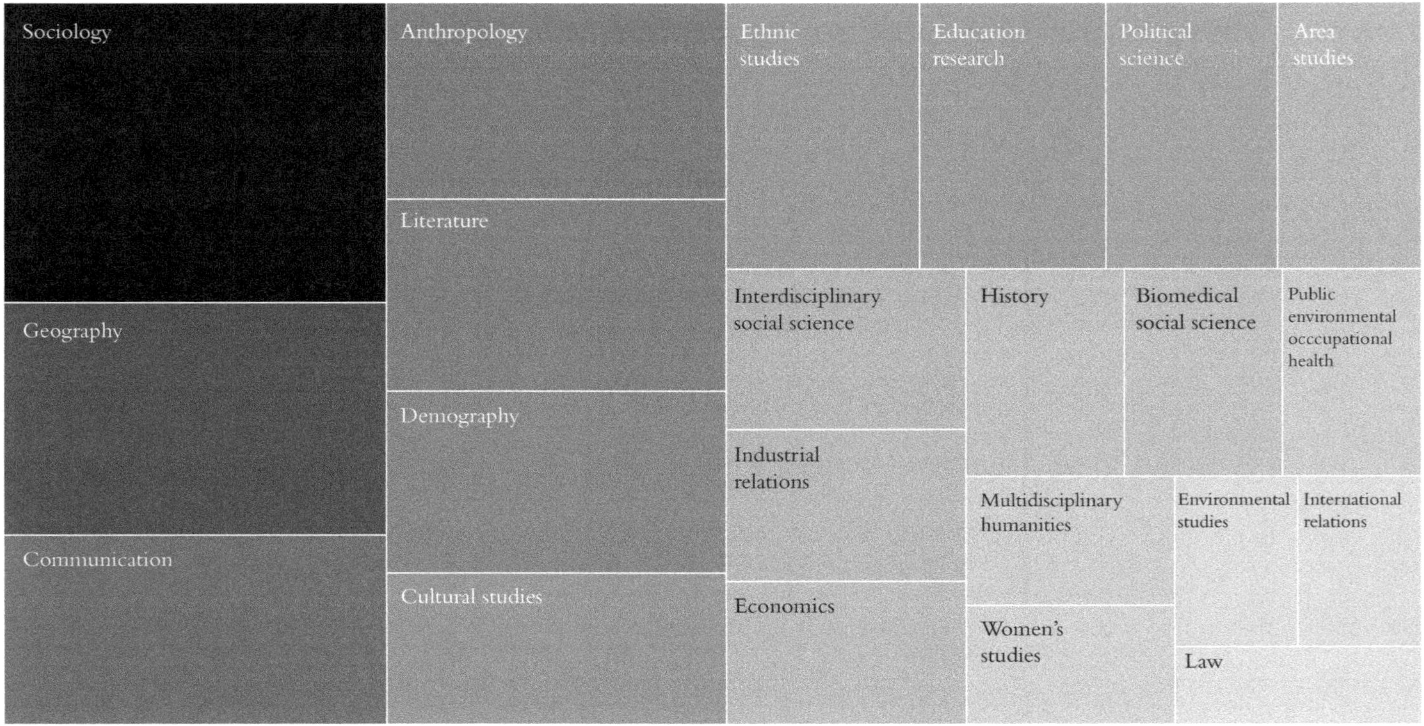

Source: *Web of Science*

explaining these patterns requires reconsideration of the political economy of labour markets, viewed contextually and analyzed at multiple levels of abstraction, drawing on a Marxist approach to the hiring and mobilization of labour-power.

A parsimonious definition

In earlier work, I followed Thomas Prosser (2016) in seeking to develop a 'parsimonious definition' of precarious employment.[1] This takes as its starting point literature presenting precarity as an emergent condition of increasingly contingent employment, developing under neoliberalism. The focus here is on the advanced capitalist economies of the Global North, as, elsewhere, nothing resembling the putative 'standard employment relationship' prevailed historically (Munck, 2013). I distinguish precarious employment from 'job tenure insecurity', the perception of contingency among workers.[2] The latter is explored in existing studies of insecurity that should be considered in parallel with those of precarious employment (Gallie et al, 2017; Choonara, 2020b). Thus defined, precarious employment can be explored quantitatively through two measures. The first traces the growth of temporary work that renders employment easily terminable. This is the approach taken by Prosser's (2016) study of eight European countries. However, as he suggests, one limitation of this approach is that economies such as the US and UK, viewed as having the most liberal employment relations, show little sign of an increase in temporary work, presumably because non-temporary employment is already quite easily terminable. Therefore, I add a second measure: job tenure – the time workers have spent in their current job.

Elsewhere I have measured both indicators for the UK, demonstrating the limits to precarious employment (Choonara, 2019). Between the early 1980s and 2015 the extent of work deemed temporary by those undertaking it had risen by, at most, 4 per cent of those employed; the average worker could, in 2015, expect their job to last about 16 years, a similar period to in 1975. Mean male tenure fell slightly from the 1970s, mainly due to one-off reorganization of jobs formerly characterized by extremely long tenure in areas such as banking. Mean female tenure rose, partly due to changes in maternity legislation. This was accompanied by a rise in the tenure of part-time work – by 2015 there was a gap of less than six months in the mean tenure of women in part-time and full-time work.

Here I examine five major OECD economies (the US, the UK, Germany, France and Italy), exploring the extent of temporary work, the distribution of tenure and the level of employment protections over recent decades.

Precarious employment in selected OECD countries

Figure 7.3 shows the temporary employment share for the five economies; Figure 7.4, job tenure bands; and Figure 7.5, employment protection indicators.[3]

The US and UK are both characterized by low but stable levels of employment protection and, particularly in the case of the UK, a tradition of 'voluntarism' based on an adversarial relation between unions and employers (Rubery and Grimshaw, 2003: 149–50, 155–6). Given the relative decline of union strength, one might expect to see the prerogatives of business find their fullest expression here. The stability of employment in the UK is therefore noteworthy. There is no long-term increase in temporary work, although it tends to be used more extensively in the wake of recessions. These recovery periods also see a rise in short-tenure jobs. The heavily interpolated data from the US shows low levels of temporary work, fluctuating within narrow margins, along with a modest decline in short-tenure employment. In these archetypical neoliberal contexts, there is little evidence of a burgeoning of precarious employment. Job tenure data remains shaped by voluntary quits; in moments of economic distress, tenure increases, declining in recoveries as people are drawn into work and people with existing jobs feel more confident about seeking new roles (Choonara, 2019: 136–43).

This does not imply an absence of precarious employment. A valuable literature documents the conditions of precarious workers, capturing their experiences in a way that aggregate quantitative analysis cannot (Choonara, 2019: 64–71). Younger people in countries such as the UK are disproportionately subject to precarious employment, although, again, the degree to which this is the case has been relatively stable in recent decades (Choonara, 2019: 89–93, 156–7). However, these conditions have not *generalized* across the labour force. This does not mean that all is well in the world of work. 'Stability' here can also mean 'stagnation'. People clinging to their existing jobs does not demonstrate contentment, particularly if stagnation coincides with periods such as that following the 2008–9 crisis, in which employee discontent has grown. This is reflected, for instance, in rising 'job status insecurity' – concern about the loss of valued features of employment (Gallie et al, 2017; Choonara, 2019: 199–221; Choonara, 2020b). However, the lens of precarious employment, as I have presented it, is too narrow to capture the range of discontents at play. Of course, one can present precarity as a 'multidimensional' concept capacious enough to capture all these ills – but only at the price of losing a focus on specifically contingent forms of employment and at the risk of arrogating decades of research on working conditions conducted under other labels.

Germany, in contrast with the Anglo-Saxon economies, has been characterized by 'highly formalized' relations between unions and employers'

Figure 7.3: Temporary employment as a percentage of dependent employment

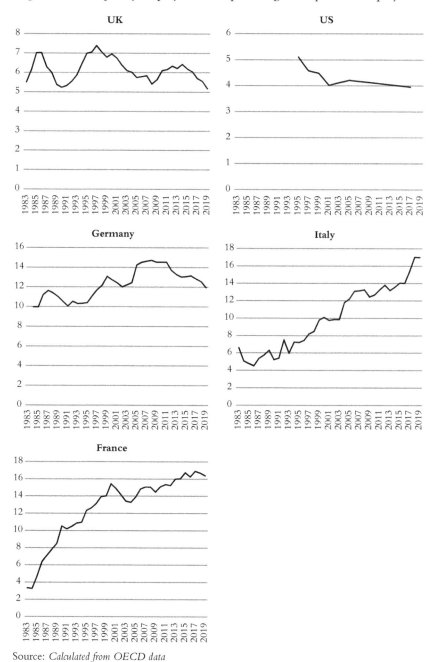

Source: *Calculated from OECD data*

Figure 7.4: Job tenure bands for employees[4]

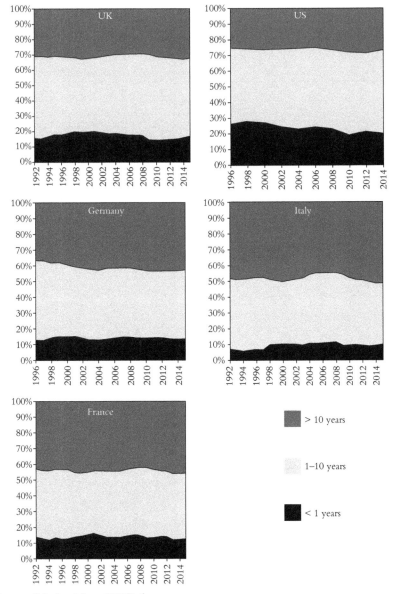

Source: Calculated from OECD data

organizations, with the state acting as 'guarantor and referee' alongside a system of works councils (Rubery and Grimshaw, 2003: 151–2). Historically there were high levels of employment protection, with temporary work tightly restricted until the 1980s (Holst and Dörre, 2013).[5] From the mid-1980s

Figure 7.5: Index of employment protection (higher number = more protection)

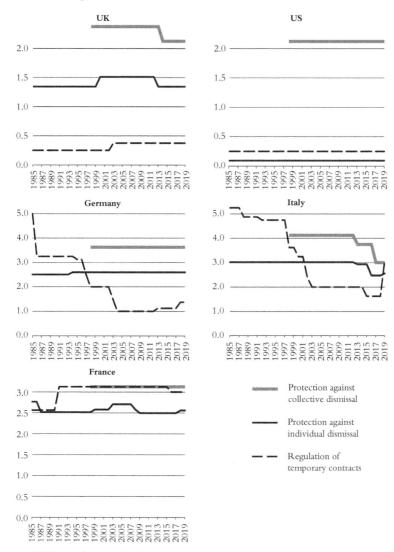

Source: OECD employment database

deregulation focused on temporary and agency work, culminating in the 2003–5 Hartz reforms. As well as promoting 'workfare' and strengthening market forces in the public sector, these reforms removed restrictions on the length of temporary contracts and extended temporary work into the construction industry (Jacobi and Kluve, 2006). Temporary workers were guaranteed equal pay or incorporation into collective pay bargaining, the latter having the perverse outcome of allowing agencies to conclude their own collective agreements with lower pay (Eichhorst, 2015).

Manufacturing, the core of the economy, but only constituting a quarter of employment, remains dominated by permanent work, with agencies used to achieve numerical flexibility in lower-skilled areas (Eichhorst, 2015). Much of the recent jobs growth occurred elsewhere. As Werner Eichhorst (2015) argues: 'the German service sector is characterized by highly diverse working conditions that show a varying use of flexible forms of employment mirroring labour and skill supply and demand patterns, as well as industrial relations'. This includes highly paid jobs, integrated into collective bargaining systems, alongside an increase in temporary employment. Overall, while there are areas of precarious employment in Germany, some of which have grown, this has not permeated through the labour force. Temporary work rose by about 4 per cent from the mid-1990s, peaking in the late 2000s, but half of this growth has since been reversed. Other studies affirm that, while the tendency has been wage stagnation and weakening social protections for those who lose their job, there has been no intensification in the growth of 'atypical employment' since the 2008–9 crisis (Jaehrling et al, 2016).

Moreover, longer-term employment has risen, with over 40 per cent of employees in a job for over a decade. Mean tenure rose gradually both in the early 2000s and in the years following the 2008–9 crisis, approaching an average of ten years – although this coexists with a fall in job tenure among those aged 24–34 and, to a lesser extent, those under 24 (Bachmann and Felder, 2018). Again, areas of precarious employment can coexist with stagnation of employment, with long-term jobs remaining the norm.

France and Italy have both been characterized historically as having highly regulated employment. French employment relations were historically based on *étatisme*, with the state seen as a guarantor of employment rights and unions seeking to shape and contest policy in spite of relatively low levels of union density. Italy is a more complex case, combining voluntarism in collective bargaining, as in the UK, with extensive, complex and often 'poorly defined' forms of regulation (Rubery and Grimshaw, 2003: 152–3, 154).

Italy, as in Germany, but starting later, witnessed extensive deregulation of temporary work. This was exceptionally tightly regulated until the centre-left Prodi government, with union support, introduced its *Pacchetto Treu* reforms in 1997. These reforms legalized limited use of agency work and fixed-term contracts, and were extended by the 2003 *Legge Biagi* introduced by Silvio Berlusconi's government. The result was a confusing process of partial deregulation through the creation of new contractual forms – leading, by one estimate, to the coexistence of 46 different types of non-permanent contract (Ferragina and Arrigoni, 2021). The initial response to the 2008–9 crisis was the further deregulation of both temporary and open-ended employment. The 2014 Jobs Act weakened employment protections for permanent workers and created a new category of workers with fewer protections against dismissals (Cirillo et al, 2017).

It is easier to make a case for the growth of precarious employment in Italy. In the mid-1990s there was a modest leap in short-tenure jobs, and from this point the proportion of temporary employment grew steadily, from 6 to 16 per cent. This growth focused on young people; 60 per cent of employees under 25 had temporary contracts by 2015. However, this has, despite its pronounced aims, failed to reverse growing levels of youth unemployment or low participation rates among women in the south (Cirillo et al, 2017). Prospects for young people are reflected in a 5.9-year gap between the age at which half of Italians are in education and the age at which half are in work; figures for the US, UK, Germany and France range between 1.8 and 2.5 years (Quintini and Martin, 2014). Temporary work in this context cannot be viewed straightforwardly as a 'stepping-stone' into open-ended employment or a 'trap' precluding transition into it. There are substantial variations in trajectories between sectors and roles, and with different types of temporary contract. Unsurprisingly, in most contexts, those in temporary work are less likely to transition to a permanent job than those already in a permanent job but are more likely to transition to a permanent job than the unemployed. It might be better, therefore, to see these roles as creating a 'bottleneck', which in the Italian case has become extremely elongated (see Bosco and Valeriani, 2018). Some young people do eventually find permanent work; indeed, given that permanent jobs growth has been negative in many years, regularization of informal jobs is often the only route to achieve this. However, many can expect several years working on short-term contracts, interspersed with periods of unemployment and underemployment.

Despite this, even more than in the other countries discussed, if people do transition into long-term employment, they will join a labour force characterized by stagnation – both of wages and mobility between jobs. Italy retains exceptional levels of long-term employment, even more so since the 2008–9 crisis. Mean job tenure exceeds that of countries such as Germany and the UK (Bachmann and Felder, 2018). Again, this reflects weak economic performance and pessimism among workers, not strength and optimism. It is also noteworthy that in 2018, for the first time since the 1990s, there was significant re-regulation of temporary work in Italy, reducing the maximum duration of various temporary contracts, increasing the costs associated with their renewal and placing restrictions on the conditions under which temporary contracts can be used for more than a year (Patrizi and D'Amora, 2019). It remains to be seen whether this slows the growth of temporary work.

France, like Italy, has seen a dramatic rise in temporary employment, but in the French case this appears to have moderated in the 2000s. The to and fro of deregulation and re-regulation is a complex tale (Lokiec, 2010; Marx 2012). *Contracts à durée determinée* (CDD), fixed-term contracts, were introduced in 1979, their use encouraged by offering them a stable legal basis. There followed a series of attempts at regulation, including, in 1982, a requirement that their use be justified and limited to 6–12 months in duration. However, faced with rising unemployment and demands for greater 'flexibility' from employers, the governing Socialist Party performed a *volte face* in the mid-1980s, seeking, unsuccessfully, to drive through a relaxation of rules. This paved the way for the incoming Chirac administration to allow CDDs to be used for up to two years, as well as weakening restrictions on dismissing employees. This was followed by further re-regulation, cutting the maximum duration of CDDs to 18 months. Regulation in 1990 also decreed that CDDs could only be used under one of four conditions: replacing employees on leave, temporary increases in activity, seasonal activities or through special contracts aimed at groups such as the long-term unemployed. Moreover, CDDs now attracted a *prime de précarité* – a payment to the worker if their contract expired rather than being made permanent. This was initially set at 6 per cent of the total salary received (Blanchard and Landier, 2002). Despite the restrictions, the use of temporary work increased and included some 'creative circumvention of the rules' by employers (Marx, 2012). As in Italy, growth was concentrated among younger employees.

As the growth of CDDs moderated in the 2000s there was further regulation, with, for instance, the *prime de précarité* raised to 10 per cent in 2002. Contributions to unemployment insurance for temporary workers also rose from 2013 (Eichhorst et al, 2017). Some deregulation of employment has been driven through since the 2008–9 recession, in the face of fierce opposition from workers. However, the focus here, in the 2016 El Khomri law and in the subsequent extensive reforms under the Macron presidency, has been to weaken the power of unions, decentralize collective agreements and render open-ended employment more flexible, for instance by making it easier for businesses to introduce redundancies for economic reasons.

Throughout all this, the distribution of tenure has been remarkably stable, with mean tenure remaining over 11 years, higher than in Germany or the UK. The deregulation that has taken place seems to have created a pool of mainly younger workers with temporary statuses without affecting the distribution of tenure across the workforce – or even, surprisingly, the mean tenure of younger workers as a whole (Bachmann and Felder, 2018).

The political economy of labour markets

What can be learnt from this telegraphic survey of precarious employment? First, the growth of precarious employment is not a straightforward reflex of the imposition of a neoliberal policy regime. There may well be imperatives to deregulate employment, particularly where employment relations are viewed as exceptionally rigid, but there can also be moves to (re-)regulate. Contrary to the ideological commitments of neoliberal theory, markets are, to borrow Karl Polanyi's (1957) phrase, 'instituted processes', not spontaneous entities. That is not to say that the state *opposes* the imperatives of capital, merely that those imperatives can point in contradictory directions as well as being subject to pressure from workers. Second, reflecting these different imperatives, legal toleration of practices does not mean that employers will adopt them. There is no legal barrier to UK firms offering only temporary contracts to employees, but few do. In the US it is often straightforward to make employees redundant, but the average worker can expect their job to last well in excess of a decade. Third, we find that pools of precarious employment, often concentrated among younger workers, can coexist with stable – or stagnating – employment, in which workers experience numerous ills that are poorly captured by the concept of precarious employment as defined here.

In short, because the tendencies at work are neither unidirectional nor universal, little more can be understood without a concrete analysis of the factors shaping employment. Even the brief survey here suggests an array of potential determinants, including the institutional setting, legislation and the prevailing industrial relations; specificities of industry, sector and occupation; demographics; education, training and skill levels; forms of discrimination; the broader state of the economy; and the struggles of workers. The question is how best to integrate the different determinants.

Existing approaches to precarious employment tend to draw, explicitly or implicitly, on dual labour market theory. In its initial formulation (Doeringer and Piore, 1970), this sought to distinguish between 'insiders' in primary labour markets, often identified with enterprises' internal labour markets, and 'outsiders' in secondary labour markets, who experience discrimination or have limited education and training. This approach has several pitfalls. As Blackburn and Mann (1979) suggest, the importance of internal labour markets is highly contextual, and those in 'external' labour markets (such as highly skilled but mobile professionals) may not be disadvantaged 'outsiders'. Moreover, dual labour market approaches have taken wildly differing approaches to distinguishing the 'primary' and 'secondary' labour markets. As this dichotomy comes under pressure, the temptation is to offer more fine-grained typologies (Doogan, 2015). This is reinforced in discussions of precarity because the overlap between contingency and other elements determining job quality is never precise (Choonara, 2019: 48).

One response to these limitations has been the development of segmented labour market theories, which explicitly extend the dualism into an overlapping array of labour market segments. However, even according to their advocates, such theories tend to form 'middle-range conceptualisations ... developed inductively as a set of generalisations based on research findings' (Apostle et al, 1985). There are two resulting problems. First, absent of any broader paradigm, determinations tend to be applied in an ad hoc manner, resulting in 'analytical chaos ... reflecting the diversity of approaches, variables and empirical material' (Fine, 1998: 149, 171). Second, segmentation tends to present distinctions *within* a labour market rather than acknowledging, as Ben Fine (1998) argues, that 'structuring is itself different from one sector to another. Only in a limited sense do labour market segments belong to the same labour market'.[6]

Another effort to extend traditional dualization is offered by theorists such as Werner Eichhorst and Paul Marx (2021), who explicitly focus on segmentation into temporary and open-ended work. They distinguish patterns of *dualization* (promoting temporary work), *liberalization* (weakening protections for employees of both groups), *de-dualization* (increasing protections for temporary workers while possibly weakening those for open-ended work) and *regulation* (enhancing protections for both groups). This typology offers a useful corrective to the assumption of a straightforward deregulation of employment in the neoliberal era and allows authors to describe different outcomes at an aggregate level. Moreover, it can capture the intent of legislation and policy, provided this is, in fact, clear and consistent. However, in offering explanations for concrete patterns, it suffers similar challenges to those discussed earlier, particularly the questions of which determinants to include and how best to integrate them into a coherent picture. Eichhorst, Marx and Wehner (2017) note that, while in its initial formulation 'segmentation was seen as a consequence of employer strategies', since the 1990s 'the dominant perspective has been to explain segmentation as a result of labour market institutions'. Rather than choosing between these alternatives, the challenge is surely to integrate both determinants on a consistent theoretical basis.

The approach suggested here draws on a specifically Marxist political economy to theorize labour markets. This confers two advantages. First, it places labour markets in the context of a broader account of the capitalist mode of production, characterized by an emphasis on class antagonism, exploitation and accumulation. Second, it draws on Karl Marx's method, in particular as exhibited in *Capital*: ordering determinants through abstraction to the simplest, followed by the successive integration of more concrete concepts, which build on, but also modify, the preceding analysis (Callinicos, 2014).

In seeking an understanding of labour market structure in this manner, care must be taken to heed Fine's (1998: 194–8) advice to distinguish *differentiation* (a general feature of labour markets) and the *structuration* of specific labour markets, which leads to them functioning and being reproduced in a distinctive manner.

Figure 7.6: The employment relation in abstraction

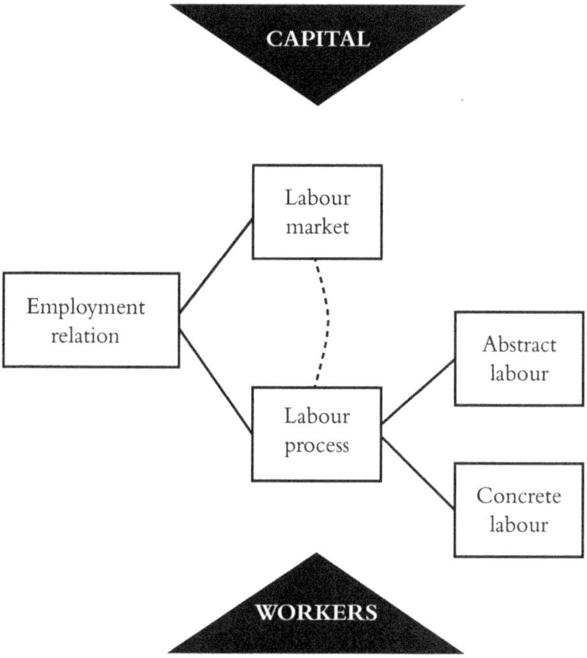

At the most fundamental level, the employment relation is a class relation between capital and labour (Figure 7.6). The relation encompasses both a market relationship and a particular labour process. While the former ostensibly involves a meeting of equals, this is illusory; one party has effective control over the means of production, the other merely brings to market commodified labour-power. Even this illusory freedom dissipates within the 'hidden abode of production' in which capital commands labour-power (Marx, 1990: 279–80). The resulting labour process is both 'abstract', an exercise of labour in general that yields value (the appropriation of a portion of which is a main goal of capitalist production), and 'concrete', a specific process leading to a specific 'use-value' (Marx, 1990: 283–306). The labour process and labour markets, through which the relation is consummated, are separate but interrelated dimensions – as indicated in Figure 7.6 by the dotted line.

Already, at this extremely abstract level, there are some apparent consequences for labour markets. First, while workers depend on capital for their livelihood, capital also relies on (collective) labour to ensure the creation and appropriation of value. This is an exploitative relation, hence one combining antagonism with interdependence. This fact underpins expressions of workers' resistance, such as strikes. Second, because the labour process has a concrete dimension, it relies on commanding specific types of labour-power. These will be more or less readily available within labour markets, and the specifics affect the balance between a desire for numerical flexibility and the desire to retain labour power, shaping particular labour markets. Here, the contextual working out of the dialectic between, on the one hand, sectoral and occupational specialization and, on the other, automation and the inculcation of generalizable skills will play a role in determining the extent of precarious employment. Third, there is the 'temporality' of the labour process. In its idealized form, labour is continuous through the working day and repeated daily. Yet this need not be the case. Examples of non-continuous labour processes include driving taxis and providing social care in people's homes. In such areas, bogus self-employment or zero-hour contracts have been used to subdivide working days into paid and unpaid components (Grimshaw et al, 2015). Similarly, university teaching suffers a double temporality: contact with students is episodic through the day and concentrated on certain times in the academic calendar.

Beyond this abstract level, additional factors emerge as we consider the peculiarities of labour-power as a commodity. First, labour-power is not sold outright to employers; it is hired for a period of time. It must be regularly reproduced, with these reproduction processes taking place predominantly outside the direct capital–labour relation. This has led to a rich literature on social reproduction (Vogel, 2013), highlighting, in particular, its gendered nature. Illustrative of one of Fine's (1998, 195) points, gender discrimination can lead to differences *or* structuration. An example of the former might be wage discrimination faced by women working alongside men, whereas the latter might involve women being pushed into particular occupations or sectors. More generally, social reproduction involves developing specific forms of labour-power, embedding labour markets in 'systems of provision', through which groups of workers reproduce themselves; empirical investigation can reveal the boundaries of the resulting, distinctly structured labour markets and their overlaps (Fine, 1998: 197–8). The reproduction of labour-power also involves systems of education that not only configure the types of labour-power available but also, more prosaically, create pools of students combining studies with casualized work (Doogan, 2009: 161–5).

The imperative for social reproduction helps shape the institutional structure imposed on labour markets, with the state playing a key role. This is already implied in Marx's famous discussion of the early 19th-century struggle over the working day in British factories. Marx's focus is on the antagonism between capitalists and workers, and the efforts of the former to circumvent and overturn successive Factory Acts. Yet Marx (1990: 348) also noted that a 'state ruled by capitalist and landlord' had limited the working day, comparing this to the necessity of using guano to revitalize farmland exhausted of nutrients through the 'blind desire for profits'. This implies the possibility of regulation, not through altruism but through a combination of a desire

Figure 7.7: Rising from the abstract to the concrete

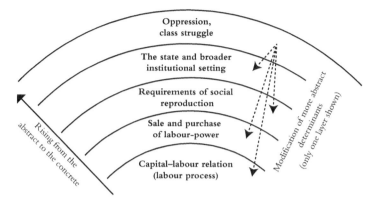

to undercut struggle and to secure a degree of 'rationality and order' amid 'the irrationality engendered by ... compliance with market forces' (Doogan, 2009: 112). This can involve rules constraining firms' ability to dismiss employees or making it costly or disruptive to do so. In combination with the wider system of employment relations, whatever national and sectoral form this takes, this process of institutionalization tends to make labour markets 'insulators' as well as 'conductors': they are an 'imperfect conduit through which new employment relations might be transmitted' (Doogan, 2009: 113).

This context of instituted labour markets, riven with contradictory imperatives, forms the terrain on which a further layer of concrete social and political phenomena can be understood. These include myriad forms of oppression imbricated with the logic of capitalism. Racism, for instance, can lead both to differences within labour markets, such as discrimination resulting in lower wages or worse conditions within workplaces, and can also structure labour markets, as, for instance, when border controls create specific types of workers deprived of legal protections in employment (Choonara, 2020a). Finally, it is important to emphasize that labour markets are contested by participants within them, by capitalists and workers. Workers are not passive victims of precarious employment but have fought, and continue to fight, to transform their conditions (Chapter 15, this volume).

The resulting ordering of determinations, provisionally depicted in Figure 7.7, is open to extension, refinement and modification, but it at least offers an attempt to systematize the study of labour markets and precarious employment, avoiding the pitfalls of dual labour market approaches.

Conclusion

The opening line of Leo Tolstoy's *Anna Karenina* reminds us that 'each unhappy family is unhappy in its own way'. The same might be said of workers: there are a range of discontents within the contemporary world of work. Sometimes this takes the form of precarious employment. Precarious employment has expanded in some countries, particularly focused on newer entrants into work. Yet this is far from a universal experience and, where it happens, it can coexist with employment stagnation, in which workers remain in their jobs for long, in some cases increasing, periods of time.

This chapter has explored some of the limits to precarious employment in five national contexts. This led to an appeal for claims about precarious employment to be situated in a systematic exploration of labour market structures, integrating a range of determinants, starting from the most abstract and rising to the concrete. Such an approach can both strengthen critical accounts of contemporary employment conditions and arm efforts to transform them for the better.

Notes

[1] Prosser (2016) uses 'precarious work' synonymously with 'precarity'.
[2] There is a specific usage of precarity to which I am more sympathetic, originating in Pierre Bourdieu's work and adopted by Kevin Doogan (2009). Precarity is here understood as a 'manufactured uncertainty' used to induce insecurity (Choonara, 2019: 202–3).
[3] Comparisons between temporary employment data should be made cautiously due to lack of harmonization of measurement and, particularly in the US and UK, reliance on subjective conceptions of surveyed employees (OECD, 2002: 127–85). Tenure data also offer a range of challenges (Choonara, 2019: 243–6). In this chapter it is simply broken down into three bands. Levels of employment protection are presented using the OECD's indices.
[4] US estimates exclude tenures under one month and include only 'dependent' employees.
[5] There is no space to discuss the distinctive employment relations in East Germany prior to reunification. OECD data are for West Germany prior to 1990.
[6] For longer discussions, see Blackburn and Mann, 1979: 21–9; Fine, 1998: 107–15; Doogan, 2009: 148–50; Choonara, 2019: 50–6.

References

Apostle, R., Clairmont, D. and Osberg, L. (1985) 'Segmentation and wage determination', *Canadian Review of Sociology*, 22(1): 30–56.

Bachmann, R. and Felder, R. (2018) 'Job stability in Europe over the cycle', *International Labour Review*, 157(3): 481–517.

Blackburn, R.M. and Mann, M. (1979) *The Working Class in the Labour Market*, London: Macmillan.

Blanchard, O. and Landier, A. (2002) 'The perverse effects of partial labour market reform: fixed-term contracts in France', *The Economic Journal*, 112(480): F214–44.

Bosco, M.G. and Valeriani, E. (2018) 'The road to permanent work in Italy: "It's getting dark, too dark to see"', *Italian Economic Journal*, 4: 385–419.

Butler, J. (2016) *Frames of War: When is Life Grievable?*, London: Verso.

Callinicos, A. (2014) *Deciphering Capital: Marx's Capital and its Destiny*, London: Bookmarks.

Choonara, J. (2019) *Insecurity, Precarious Work and Labour Markets: Challenging the Orthodoxy*, London: Palgrave Macmillan.

Choonara, J. (2020a) 'The precarious concept of precarity', *Review of Radical Political Economics*, 52(3): 427–46.

Choonara, J. (2020b) 'The evolution of generalised and acute job tenure insecurity', *Work, Employment & Society*, 34(4): 713–25.

Cirillo, V., Fana, M. and Guarascio, D. (2017) 'Labour market reforms in Italy: evaluating the effects of the Jobs Act', *Economica Politica*, 34: 211–32.

Doeringer, P.B. and Piore, M.J. (1970) *Internal Labor Markets and Manpower Analysis*, Washington, DC: Department of Labor.

Doogan, K. (2009) *New Capitalism? The Transformation of Work*, Cambridge: Polity.

Doogan, K. (2015) 'Precarity – minority condition or majority experience?', in D. Della Porta, S. Hänninen, M. Siisiäinen and T. Silvasti (eds) *The New Social Division: Making and Unmaking Precariousness*, Houndmills: Palgrave Macmillan, pp 43–62.

Eichhorst, W. (2015) 'The unexpected appearance of a new German model', *British Journal of Industrial Relations*, 54(1): 49–69.

Eichhorst, W. and Marx, P. (2021) 'How stable is labour market dualism? Reforms of employment protection in nine European countries', *European Journal of Industrial Relations*, 27(1): 93–110.

Eichhorst, W., Marx, P. and Wehner, C. (2017) 'Labor market reforms in Europe: towards more flexicure labor markets?', *Journal for Labour Market Research*, 51(3): 1–17.

Ferragina, E. and Arrigoni, A. (2021) 'Selective neoliberalism: how Italy went from dualization to liberalisation in labour market and pension reforms', *New Political Economy*, 26(6): 964–984.

Fine, B. (1998) *Labour Market Theory: A Constructive Reassessment*, London: Routledge.

Gallie, D., Felstead, A., Green, F. and Inanc, H. (2017) 'The hidden face of job insecurity', *Work, Employment & Society*, 31(1): 36–53.

Grimshaw, D., Rubery, J. and Ugarte, S.M. (2015) 'Does better quality contracting improve pay and HR practices? Evidence from for-profit and voluntary sector providers of adult care services in England', *Journal of Industrial Relations*, 43(3): 293–310.

Holst, H. and Dörre, K. (2013) 'Revival of the "German model"? Destandardization and the new labour market regime', in M. Kock and M. Fritz (eds) *Non-Standard Employment in Europe*, Houndmills: Palgrave Macmillan, pp 132–49.

Ivancheva, M., Lynch, K. and Keating, K. (2019) 'Precarity, gender and care in the neoliberal academy', *Gender, Work & Organization*, 26(4): 448–62.

Jacobi, L. and Kluve, J. (2006) 'Before and after the Hartz reforms: the performance of active labour market policy in Germany', Institute for the Study of Labor (IZA) discussion paper no. 2100.

Jaehrling, K., Wagner, I. and Weinkopf, C. (2016) 'Reducing precarious work in Europe through social dialogue: the case of Germany', Institut Arbeit und Qualifikation, University of Duisburg-Essen. Available from: https://www.researchgate.net/publication/311102911_Reducing_precarious_work_in_Europe_through_social_dialogue_The_case_of_Germany [Accessed 18 March 2022].

Joronen, M. and Griffiths, M. (2019) 'The affective politics of precarity: home demolitions in occupied Palestine', *Environment and Planning D: Society and Space*, 37(3): 561–76.

Lain, D., Airey, L., Loretto, W. and Vickerstaff, S. (2019) 'Understanding older worker precarity: the intersecting domains of jobs, households and the welfare state', *Ageing and Society*, 39(10): 2219–41.

Lancione, M. (2019) 'The politics of embodied urban precarity: Roma people and the fight for housing in Bucharest, Romania', *Geoforum*, 101: 182–91.

Lokiec, P. (2010) 'Fixed-term contracts in France', in R. Blanpain (ed) *Regulation of Fixed-term Contracts: A Comparative Overview*, Alphen aan den Rijn: Kluwer Law International.

Marx, K. (1990) *Capital Volume I*, London: Penguin.

Marx, P. (2012) 'Labour market dualisation in France', *European Societies*, 14(5): 704–26.

Munck, R. (2013) 'The precariat: a view from the South', *Third World Quarterly*, 34(5): 747–62.

OECD (2002) *OECD Employment Outlook 2002*. Available from: www.oecd.org/els/emp/oecdemploymentoutlook2002.htm [Accessed 26 March 2021].

Patrizi, A. and D'Amora, F. (2019) 'Recent developments in employment disputes in Italy', Studio Legale Associato Quorum. Available from: www.lexology.com/library/detail.aspx?g=c4a1fcba-54d8-478d-8a6b-ea0bd7723656 [Accessed 26 March 2021].

Polanyi, K. (1957) 'The economy as instituted process', in K. Polanyi, C.M. Arensberg and H.W. Pearson (eds) *Trade and Market in the Early Empires*, London: Collier Macmillan, pp 243–70.

Portacolone, E., Rubinstein R.L., Covinsky, K.E., Halpern, J. and Johnson, J.K. (2019) 'The precarity of older adults living alone with cognitive impairment', *The Gerontologist*, 59(2): 271–80.

Prosser, T. (2016) 'Dualization or liberalization? Investigating precarious work in eight European countries', *Work, Employment & Society*, 30(6): 949–65.

Quintini, G. and Martin, S. (2014) 'Same same but different: school-to-work transitions in emerging and advanced Economies', OECD Social, Employment and Migration working paper no. 154.

Robinson, R.N.S., Martins, A., Solnet, D. and Baum, T. (2019) 'Sustaining precarity: critically examining tourism and employment', *Journal of Sustainable Tourism*, 27(7): 1008–25.

Rubery, J. and Grimshaw, D. (2003) *The Organization of Employment*, Houndmills: Palgrave Macmillan.

Standing, G. (2011) *The Precariat: The New Dangerous Class*, London: Bloomsbury.

Virno, P. (2004) *A Grammar of the Multitude*, Cambridge, MA: Semiotext(e).

Vogel, L. (2013) *Marxism and the Oppression of Women*, Chicago: Haymarket.

8

The Social Foundations
of Precarious Work: The Role
# of Unpaid Labour in the Family

Valeria Pulignano and Glenn Morgan

Introduction

Precarious work in the advanced capitalist economies is characterized by
insecurity, which manifests itself through unpredictable hours, unstable
rewards, and lack of rights to sick pay, pension and holiday entitlements
(Kalleberg, 2009).[1] This situation is contrasted with work that is conducted
under what has been described as the standard employment contract, where
workers are employed for a set number of hours per week, at specified wage
rates, with predictable earnings and a range of benefits, such as sick pay,
holiday entitlement and so on (Bosch, 2004). In this chapter, we argue that
in order to understand this change it is necessary to see precarious work as
part of what Glucksmann (2005) describes as 'the total social organization
of labour', by which she means the connections and interdependencies
between paid and unpaid work, between market and non-market relations,
and between the family, the state and the economy. We therefore shift the
focus of the debate on precarious work from the paid area of employment
towards these interconnections between paid and unpaid work in the public
and private spheres. We argue that precarious work increasingly creates a
grey zone of activities that are unpaid and unacknowledged by employers.
Workers have to perform these activities in order to gain access to paid
employment. In turn, workers can only perform these grey zone activities
if the family and household sphere is also reorganized in order to support
them. We argue that these interconnections are, as Glucksmann suggests,
endemic in the structure of capitalism, but their actual form varies across

different regimes of accumulation and production. The particular growth and extension of grey zone activities and restructuring of households in the current period has been brought about as the Fordist and Keynesian regime of accumulation, and the associated pattern of the standard employment contract, has declined and been replaced by the emergence of neoliberal market deregulation and the rise of precarious work.

The chapter consists of three sections. First, we place the argument within theoretical debates about work inside (public sphere) and outside (private sphere) the market from a critical political economy of capitalism approach, encompassing both an (historical) employment and domestic labour perspective. Secondly, we examine the micro-social foundations of ongoing macro-structural changes, which we identify in the rise of precarious work and the emergence and growth of grey zones of unpaid but necessary work in and around the household in order to access the paid labour market. Thirdly, and in conclusion, we explore the theoretical and empirical implications of this shift in focus.

Moving 'work' beyond the inside and outside the market debate

We begin by locating precarious work in the processes whereby the standard employment contract has been undermined (Rubery et al, 2018). We recognize that the speed, extent and nature of such processes are fundamentally affected by different institutional configurations (Baccaro and Howell, 2017; Doellgast et al, 2018) and relationships of power in the state (Howell, 2021) and in the economy, alongside variations by sector and by firm-level strategy (Alberti et al, 2018). Highly flexible employment contracts and precarious work are particularly present in hospitality and retail services, personal and social care sectors, entertainment and creative industries, and logistics and delivery (Rubery et al, 2015; Umney and Kretsos, 2015; Moore and Newsome, 2018; Wood et al, 2018), but this is not to say that they are absent in other sectors (Pulignano and Doerflinger, 2018). However, these flexible employment contracts share in common the manner in which they have undermined the standard employment contract and have established precarious work (Rubery et al, 2018). In particular, they have generated the fragmentation of tasks (by time and by function), often leading to poor-quality jobs, increasing unpredictability and extreme variability in working hours and pay, as well as providing little in the way of benefits such as sick pay, pension rights and so on. Flexibilization is also associated with an increasing number of independent contractors or self-employed freelancers, who usually find themselves experiencing a loss of control despite the worker being, in theory, able to pick and choose when to work. Research on the platform economy, especially, illustrates that algorithmic controls shape when work might be available for the self- employed contractor, how their performance will be monitored and evaluated, and what level of reward is available. Algorithmic controls are therefore a kind of 'cybernetic control' (Huws, 2001) because at each fold of the feedback loop accountability can be deflected and denied (Stark and Pais, 2021). The generation of algorithmic controls involves non-bureaucratic means of control in the sense that workers are not told what to do by managers but by the algorithm. This is important because, as Rahman and Thelen (2019) argues, subjecting workers to bureaucratic control would damage the platform owner's claims that workers are independent contractors or self-employed and therefore are not eligible for the protections of employee status. Algorithmic control thus underpins a distinctive form of precarious work that is highly individualized and for which there is little opportunity to share experiences and organize (though efforts have been ongoing in this area). An increasing number of people juggle multiple jobs and tasks within the platform economy and the wider labour market (Ilsøe et al, 2021) while shouldering familial responsibilities for the care of children and the elderly, and supporting each other in coping with the risks of low pay, unemployment and unsociable hours (Smith and McBride, 2020).

In our view, a key aspect of this process is the restructuring of the 'total social organization of labour' (Glucksmann, 2005), and for this reason it is helpful to return to the early origins of this discussion, through which arguments emerged to address unwaged forms of work found within the family and the household (for example, Federici, 1974, 2012; Molyneux, 1979). These discussions emphasized the need to understand the unpaid work done, mainly by women, that was outside the market but was necessary for capitalism in the process of social reproduction, that is, recuperating workers' energies on a daily basis, developing a new generation of workers through the rearing of children and meeting the needs of care for workers as they progressed through a lifetime of labour and into old age. Wages in the formal economy were necessary for these processes of social reproduction but not sufficient; labour and work within the household was required and this was predominantly supplied by women. In this way, this system is integrally connected to the gendered division of labour in the household and the economy in so far as the family is considered the primary unit for absorbing the task of socially reproducing labour. This domestic labour is deemed as not 'work' and as lacking in skills despite its *economic* contribution to maintaining the capitalist system by providing labour necessary for the reproduction of labour power.

Domestic work was instead wrapped up in multiple layers of ideology that emphasized the moral obligation of the woman, in particular, to undertake this work (see McIntosh, 1978). The moral obligation of the man was to support the family by paid work inside the market. The idea of the 'family wage' (see, for example, the early discussions in Land, 1980 and Horrell and

Humphries, 1992) was used to support the demands of male workers for a wage that reproduced labour on a day-to-day basis and over generations, with the assumption that the woman would be mainly responsible for the home and the tasks of reproduction, including child birth and child rearing. Moral and religious justifications for the 'family wage' could be influential in providing employer and middle-class support for working-class struggles to achieve increased income, as they lay the basis for a 'respectable' working class integrated into society through trade unions, cooperatives, friendly societies, religion and social democratic mass parties. Over the 19th and early 20th centuries, nation states, often prompted by war and the need to field a physically adequate military instilled with a strong nationalist ideology, also took over or worked in conjunction with these institutions to support processes of social reproduction through the provision of education, housing, unemployment and old-age benefits and health services (Mann 1993). If, as was often the case, women did enter the labour force, they could, by the same moral yardstick, be 'justifiably' paid lower wages on the basis that men were the main supporters of the family income. They could also be subjected to marriage bars, requiring them to resign on marriage or on the birth of children. Women working for 'pin money' (Zelizer, 2017) with limited expectations about careers or employment rights were helpful for employers using large numbers of female workers to reduce costs, not just in some areas of manufacturing such as textiles, packaging and food but also in the growing retail, health and social care, and secretarial sectors of the first half of the 20th century. The fact that many women might be single or widowed, and therefore lacking any male 'breadwinner' support, was irrelevant to this framing. State welfare structures tended to mirror these differences, with women primarily dependent on men for access to universal (as opposed to means tested) benefits, though countries differed according to the degree to which they encouraged women into the labour force and made institutional arrangements to ensure that this was possible (Esping-Andersen, 1990, 1999). These debates, nevertheless, reflected a broader set of moral values that placed women primarily in the home with the responsibility of the care of family members (Finch, 1989). As the domestic labour and 'wages for housework' debate pointed out, work in the sense of the physical and mental effort involved in these tasks of social reproduction was made invisible and the skills necessary for undertaking them devalued and denigrated in comparison to 'real work' in the public sphere. The struggles of women and men to survive under these conditions were obvious in the late 19th and early 20th centuries when employment was unstable, wages were low and state support was limited (see, for example, Seccombe, 1993). Nevertheless, in some form or other, depending on the institutional context, the 'family wage' and all the gender power relations that underpinned it survived up to the 1970s.

The notion of the appropriate 'family wage' was, in reality, determined by the relative bargaining position in the labour market of employees and their representatives, as well as the role of the state in supporting women to prioritize motherhood roles and social reproduction (for instance, through pro-natalist policies that involved keeping married women at home to have as many children as possible: Skinner, 2011) or, alternatively, encouraging them into the labour market (Fleckenstein and Seeleib-Kaiser, 2011). In the Fordist era of Keynesian macro-economic management, the requirement to boost production, brought about by growing consumption (due to rising living standards and new forms of credit) coupled with increased productivity in manufacturing and the rise of service sector employment, drew more women into the labour force. While there were various moral panics associated with this during the 1950s and 1960s, for instance, regarding declining fertility (Seccombe, 1993) and children going home to empty houses, the limited and varied nature of state expansion into early years nursery education or after school activity, or into providing adequate care for the elderly, meant that most of the pressure for change was on women who had to be perfect housewives and consumers, managing the household economy but under the financial and physical power of the husband. The ubiquity of the standard employment contract based on the idea of the family wage, therefore, supported the clear distinction between the public world of work and the private sphere of the family, which was intermediated by state institutions providing certain services for social reproduction under the Keynesian regime of accumulation.

There were, however, other economic, political and social changes during the 1960s and 1970s, which created strains on this system and challenged the gendered division of labour in the economy and in the household. This included, for example, the growing education and employment opportunities for women, and the declining job opportunities for traditional male working-class jobs; feminist demands for greater equality; legislation on equal pay and equal opportunities; new patterns of household formation related to changes in reproductive technologies; the declining significance of marriage and the increasing frequency of divorce; and the availability under certain conditions of welfare and housing benefits to support single-parent female households. Many of these tensions came about as political parties, pushed by their electorates, demanded an increased role for the state in ameliorating the impact of markets and controlling and regulating market processes in the name of fairness and basic standards for all citizens (whether men or women). State employment augmented by these processes became a crucial labour market for many jobs associated with women's caring functions, and as state services expanded and brought more women into the labour market, demands for greater equality in pay and employment opportunities grew, prompting, in turn, more demand for state services, for instance, to provide nurseries, schooling and higher education, to expand health and social services, and to fill the bureaucratic and operative roles associated with the expansion of the state (see, for example, Crouch, 1999).

The rise of neoliberalism as a governmental policy frame from the 1970s explicitly challenged aspects of this regime by emphasizing the beneficial effects of free markets and the deleterious effects of government intervention, together with the need for more family and individual responsibility for issues of social reproduction, potentially allowing a reduction in state expenditure and taxation rates. Cooper, for example, argues that neoliberalism and social conservatism 'both agreed ... that the private family (rather than the state) should serve as the primary source of economic security' (Cooper, 2017: 69). The continuous expansion of the state, which had been seen in most developed economies during the Keynesian era, lost its legitimacy under this attack, even if it was more difficult for neoliberal governments to drastically prune services that by now had become part of the taken-for-granted institutional infrastructure of most societies.

The result has therefore been a long-term ideological shift against the state and the functions in the area of social reproduction, which it could be said took over from families during the Keynesian era. This has been reflected in different forms of state restructuring in the advanced economies, reflected in variations in degrees of privatization, contracting out, retrenchment and austerity over the last few decades (Hay and Wincott, 2012; Hemerijck, 2013; King and LeGales, 2017). Neoliberal policies towards work emphasized that social reproduction was best managed within the family household and that the services required to supplement this should be mainly provided through market mechanisms, with state involvement limited to areas of 'market failure'. State regulation of the labour market or the provision of services and welfare benefits as a right would be reduced to different degrees across European societies (Häusermann and Palier, 2008; Dolvik and Martin, 2015).

Under neoliberalism, as the standard employment contract is challenged and the welfare state reduced, employers rely on the family to fill the gaps, with the state increasingly acting as a backstop, disciplining failing families through educational and social welfare services and developing mechanisms to control deviance (for instance through growing incarcerations of the 'dangerous classes'). Those who are employed on part-time flexible contracts or undertake relatively stable part-time work under an open-ended contract, which is grounded in inegalitarian gender relations, find it difficult to earn a reliable and stable amount of earnings that can support an adequate standard of living. They need to be supported during periods when they are not working or only earning small amounts. Such periods are often out of their own control as a result of decisions taken by managers or, increasingly, by algorithms; the unpredictability makes it difficult for support to be routinized. Therefore, family support is often called upon at short notice in the form of a request for urgent emergency aid. However, pre-existing inequalities mean that the resources families can bring to this change are already pre-structured by the socio-economic conditions of class. As Molyneux (1979) noted, 'it is precisely where the value of labour power is lowest that the input of domestic labour is often most minimal' (11). Thus, those likely to be found in precarious jobs may have to accept lower standards of wage income while having less capacity to mitigate the impact of this by the use of home-based resources as family members may likely all be in relatively precarious employment or dependent on state benefits, so possessing little slack to help each other in financial terms or in terms of time and space. It is by following this analysis that Supiot claims for the need to establish a closer tie between work inside and outside the market as the way to provide social protection: 'The difficulties nowadays is to perceive the occupational status of persons as extending beyond the immediate contractual commitment to their work to cover the diverse forms of work experienced during one's life' (2001: 53). In contrast to the situation under the standard employment contract, where wages flowed across the boundaries between formal paid work in the public sphere and work in the private household sphere, under these new conditions, the private household sphere has to become much more active in supporting paid work and more oriented to the marketability of its participants.

Unpaid in paid work: implications for the household

In this section, we explore in more detail the way in which employers are able to design precarious work in ways which rely on families and households covering gaps that are created by the withdrawal of the support afforded by the standard employment contract and the welfare state. Employers have been able to effectively push elements of paid work, which might in the past have been included in normal working hours and paid accordingly, into the grey zones of unpaid labour, even though these elements necessarily have to be done in order to access precarious work. Following Baccaro and Howell (2017), we emphasize that as employer discretion over the employment relationship increased due to processes of deregulation and legislation weakening workers' rights collectively, this opened up a range of strategies about how to organize business and labour. The sectors that moved most directly towards establishing the sorts of highly flexible arrangements associated with precarious work involved goods and services where controlling labour costs was a major part of achieving profitability and where demand varied over the course of a day, a week or a more extended period of time. As discussed earlier, therefore, highly flexible employment contracts and precarious work are particularly present in hospitality and retail services, personal and social care sectors, entertainment and creative industries, and logistics and delivery. The particular way in which these sectors organize work has been discussed widely (Rubery et al, 2015; Umney and Kretsos, 2015; Alberti et al, 2018; Moore and Newsome, 2018; Pulignano and Doerflinger, 2018; Wood et al, 2018). In this section, we focus our attention on the broad impact of these different forms of flexibilization on unpaid work undertaken in families and households to support participation in these varied work arrangements. It is our contention that the emergence of these grey zones of unpaid labour extend the responsibilities of families and households when it comes to the preparation of labour in the form and type required for these new precarious positions. In principle, resources might come from the state supporting the workforce when the latter is either not employed or too low paid to be able to fully support themselves. However under the restructuring of the welfare state that has occurred under neoliberalism, access to such state benefits has become more complex and has in fact led to new forms of semi-voluntary and compulsory unpaid work activities (such as internships, work experience and participating in training programmes, not to mention the considerable work required to fill in complex bureaucratic forms and provide appropriate documentation, a process which may particularly impact on recent migrants and their families or on second generation families, as in the UK Windrush scandal). Only by conforming to these requirements and engaging in these sorts of unpaid work is it possible to maintain eligibility for access to benefits that can cushion irregular, low paid work (Girardi et al, 2020). People thus have to engage in learning how to train themselves by following online courses and projecting their curriculum vitae and their self to potential employers and customers (Greer, 2016). They also have to show their ability to be a disciplined employee, from the point of view of turning up on time, regularly and in a condition to work, and they are expected to be willing to take jobs even if these do not provide sufficient money to live on. In doing so, such schemes have succeeded in subsidizing low paying employers and their policies of precarious work.

Importantly, resources may come from expectations for cross-subsidization and responsibilities within the nuclear family and beyond. For instance, Schor (2020) describes individuals who undertake un- (or under)paid work as a necessary requirement for accessing paid work as they are trapped in *economic dependency*. Such work will, in turn, be dependent on hidden and unacknowledged support from others in the household (Joyce et al, 2020). For example, being available for paid work as determined by market demand, the worker will have indeterminate periods of time without pay and other benefits such as holiday pay, pension contributions and sickness benefits. This time of waiting for the opportunity to earn, which is unpaid, requires that the household can manage its finances sufficiently to deal with the irregularity of income of the precarious worker. This may be through individuals in the household subsidizing each other in various ways, such as adult children living rent-free with their parents for much longer than previously because they do not have the income required to have their own accommodation. It could also embrace parents living with their adult children because of the difficulties of the latter to provide care work in terms of child rearing when coping with the new flexible and precarious work patterns, which includes working unsocial hours during weekends and evenings. Hence, the result can be a change in family structures, with different approaches and capacities for domestic labour to supplement inadequate wage income. This is because 'precarious work needs labour' (Standing, 2011) and precarious workers are found to be the ones struggling the most when attempting to reconcile their daily life with insecure jobs (Ba', 2019).

This links into the third important resource for the use of unpaid labour in precarious paid work by employers, which is the individual who accepts reduced expectations in relation to acceptable standards of living relative to prevailing norms. This is because precarious workers who have to give time and money to be ready for work are likely the ones who then reorganize their home lives in the light of their expectations of income and income stability (for a wide range of examples see Pulignano and Morgan, 2021). Whiting and Symon (2020), for example, discuss 'digi-housekeeping', the unpaid work required to maintain the digital tools that are necessary to participate in the gig economy. Organizations such as Amazon and Uber expect workers to equip themselves with cars and vans and to maintain their upkeep and costs out of their earnings, often requiring significant capital outlays from individuals and families if they are going to take part in deliveries or taxi work (Alimahomed-Wilson and Reese, 2020; Woodcock and Graham, 2020).

Overall, it is possible to argue that it is not only work in the public sphere of paid employment but also families associated with household arrangements that are becoming more precarious. As we have discussed, managing the household finances under conditions of unpaid labour in precarious work leads to multiple potential disruptions to families, which have to be borne as a cost by the individual and the household. Such costs are revealed in household breakups, in mental health and addiction issues, low levels of criminality and ultimately, as described by Case and Deaton (2020), 'deaths of despair'. Middle-class families with resources may be able to supply this support, but overall, we suggest this process is deepening and intensifying inequalities between households. This particularly relates to individuals who lack any household support, including financial and domestic labour, and who then may be pushed further towards food banks and charities, with the potential to lead to homelessness and poverty. As Molyneux (1979) argued:

> Single workers, and migrants, whose labour power is usually reproduced on a daily basis without the benefit of female domestic

labour, are invariably paid below average wages. Even supposing that they were able and willing to afford the necessary appliances, such categories of workers live in conditions (slums, hostels, shanties) which make it difficult for them to perform their own domestic labour; as a consequence they tend to rely on services and food obtained on the market. (Molyneux, 1979: 11)

As we will illustrate in the following section, this opens up the possibility for new thinking about how precarious work increases the costs of reproductive labour by family members, in particular women, who have to bear the costs of social reproduction in the first place.

Unpaid in paid work: implications for reproductive labour

Parry (2005: 10) states that it is limiting to consider 'work today merely as a discrete activity carried out in exchange for remuneration and dependency'. Instead, we argue, there exists between home and work a range of grey zones where the boundaries between work and home blur, and where unpaid work emerges. This blurring can take different forms and it can reveal a variety of ways in which work can been shifted out of the responsibility of the employer and create new (inter)-dependencies within and between the sphere of public (paid) and private (domestic) work that are now the responsibility of the individual and the household (see also Pulignano and Morgan, 2021). Hence, unpaid work is likely to occur and to account for precarity within the emerging and broad realm of *dependency*, which reflects individual *necessity* within paid employment.

This statement paves the way for further reflections on the new ways in which the capacities for socially reproductive labour within the home can supplement unpaid labour in precarious paid employment. One possibility is the reassertion of hegemonic structures of male dominance, reinforcing old disparities based on gender within the household. For example, by continuing to expose women to occupational segregation in flexible, devalued and unpaid (or low paid) jobs because the sphere of domestic work (and with it, primarily the activities undertaken by women in the home) is extending again to cope with the increasingly precarious work situations of some members of the family. Traditional domestic labour debates about commodifying housework through the 'wages for housework' campaign went along with arguments for *de*-commodifying forms of socially necessary work, such as care and parenting work, by making them an obligation of the state. Neoliberalism, however, makes people work all the harder by persuading them that there is adequate compensation for the loss of individual lived time through the freedom to enjoy more autonomy in the work process alongside increased consumer goods for the self and the family, thus encouraging families to adapt to the new context (Everingham, 2002). By contrast, it can be argued that by heightening the demands on the private sphere of home and the family, the unpaid element in paid precarious work fosters societal crisis precisely because of the pressures placed on families. Undertaking care responsibilities risks limiting the capacity of individuals and family members – particularly women – to take advantage of all the promise the new freedoms under neoliberalism theoretically claim to offer (Berg, 2019).

Proposals based on women's assumed preferences for care – even via the 'dual roles' model based on the 'flexible family' (Streeck, 2009) – have often made it unlikely that women could avoid the 'entrapment' of responsibility for care work. The goal of gender equality is historically an ambitious one, and existing studies argue that it is unlikely to be achieved unless something can be done about the nature of employment (Crompton, 2006). Our discussion reinforces this statement by rejecting assumptions that are grounded in shaky theories about women's preferences. Within a situation where paid workers are left having to continuously re-negotiate their time with employers and with household members in order to engage in multiple and often diverse tasks in between the public and the private spheres of work (Brannen, 2005), it is important to recognize that the commitment of the individual to undertake work for which s/he is indeed often not paid may increase, for example in care work or in the creative sector, as issues of duty, responsibility and achievement over-ride instrumental wage-driven logics. This in turn enhances the costs for social reproductive labour in terms of gender inequality. This is because most care work is still carried out within the household directly by women and/or supported by public funds. However, even in the last case, caregiver parity would be very unlikely to result in income equality and would tend to consolidate the gender division of domestic labour. As Fraser (1994) observes, in order for gender equity to occur the shift should take place in the private sphere of home and the family and the household. Conversely, as we have attempted to illustrate in this chapter, we see that contemporary neoliberal forces are nowadays curbing much more deeply the 'social bonds of care' (Fraser, 2016) by squeezing social resources within families and households. Paradoxically, neoliberal capitalist regime justifies this as an extension of the freedom of the individual and the family to organize their lives on their own time. However, as we have argued, neoliberalism refuses to recognize the value of socially reproductive work by piling more work into the grey zone of unpaid work. Neoliberalism does it by imposing flexible (unpaid) work schedules in terms of working hours, which dictates how the allocation of such (mostly) unpaid work will occur. In so doing, it intensifies the difficulty for individuals to predict whether the choices they make will provide them with the income they want (Ravenelle, 2019; Acevedo, 2020).

Conclusion

This chapter has illustrated how and why studying precarious work at the interface between (marketable activities) work and (non-marketable) home, and where unpaid work is revealed, can open up new theoretical perspectives, which may potentially have relevant implications for empirical and policy research. From a theoretical perspective, we have illustrated how a perspective of precarious work that moves beyond the inside and outside of the market – or paid and unpaid – work debate can be novel in how it systematically links the understanding of the 'precarious' not only to working patterns but also to the realities of households. This may better help in understanding the effects and implications of neoliberal capitalism at the micro level of families and processes of social reproduction. This suggests a new research agenda on precarious work that brings the household and family dimension much more into a central focus, showing how different forms of precarity require a range of adjustments and changes in household and family arrangements. It may be expected that such adjustments can be managed more smoothly where middle-class families have access to financial, social and cultural capital, though even here tensions can arise because of the amounts of human capital investment that are required to get children into the best schools, the best universities and the most prestigious positions in corporations, professions and public service (Sherman, 2017). Where such resources are not available, a wide range of responses may emerge in terms of individuals taking on multiple precarious jobs while others in the family concentrate on the care of children and the elderly, supported by a do-it-yourself economy for many aspects of everyday living. Alternatively, such families may turn to the state to support them at times of crisis, but under conditions of austerity, this leads to more direct control over the family, its behaviours and its way of life – all of which may put further pressure on the cohesion of families already under pressure as a result of lack of money and lack of steady work. The result may be the sort of disintegration of families that characterized the poor in the 19th-century industrialization process.

Another important conclusion this chapter indicates is related to the reassertion of hegemonic structures of male dominance and the reinforcement of old disparities based on gender that may derive from precarious work that is unpaid. This is because the sphere of domestic labour, which is primarily gendered and devalued, is extending again to cope with the increasingly precarious work situations of some members of the family. This all implies that there are important policy implications and political recommendations that need raising about how to re-dignify, re-humanize and re-value work and the worker. This further reinforces our commitment to an integrated research agenda that can help identify key policy interventions and key areas and issues that are in need of future regulation.

Note

[1] Acknowledgements for funding: European Research Council – ERC Advanced Grant 'ResPecTMe' – under the European Union's Horizon 2020 research and innovation programme (Grant agreement n. 833577). We would like to express our thanks to Joseph Choonara, Arne Kalleberg and Jill Rubery for very useful comments on a previous version of this paper.

References

Acevedo, D.D. (2020) (ed) *Beyond the Algorithm: Qualitative Insights for Gig Work Regulation*, Cambridge: Cambridge University Press.

Alberti, G., Bessa, I., Hardy, K.R., Trappmann, V. and Umney, C. (2018) 'In, against and beyond precarity: work in insecure times', *Work, Employment and Society*, 32(3): 447–57.

Alimahomed-Wilson, J. and Reese, E. (eds) (2020) *The Cost of Free Shipping: Amazon in the Global Economy*, London: Pluto.

Ba', S. (2019) 'The struggle to reconcile precarious work and parenthood: the case of Italian "precarious parents"', *Work, Employment and Society*, 33(5): 812–28.

Baccaro, L. and Howell, C. (2017) *Trajectories of Neoliberal Transformation: European Industrial Relations since the 1970s*, Cambridge: Cambridge University Press.

Berg J. (2019) *Protecting Workers in the Digital Age: Technology, Outsourcing and the Growing Precariousness of Work*, Geneva: International Labour Organization.

Bosch, G. (2004) 'Towards a new standard employment relationship in Western Europe', *British Journal of Industrial Relations*, 42(4): 617–36.

Brannen, J. (2005) 'Time and the negotiation of work-family boundaries: autonomy or illusion?', *Time & Society*, 14(1): 113–31.

Case, A. and Deaton, A. (2020) *Deaths of Despair and the Future of Capitalism*, Princeton: Princeton University Press.

Cooper, M. (2017) *Family Values: Between Neoliberalism and the New Social Conservativism*, New York: Zone Books.

Crompton R. (2006) *Employment and the Family*, Cambridge: Cambridge University Press.

Crouch, C. (1999) *Social Change in Western Europe*, Oxford: Oxford University Press.

Doellgast, V., Lillie, N. and Pulignano, V. (eds) (2018) *Reconstructing Solidarity: Labour Unions, Precarious Work and the Politics of Institutional Change in Europe*, Oxford: Oxford University Press.

Dolvik, J.E. and Martin, A. (eds) (2015) *European Social Models: From Crisis to Crisis*, Oxford: Oxford University Press.

Esping-Andersen, G. (1990) *The Three Worlds of Welfare Capitalism*, Cambridge: Polity.

Esping-Andersen, G. (1999) *Social Foundations of Postindustrial Economies*, Oxford: Oxford University Press.

Everingham, C. (2002) 'Engendering time: gender equity and discourses of workplace flexibility', *Time & Society*, 11(2–3): 335–51.

Federici, S. (1974) *Wages Against Housework*, New York: Spring.

Federici, S. (2012) *Revolution at Point Zero: Housework, Reproduction, and Feminist Struggle*, Brooklyn: PM Press.

Finch, J. (1989) *Family Obligations and Social Change*, Cambridge: Polity.

Fleckenstein, T. and Seeleib-Kaiser, M. (2011) 'Business, skills and the welfare state: the political economy of employment-oriented family policy in Britain and Germany', *Journal of European Social Policy*, 21(2): 136–49.

Fraser, N. (1994) 'After the family wage: gender equality and the welfare state', *Political Theory*, 22(4): 591–618.

Fraser N. (2016) 'Contradictions of capital and care', *New Left Review*, July/August.

Girardi S., Pulignano V. and Maas R. (2020) 'Activated and included? The social inclusion of social assistance beneficiaries engaged in "public works"', *International Journal of Sociology and Social Policy*, 39(9–10): 738–51.

Glucksmann, M.A. (2005) 'Shifting boundaries and interconnections: extending the "total social organisation of labour"', *The Sociological Review*, 53(2): 19–36.

Greer, I. (2016) 'Welfare reform, precarity and the re-commodification of labour', Work, *Employment and Society*, 30(1): 162–73.

Häusermann, S. and Palier, B. (2008) 'The politics of employment-friendly welfare reforms in post-industrial economies', *Socio-Economic Review*, 6(3): 559–86.

Hay, C. and Wincott, D. (2012) *The Political Economy of European Welfare Capitalism*, London: Palgrave Macmillan.

Hemerijck, A. (2013) *Changing Welfare States*, Oxford: Oxford University Press.

Horrell, S. and Humphries, J. (1992) 'Old questions, new data, and alternative perspectives: families' living standards in the Industrial Revolution', *The Journal of Economic History*, 52(4): 849–80.

Howell, C. (2021) 'Rethinking the role of the state in employment relations for a neoliberal era', *Industrial and Labor Relations Review*, 74(3): 739–72.

Huws, U. (2001) 'The making of a cybertariat? Virtual work in a real world', *Socialist Register*, 37, 1–23.

Ilsøe, A., Larsen, T. and Bach, E. (2021) 'Multiple jobholding in the digital platform economy: signs of segmentation', *Transfer: European Review of Labour and Research*, 27(2): 201–18.

Joyce, S., Stuart, M., Forde, C. and Valizade, D. (2020) 'Work and social protection in the platform economy in Europe', *Industrial and Labor Relations*, 25: 153–84.

Kalleberg, A.L. (2009) 'Precarious work, insecure workers: employment relations in transition', *American Sociological Review*, 74(1), 1–22.

King, D. and LeGales, P. (eds) (2017) *Reconfiguring European States in Crisis*, Oxford: Oxford University Press.

Land, H. (1980) 'The family wage', *Feminist Review*, 6: 55–77.

Mann, M. (1993) *The Sources of Social Power Vol. II: The Rise of Classes and Nation-states, 1760–1914*, Cambridge: Cambridge University Press.

McIntosh, M. (1978) 'The state and the oppression of Women', in A. Kuhn and A.M. Wolpe (eds) *Feminism and Materialism*, London: Routledge and Kegan Paul, pp 254–90.

Molyneux, M. (1979) 'Beyond the domestic labour debate', *New Left Review*, 116: 3–27.

Moore, S. and Newsome, K. (2018) 'Paying for free delivery: dependent self-employment as a measure of precarity in parcel delivery', *Work, Employment and Society*, 32(3): 475–92.

Parry, J. (2005) 'Care in the community? Gender and the reconfiguration of community work in a post-mining neighborhood', *Sociological Review*, 53(2): 149–66.

Pulignano, V. and Doerflinger, N. (2018) 'Labour markets, solidarity and precarious work: comparing local unions' responses to management flexibility strategies in the German and Belgian metalworking and chemical industries', in V. Doellgast, N. Lillie and V. Pulignano (eds) *Reconstructing Solidarity*, Oxford: Oxford University Press, pp 104–23.

Pulignano, V. and Morgan, G. (2021) 'Emerging "grey zones" at the interface of work and home. Advancing research and theory on precarious work', paper presented at the SASE Conference, July 2021. Available from: https://sase.org/event/2021-sase-conference/ [Accessed 19 April 2022].

Rahman S.K. and Thelen K. (2019) 'The rise of the platform business model and the transformation of twenty-first-century capitalism', *Politics & Society*, 47(2): 177–204.

Ravenelle, A. (2019) *Hustle and Gig: Struggling and Surviving in the Sharing Economy*, Oakland: University of Chicago Press.

Rubery, J., Grimshaw, D., Hebson, G. and Ugarte, S. (2015) '"It's all about time": time as contested terrain in the management and experience of domiciliary care work in England', *Human Resource Management*, 54(5): 753–72.

Rubery, J., Grimshaw, D., Keizer A. and Johnson, M. (2018) 'Challenges and contradictions in the "normalising" of precarious work', *Work, Employment and Society*, 32(3): 509–27.

Schor, J. (2020) *After the Gig. How the Sharing Economy got Hijacked and how to Win it Back*, Oakland: University of California Press.

Seccombe, W. (1993) *Weathering the Storm: Working Class Families from the Industrial Revolution to the Fertility Decline*, London: Verso.

Sherman, R. (2017) *Uneasy Street: The Anxieties of Affluence*, Princeton: Princeton University Press.

Skinner, Q. (ed) (2011) *Families and States in Western Europe*, Cambridge: Cambridge University Press.

Smith, A. and McBride, J. (2020) '"Working to live, not living to work": low-paid multiple employment and work-life articulation', *Work, Employment and Society*, 35(2): 256–76.

Standing, G. (2011) *The Precariat: The New Dangerous Class*, London: Bloomsbury.

Stark, D. and Pais, I. (2021) 'Algorithmic management in the platform economy', *Sociologica*, 14(3): 47–72.

Streeck, W. (2009) *Re-forming Capitalism: Institutional Change in the German Political Economy*, New York: Oxford University Press.

Supiot, A. (2001) *Beyond Employment: Changes in Work and the Future of Labour Law in Europe*, Oxford: Oxford University Press.

Umney, C. and Kretsos, L. (2015) '"That's the experience": passion, work precarity, and life transitions among London Jazz Musicians', *Work and Occupations,* 42(3): 313–34.

Whiting, R. and Symon, G. (2020) 'Digi-housekeeping: the invisible work of flexibility work', *Employment and Society*, 34(6): 1079–96.

Wood, A., Graham, M., Lehdonvirta, V. and Hjorth, I. (2018) 'Good gig, bad gig: autonomy and algorithmic control in the global gig economy', *Work, Employment and Society*, 33(1): 56–75.

Woodcock, J. and Graham, M. (2020) *The Gig Economy: A Critical Introduction.* Cambridge: Polity Press.

Zelizer, V.A. (2017) *The Social Meaning of Money: Pin Money, Paychecks, Poor Relief, and Other Currencies*, Princeton: Princeton University Press.

9

Precariousness in the Platform Economy

Agnieszka Piasna

Introduction

Labour practices in the platform economy have become a significant legal and political issue, even though the platform economy still only involves a relatively small proportion of the workforce, with an estimated 0.2 per cent to 10 per cent of adults engaging in platform work on a regular basis (see, for example, Piasna and Drahokoupil, 2019; Piasna, 2020a). The main controversy arises around the roles and responsibilities adopted by key actors involved in the platform-driven economy (Berg and De Stefano, 2017; Graham et al, 2017). The market is organized by digital labour platforms, which are companies functioning as technological intermediaries that connect clients, either companies or individual consumers, with workers willing to provide a requested service (Drahokoupil and Piasna, 2017). Workers in the platform economy are generally employed by neither of the parties of this economic exchange and work as self-employed or independent contractors. Jobs are dissolved into tasks, which are then 'sold' to workers competing to acquire paid work, who usually receive piece-rate remuneration.

Labour platforms operate in various sectors, ranging from on-location services such as transportation, delivery or handyperson work, to remotely provided IT or creative work (Pesole et al, 2018; Piasna and Drahokoupil, 2019). Insofar as the sectoral classification of labour platforms is helpful in identifying specific challenges facing the workforce, there is a marked commonality in many of the features of platform work, notably erratic and low earnings, absence of labour and social protection, and job instability (Bergvall-Kåreborn and Howcroft, 2014; Berg, 2016; Scholz, 2016; Piasna and Drahokoupil, 2019). These are the features usually used to identify precarious employment (Kalleberg, 2009; Kalleberg and Vallas, 2017; Piasna, 2017). Such conditions largely result from shifting the risks and costs involved in doing business onto the workforce. Platforms cede most of the responsibilities of employers to workers, thus depriving them of employment rights and protections, but they also do not allow genuine autonomy and self-determination of employment conditions (De Stefano, 2018; Piasna and Drahokoupil, 2021).

The platform economy, then, can be approached as the next stage of the ongoing process of individualization of risk and precarization of labour, following a proliferation of employment forms that fall outside of the standard employment relationship and a weakening of the pillars on which this normative model of employment has rested (Bosch, 2004; Stone and Arthurs, 2013; Rubery, 2015; Fudge, 2017). In that sense, labour platforms risk exacerbating many existing inequalities by rendering those most in need of protection more vulnerable to market pressures and exploitation (Rubery and Piasna, 2016; Piasna and Drahokoupil, 2021). Moreover, through their sectoral diversity and the fact that they organize not only low-skilled manual work but also white-collar professions, digital labour platforms have the potential to expand precarious conditions across all occupational classes.

Employment relations in the platform economy

Despite the novelty of the digital technology used to match labour demand and supply and to manage the work process, employment conditions in the platform economy are better understood when considered as part of a larger structural trend towards market-based orientation in managing and remunerating labour (Drahokoupil and Piasna, 2017; van Doorn, 2017; Rahman and Thelen, 2019). At the centre of this decades-long process has been a hollowing out of the standard employment relationship, or more generally, a weakening of the social contract that afforded considerable job and income security to workers. Relatively secure, full-time jobs that provided access to labour rights, social protection and various benefits were never universal, but they constituted a normative reference point for much of the 20th century. They provided workers with protections against pure market relationship and supported the decommodification of labour (Bosch, 2004). In contrast, neoliberal labour market policies, aimed at increasing labour supply, and the process of firm restructuring led to increasingly flexible and non-standard employment models (Kalleberg, 2003; Rubery, 2015; Weil, 2019). This manifested in the proliferation of outsourcing, sub-contracting, and a variety of non-standard and precarious forms of employment (Kalleberg, 2000).

Digital labour platforms, although they vary in the specificities of their business models and the sector in which they provide services, tend not to employ the workforce on which they rely. Thus, instead of establishing the employment relationship and hiring employees, for the most part, platforms use self-employed or independent contractors (De Stefano, 2018). The avoidance of an employer role is accentuated with the use of terminology that removes any association with employees or waged labour. Platform workers are often referred to as partners, and payslips are called invoices. There is nothing fundamentally new in companies structuring their workforce as a pool of self-employed micro-entrepreneurs, but technology makes such models easier and more efficient for engagers of labour (Adams et al, 2018). For workers, however, this translates into lack of reciprocal rights and obligations that are created by a legal link between employers and employees. In this respect, the platform economy represents a further step towards increasing precariousness of work.

The shifting of risks

In a situation whereby no actor assumes the role of an employer, risks, responsibilities and costs are effectively shifted onto workers (Drahokoupil and Piasna, 2017). Most institutions of worker protection, such as minimum wages, collective rights and social insurance, are linked to the employment relationship. Platform workers are thus excluded from these safety nets and the scope of labour law protection. A drop in demand, a work equipment failure and incapacity to work due to sickness or an accident at work are all risks usually shouldered by platform workers. This has become apparent in the COVID-19 crisis that forced food delivery platform workers to choose between sustaining income and protecting their health (Fairwork, 2020).

In the absence of an employment relationship, access to practices of labour representation, such as that offered by trade unions, is inhibited, which limits the capacity to voice concerns and seek support (Vandaele et al, 2019; Wood et al, 2019a). At the same time, by renouncing the role of the employer, platforms evade responsibilities and costs usually involved in employing people. The cost efficiency of matching labour supply with demand by platforms is thus largely achieved not so much by lowering costs but by shifting them from engagers of labour onto the workforce.

The uncertainty and insecurity faced by platform workers is further augmented by a lack of promise of a continuation of work in the future, even in the shortest time horizon. Workers can be disconnected by the platform at any point in time, without a notice period or warning (Drahokoupil and Piasna, 2019; Shanahan and Smith, 2021). While this is a reality also faced by solo self-employed people or entrepreneurs in the traditional (offline) economy, in contrast to these groups, platform workers have very limited scope for determining the terms and conditions of their work, including prices for their services (De Stefano, 2018; Wood et al, 2019a). In many on-location labour platforms, notably in transport and delivery, a choice of clients or a possibility to reject orders are constrained or negatively sanctioned. One important means used by labour platforms to exert control and discipline workers is a reliance on clients' ratings. Good ratings increase chances of being assigned new tasks in the future, while bad ratings can lead to a worker's account being suspended or deactivated (for instance, Wood et al, 2019a). Continuation of work thus largely depends on clients' reviews that can be biased or unfair but can hardly be disputed by workers, thus adding to their powerlessness vis-à-vis a platform. Securing positive ratings was also found to compel workers to perform additional work, usually without compensation, to keep clients satisfied (Pulignano et al, 2021). Despite their importance and efforts invested in securing positive ratings, they are not portable between platforms, thus locking-in workers on a particular platform, on which they become increasingly dependent. In addition, platforms have been found to unilaterally change conditions, which leads to feelings of precarity and anxiety among workers (Piasna and Drahokoupil, 2021). Unilateral changes to rates, rules of task allocation or switching between legal forms are a source of discontent, but workers have little means to contest platforms' decisions and hold them accountable (Shapiro, 2018; Drahokoupil and Piasna, 2019; Schor et al, 2020).

Employment conditions in the platform economy thus generate a power asymmetry to the disadvantage of workers. The perceptions of powerlessness of workers vis-à-vis platforms clearly surface in recent scholarship. For instance, TaskRabbit workers in the US, interviewed by Schor and colleagues (2020: 849), described their situation on the platform thus: "[w]e really are just cannon fodder", while Deliveroo riders in Belgium, cited by Piasna and Drahokoupil (2021: 1410), portrayed their work in terms of a "modern slavery" and felt that they were "not perceived or treated as human beings" by the platform. Platform work thus carries features of a highly commodified form of labour, producing subjective experiences and perceptions of precariousness among its workforce. By rejecting the role of an employer, platforms approach labour as a disposable commodity that can be effectively bought and sold in a market-based transaction.

Regulatory avoidance

The avoidance by platforms of assuming the role of employer has been the source of much controversy. Platforms argue that they offer a highly flexible work model that responds to the needs and preferences of their workforce. Not only is such a high level of flexibility not compatible with an employment relationship, the argument goes, but people working through platforms express a clear preference for working as independent contractors rather than as employees (see the discussions in Prassl, 2018;

Dubal, 2020). This view is at odds with the increasing amount of litigation against platform companies, brought forward by workers dissatisfied with the misclassification of their employment status and arguing for a restoration of an employment relationship, with all its rights, benefits and responsibilities (Kirchner and Schüßler, 2020). Similarly, numerous bottom-up collective struggles of platform workers for better employment conditions point to an inadequacy of the current system to meet their needs from work (Tassinari and Maccarrone, 2017; Vandaele et al, 2019).

A preference for an independent contractor status among platform workers was indeed revealed in several empirical studies, notably of Uber drivers (see, for example, Hall and Krueger, 2018; Berger et al, 2019). However, these findings have been subsequently challenged on the grounds that they confused a preference for working time flexibility with that for a flexible employment status, and criticized for methodological flaws (see, for instance, Berg and Johnston, 2019; Dubal, 2020). Other studies, by contrast, found a preference for an employee status and related protections among platform workers (Piasna and Drahokoupil, 2021), as well as among non-standard workers in general (Datta, 2019). Similarly to vulnerable workers, who tend to opt for precarious self-employment to escape unemployment (Adams et al, 2018; Banerjee and Duflo, 2011), platform work tends to be undertaken out of a lack of better alternatives (Pesole et al, 2018).

Nevertheless, insofar as investigating workers' preferences is an important element of expanding our understanding of work in the platform economy, opting out of labour law protection and rules applicable to employment relations is, in principle, not a matter of one's choosing (see ETUC, 2020). In this sense, online labour platforms deploy a narrative of individualization and freedom to render their business model attractive to workers and strive to normalize precarious employment (see also Rubery et al, 2018), at the same time providing a convenient and readily available infrastructure that enables firms to externalize risks and limit their obligations towards the workforce on which they rely (see the discussion in Vallas and Schor, 2020). This leaves platform workers disembedded from systems of social protection and exposed to market uncertainties and precarity (Kalleberg and Vallas, 2017).

Fragmentation

The hallmark of precarity is the condition of perpetual job insecurity. As the platform economy does not offer stable and continuous employment, platform workers instead build their working lives by stacking up multiple 'gigs', that is, a portfolio of small tasks or somewhat larger projects (Berg, 2016; Graham et al, 2017; Wood et al, 2019a; Piasna, 2020a). The intermittent nature of work through digital platforms creates fragmented employment patterns among its workforce. Spells of work on one or more tasks simultaneously are intertwined with extensive periods of job search, either in the form of watching for tasks to appear online or waiting for orders or clients (Berg, 2016). The spells between the performance of 'gigs' are not remunerated and, in this sense, resemble periods of unemployment or inactivity in the traditional economy. Moreover, tenure in the platform economy is very short; in food delivery, for instance, it is found to be in the range of several months (Drahokoupil and Piasna, 2019). To smooth out this intermittent activity, platform workers often have other jobs in the traditional, non-platform, economy, but these are more likely to be in the form of non-standard employment (Piasna and Drahokoupil, 2019; Ilsøe et al, 2021).

According to some accounts (see, for example, Sundararajan, 2016), diversification replacing a 'job for life' has become the new normal, and, rather than leading to precarity, it opens up new opportunities for workers to have a varied, independent and fulfilling career. Somewhat contrary to these expectations, comparative empirical evidence shows that thus far it is predominantly economic and job insecurity that pushes workers to engage in multiple paid activities (Piasna et al, 2020). Juggling multiple jobs is thus largely a compensatory strategy for job quality deficits in the primary employment (Wu et al, 2009; Dickey et al, 2011).

Fragmentation of work in the platform economy is observed also on the level of work organization. Digital labour platforms break down once whole jobs into small and simplified tasks. That way they can be feasibly performed by a dispersed workforce based on brief instructions provided over the Internet and without a need for any company-specific knowledge or training. The literature has labelled this disintegration of jobs into small on-demand tasks a 'digital Taylorism' (Healy et al, 2017; Goods et al, 2019). Efficiency maximization is achieved by standardizing and routinizing tasks, and in many respects resembles old methods of worker exploitation, such as piecework. This method of organizing and managing the work process removes many of the intrinsic rewards from work, such as those derived from seeing a completed product from one's efforts at work or the possibility of developing skills. The latter, coupled with a lack of employer-provided training, can negatively affect employability and labour market prospects.

Overall, the experience of this type of work risks having long-lasting negative effects on work patterns among platform workers, although more longitudinal research is needed to ascertain such effects. Previous research in the traditional economy has shown that uncertainty and precariousness experienced by young people early on in their careers were linked to poorer job quality outcomes in their future employment trajectories (Dieckhoff, 2011). Moreover, experiences of job insecurity tend to lower expectations and change behavioural strategies in future job searches, thus reproducing fragmented employment patterns throughout a working life (Mills et al, 2006;

Drahokoupil and Piasna, 2019). While this does not apply to all platform workers without exception, the development of the platform economy may lead to the emergence of particularly precarious conditions among workers who combine platform work with other non-standard forms of employment. Such groups would have little to no access to any form of protection or safety net, and would be exposed to competition for work relatively often, which, in the absence of employer-funded skill development, can lead to the accumulation of labour market disadvantage over time (see also Rubery and Piasna, 2016).

Earnings and economic security

Digital labour platforms lower the transaction costs involved in matching labour supply and demand. However, as noted earlier, the matching service provided by platforms may in fact merely shift the transaction costs to workers. In addition to the transfer of those costs and risks that are related to an avoidance of the employment relationship and worker protections, the shifting of costs is directly perceptible in earnings from platform work. The main logic of efficiency maximization in the platform economy is similar to that in low-level non-standard jobs in conventional service sectors, where labour costs are lowered by closely matching staffing levels to fluctuations in demand. Workers are thus scheduled to work only during peak times, while any slack time when the demand is low is removed from paid working time (Wood, 2016; Piasna, 2018). This is the practice increasingly used in retail or care sectors in the traditional economy (Henly et al, 2006; Lambert et al, 2012; Piasna, 2020b), introducing instability and income insecurity into workers' lives. Due to the use of digital technology and artificial intelligence to allocate tasks to workers, labour platforms can potentially achieve an even closer match between labour demand and supply, shortening paid working time to the minimum and, in doing so, fully shifting any inefficiency in time use onto workers.

Moreover, platform workers are only paid for the tasks they complete, yet securing paid work through platforms has been found to necessitate an extensive input of time and effort that is not paid (Berg, 2016; Pulignano et al, 2021). In the absence of regulations such as minimum wages, platforms may have little incentive to invest in algorithms that allow workers to search for work efficiently and eliminate unpaid waiting or search time. Unpaid work is thus enshrined as a reality of work through platforms, adding to the social and economic unpredictability faced by platform workers – a crucial feature of precariousness (Pulignano, 2019).

Digital labour platforms do not rely on a continuous employment relationship to secure appropriate levels of labour supply. Instead, to ensure that there is always someone available to provide a service on request, platforms aim at attracting a large pool of readily available workers that exceeds the number of tasks on offer. Low entry barriers, with the recruitment process usually reduced to a straightforward registration on a website or in an app, as well as gamification mechanisms encouraging workers to stay logged in longer, are some of the inexpensive strategies used by platforms to ensure labour oversupply. This business strategy of labour platforms to attract a large supply of workers produces between-worker competition for a limited number of tasks or clients (Shapiro, 2018; Wood et al, 2019a). The outcome is an insufficient availability of work, with many workers not able to access as much paid activity as they would need to make ends meet (Schor et al, 2020; Piasna and Drahokoupil, 2021). Labour oversupply also negatively affects the market power of workers vis-à-vis a platform, propagating feelings of job insecurity and perceptions of replaceability by other workers willing to perform the same tasks for lower pay (Lehdonvirta, 2018; Wood et al, 2019b). This is particularly the case on platforms operating globally, where competition for tasks between workers from low- and high-income countries puts additional downward pressure on rates and incomes.

Finally, platforms can put downward pressure on labour costs because the use of self-employment allows firms to pay workers below the statutory minimum wage levels or collectively agreed wages applicable to employees in a given sector. Platforms are also able to avoid the costs associated with health, unemployment and retirement insurance, or education and up-skilling of workers. At the same time, the foregone protections are not compensated with worker autonomy in determining pay levels or prices for their own services, which should be the case for the self-employed or independent contractors (see the discussion in Dubal, 2020). This issue is particularly relevant in food delivery and taxi services organized by labour platforms, where information about the price for the trip is often withheld from workers before they accept a task (Rosenblat and Stark, 2016; Shapiro, 2018; Goods et al, 2019).

Overall, the architecture of online labour platforms and the algorithmic management of work can be used to exert downward pressure on wages and lower labour costs. Digital technology increases efficiency for labour engagers by closely matching labour demand and supply in real time. In the absence of institutions of income protection, platform workers need to face the costs related to fluctuation in demand and the related risk of income loss when demand is low, or when work is not possible or desirable. This is coupled with a considerable load of unpaid hours, which are needed to find and access work through platforms – a condition which is aggravated by insufficient availability of paid tasks and a limited scope for determining pay rates in many sectors. All this translates into very low, unpredictable and erratic earnings, as reported in many investigations into conditions of platform work (Berg, 2016; Piasna and Drahokoupil, 2019; Wood et al, 2019a).

Precarious work or precarious workers

Digital labour platforms that avoid the role of an employer are able to shift the costs and risks of employment onto workers. Precariousness is thus a fitting description of the conditions that platform workers confront as they strive to earn their living while compelled to assume forms and levels of risk that were previously shouldered by employers and the state (see the discussion in Vallas and Schor, 2020). And yet, digital labour platforms are also portrayed as reducing precarity.

A positive role for digital labour platforms is mainly proposed in terms of their labour market integrative function. Highly flexible work models, where time and place of work are not fixed, provide employment opportunities to individuals who might be otherwise excluded from the labour market, such as those with disabilities or with care obligations, notably women (see Rani and Furrer, 2021). Remote platform work allows workers in developing countries and from regions with high unemployment to access paid work from clients who otherwise would not recruit in their area (Wood et al, 2019a). Low entry barriers and a lack of a standard recruitment process might constitute a further advantage for workers facing discriminations in hiring. Platform work also lends itself to combination with other sources of income. Indeed, available evidence shows that platform workers typically have one or more paid jobs in addition to work they obtain through platforms (Hall and Krueger, 2018; Drahokoupil and Piasna, 2019; Piasna and Drahokoupil, 2019; Urzí Brancati et al, 2020; Ilsøe et al, 2021). If platform work, then, supplements low incomes from the main job, it can mitigate precarity by enabling a build-up of savings, paying basic expenses or reducing debt (see Vallas and Schor, 2020).

Such approaches to the platform economy view precarity as a circumstance that characterizes a person, even if the cause of this circumstance lays in the labour market. Accordingly, while a low wage and insecure job produces a precarious life, juggling two such low wage and insecure jobs reduces the initial precarity of a worker insofar as two low incomes may add up to a liveable wage. A contrasting view, however, is taken in the job quality scholarship that evaluates the features and characteristics of a job irrespective of who performs this job (Green and Mostafa, 2012; Burchell et al, 2014; Piasna et al, 2017).

This is further complicated by recent findings showing that worker outcomes are determined by the degree of economic dependence on platform earnings (Schor et al, 2020; Piasna and Drahokoupil, 2021). Accordingly, workers who do not rely on platform work to pay their basic living expenses were found to be more selective in the tasks they perform; work less on a platform, and only when it genuinely suited them; and invest less unpaid time in searching for tasks when the demand is low (Kuhn and

Maleki, 2017; Lehdonvirta, 2018). From this, it follows that platform work was not associated with precarity for workers who derived income security from other sources. When using platforms to only earn extra income, which does not need to be stable, predictable or liveable, workers are able to achieve greater satisfaction, autonomy and, in some cases, higher hourly wages from this type of work. In contrast, those who attempt to make a living out of platform work experience more precarity (Schor et al, 2020). In this sense, the platform economy can reproduce conventional inequalities, such as those related to socio-economic status.

Conclusion

The growth of digital labour platforms has created new forms of organization and outsourcing of labour. A central element of this model is that no side of the transaction assumes the role of an employer, even though labour is supplied by private individuals, not companies. This leaves workers in the platform economy without access to social security, labour law protection, training, or workers' rights, including the right to organize and bargain collectively. While it is usually easy to sign up on a platform, it is also possible to be disconnected at any time without notice. Availability of work is not guaranteed, which, coupled with platforms' strategy of creating an oversupply of workers relative to demand and very low pay rates, results in a considerable amount of unpaid time that has to be put into acquiring work through platforms. Insecurity of work and unpredictability of earnings position platform work in the realm of precarious employment.

Uncertainty and costs related to fluctuating demand are shifted towards workers. Piece rates and competition for tasks discipline workers to be available instantaneously and produce on demand. In this way, workers smooth out the market fluctuation and shoulder risks, while the platform companies and clients can profit (Snyder, 2016). The shifting of costs and risks is paired with a degree of flexibility in time and place of work that might be unavailable to workers in the traditional workplaces. This attracts workers willing to forego protections to gain freedom and autonomy. In the long run, however, workers find the uncertainty of work and unpredictability of work hours and earnings difficult to sustain (Bergvall-Kåreborn and Howcroft, 2014; Scholz, 2016; Snyder, 2016). The outcome is a high turnover and very short tenures.

If the trend towards flexibilization and deregulation of work continues, standard employment will become less prevalent and thus harder to access (Bosch, 2004; Rubery, 2015; Rubery and Piasna, 2016). Job insecurity and low wages in non-standard employment can then push more workers to look for additional income in the platform economy, tempted by the ease of joining a platform and the promise of flexibility that accommodates diverse life circumstances, such as having to care for young children, which may attract more women, in particular, to these online markets. The spread of platform work can, in turn, have a spill-over effect on conventional employers. It provides technological solutions that foster an adoption of its template of organizing work and employment on an on-demand and highly flexible basis beyond the boundaries of the platform economy itself, which in turn risks eroding employment standards and protections for a growing number of workers (Vallas and Schor, 2020).

However, these developments are not necessarily an inevitable consequence of a highly competitive global marketplace (Snyder, 2016), though they tend to be presented that way (compare Sundararajan, 2016). Regulatory avoidance and risk-shifting onto workers, which drive precariousness of work arrangements in the platform economy, are a matter of business strategy and policy choices. Alternative ways of organizing platform work are possible, such as through regular employment, guaranteed hourly wages or a minimum floor of paid activity (Lehdonvirta, 2018; Goods et al, 2019; Piasna and Drahokoupil, 2021).

The COVID-19 crisis has placed the insecurity and precarity of platform work in sharp focus. Aside from considerable public attention, the recent period has also seen substantial regulatory breakthroughs. The notable, and contrasting, examples include Proposition 22, passed in California in November 2020, which exempts app-based gig companies from having to treat their workers like employees, and the UK Supreme Court ruling of 19 February 2021, classifying Uber drivers as workers. It remains to be seen which direction for regulatory change will prevail in the years to come and whether a lasting divergence in the conditions of work in the platform companies will arise between the US and European labour markets.

References

Adams, A., Freedman, J. and Prassl, J. (2018) 'Rethinking legal taxonomies for the gig economy', *Oxford Review Economic Policy*, 34(3): 475–94.

Banerjee, A. and Duflo, E. (2011) *Poor Economics: A Radical Rethinking of the Way to Fight Global Poverty*, New York: Public Affairs.

Berg, J. (2016) 'Income security in the on-demand economy: findings and policy lessons from a survey of crowdworkers', International Labour Organization, Conditions of Work and Employment Series No. 74.

Berg, J. and De Stefano, V. (2017) 'It's time to regulate the gig economy', *Open Democracy*, 18 April. Available from: https://www.opendemocracy. net/en/beyond-trafficking-and-slavery/it-s-time-to-regulate-gig-econ omy/ [Accessed 18 March 2022].

Berg, J. and Johnston, H. (2019) 'Too good to be true? A comment on Hall and Krueger's analysis of the labor market for Uber's driver-partners', *ILR Review*, 72(1): 39–68.

Berger, T., Frey, C.B., Levin, G. and Danda, S.R. (2019) 'Uber happy? Work and well-being in the "gig economy"', *Economic Policy*, 34(99): 429–77.

Bergvall-Kåreborn, B. and Howcroft, D. (2014) 'Amazon Mechanical Turk and the commodification of labour', *New Technology, Work & Employment*, 29(3): 213–23.

Bosch, G. (2004) 'Towards a new standard employment relationship in Western Europe', *British Journal of Industrial Relations*, 42(2): 617–36.

Burchell, B., Sehnbruch, K., Piasna, A. and Agloni, N. (2014) 'The quality of employment and decent work: definitions, methodologies, and ongoing debates', *Cambridge Journal of Economics*, 38(2): 459–77.

Datta, N. (2019) 'Willing to pay for security: a discrete choice experiment to analyse labour supply preferences', CEP Discussion Papers, no. dp1632, Centre for Economic Performance, LSE. Available from: https://cep.lse.ac.uk/pubs/download/dp1632.pdf [Accessed 29 March 2022].

De Stefano, V. (2018) ' "Negotiating the algorithm": automation, artificial intelligence and labour protection', International Labour Organization, employment working paper no. 246. Available from: www.ilo.org/wcmsp5/groups/public/---ed_emp/---emp_policy/documents/publication/wcms_634157.pdf [Accessed 29 March 2022].

Dickey, H., Watson, V. and Zangelidis, A. (2011) 'Is it all about money? An examination of the motives behind moonlighting', *Applied Economics*, 43(26): 3767–74.

Dieckhoff, M. (2011) 'The effect of unemployment on subsequent job quality in Europe: a comparative study of four countries', *Acta Sociologica*, 54(3): 233–49.

Drahokoupil, J. and Piasna, A. (2017) 'Work in the platform economy: beyond lower transaction costs', *Intereconomics: Review of European Economic Policy*, 52(6): 335–40.

Drahokoupil, J. and Piasna, A. (2019) 'Work in the platform economy: Deliveroo riders in Belgium and the SMart arrangement', ETUI working paper no. 2019.01. Available from: www.etui.org/sites/default/files/ez_import/WP-2019-01-deliveroo-WEB-2.pdf [Accessed 29 March 2022].

Dubal, V.B. (2020) 'An Uber ambivalence: employee status, worker perspectives, and regulation in the gig economy', in D. Das Acevedo (ed) *Beyond the Algorithm: Qualitative Insights for Gig Work Regulation*, Cambridge: Cambridge University Press, pp 33–56.

ETUC (2020) 'ETUC resolution on the protection of the rights of non-standard workers and workers in platform companies (including the self-employed)', adopted at the Executive Committee Meeting of 28–29 October, European Trade Union Confederation. Available from: www.etuc.org/en/document/etuc-resolution-protection-rights-non-standard-workers-and-workers-platform-companies [Accessed 29 March 2022].

Fairwork (2020) *The Gig Economy and Covid-19: Looking Ahead*, Oxford: The Fairwork Project.

Fudge, J. (2017) 'The future of the standard employment relationship: labour law, new institutional economics and old power resource theory', *Journal of Industrial Relations*, 59(3): 374–92.

Goods, C., Veen, A. and Barratt, T. (2019) '"Is your gig any good?" Analysing job quality in the Australian platform-based food-delivery sector', *Journal of Industrial Relations*, 61(4): 502–27.

Graham, M., Hjorth, I. and Lehdonvirta, V. (2017) 'Digital labour and development: impacts of global digital labour platforms and the gig economy on worker livelihoods', *Transfer: European Review of Labour and Research*, 23(2): 135–62.

Green, F. and Mostafa, T. (2012) 'Trends in job quality in Europe', Eurofound report, Available from: https://www.eurofound.europa.eu/publications/rep ort/2012/working-conditions/trends-in-job-quality-in-europe [Accessed 16 July 2021].

Hall, J.V. and Krueger, A.B. (2018) 'An analysis of the labor market for Uber's driver-partners in the United States', *ILR Review*, 71(3): 705–32.

Healy, J., Nicholson, D. and Pekarek, A. (2017) 'Should we take the gig economy seriously?', *Labour & Industry: A Journal of the Social and Economic Relations of Work*, 27(3): 232–48.

Henly, J.R., Shaefer, H.L. and Waxman, E. (2006) 'Nonstandard work schedules: employer- and employee-driven flexibility in retail jobs', *Social Service Review*, 80(4): 609–34.

Ilsøe, A., Larsen, T.P. and Bach, E.S. (2021) 'Multiple jobholding in the digital platform economy: signs of segmentation', *Transfer: European Review of Labour and Research*, 27(2): 201–18.

Kalleberg, A.L. (2000) 'Nonstandard employment relations: part-time, temporary and contract work', *Annual Review of Sociology*, 26: 341–65.

Kalleberg, A.L. (2003) 'Flexible firms and labor market segmentation effects of workplace restructuring on jobs and workers', *Work & Occupations*, 30(2): 154–75.

Kalleberg, A.L. (2009) 'Precarious work, insecure workers: employment relations in transition, *American Sociological Review*, 74: 1–22.

Kalleberg, A.L. and Vallas, S. (2017) 'Probing precarious work: theory, research, and politics', *Research in the Sociology of Work*, 31: 1–30.

Kirchner, S. and Schüßler, E. (2020) 'Regulating the sharing economy: a field perspective', in I. Maurer, J. Mair and A. Oberg (eds) *Theorizing the Sharing Economy: Variety and Trajectories of New Forms of Organizing*, Bingley: Emerald Publishing, pp 215–36.

Kuhn, K.M. and Maleki, A. (2017) 'Micro-entrepreneurs, dependent contractors, and instaserfs: understanding online labor platform workforces', *Academy of Management Perspectives*, 31(3): 183–200.

Lambert, S.J., Haley-Lock, A. and Henly, J.R. (2012) 'Schedule flexibility in hourly jobs: unanticipated consequences and promising directions', *Community, Work & Family*, 15(3): 293–315.

Lehdonvirta, V. (2018) 'Flexibility in the gig economy: managing time on three online piecework platforms', *New Technology, Work & Employment*, 33(1): 13–29.

Mills, M., Blossfeld, H.-P. and Klijzing, E. (2006) 'Becoming an adult in uncertain times: a 14-country comparison of the losers of globalization', in H.-P. Blossfeld, E. Klijzing, M. Mills and K. Kurz (eds) *Globalization, Uncertainty and Youth in Society*, London: Routledge, pp 393–411.

Pesole, A., Urzí Brancati, M.C., Fernández-Macías, E., Biagi, F. and González Vázquez, I. (2018) 'Platform workers in Europe', Publications Office of the European Union, EUR29275 EN. Available from: https://publi cations.jrc.ec.europa.eu/repository/bitstream/JRC112157/jrc112157_ pubsy_platform_workers_in_europe_science_for_policy.pdf [Accessed 29 March 2022].

Piasna, A. (2017) ' "Bad jobs" recovery? European Job Quality Index 2005–2015', ETUI, working paper no. 2017.06. Available from: www.etui.org/ sites/default/files/WP-2017.06-WEB.pdf [Accessed 29 March 2022].

Piasna, A. (2018) 'Scheduled to work hard: the relationship between non-standard working hours and work intensity among European workers (2005–2015)', *Human Resource Management Journal*, 28(1): 167–81.

Piasna, A. (2020a) 'Counting gigs. How can we measure the scale of online platform work?', ETUI, working paper no. 2020.06. Available from: www. etui.org/sites/default/files/2020-09/Counting%20gigs_2020_web.pdf [Accessed 29 March 2022].

Piasna, A. (2020b) 'Standards of good work in the organisation of working time: fragmentation and the intensification of work across sectors and occupations', *Management Review*, 31(2): 259–84.

Piasna, A. and Drahokoupil, J. (2019) 'Digital labour in central and eastern Europe: evidence from the ETUI Internet and Platform Work Survey', ETUI, working paper no. 2019.12. Available from: www.etui.org/sites/ default/files/WP%202019%2012%20%20Digital%20Labour%20Web%20 version.pdf [Accessed 29 March 2022].

Piasna, A. and Drahokoupil, J. (2021) 'Flexibility unbound: understanding the heterogeneity of preferences among food delivery platform workers', *Socio-Economic Review*, 19(4): 1397–419.

Piasna, A., Burchell, B., Sehnbruch, K. and Agloni, N. (2017) 'Job quality: conceptual and methodological challenges for comparative analysis', in D. Grimshaw, C. Fagan, G. Hebson and I. Tavora (eds) *Making Work More Equal: A New Labour Market Segmentation Approach*, Manchester: Manchester University Press, pp 168–87.

Piasna, A., Pedaci, M. and Czarzasty, J. (2020) 'Multiple jobholding in Europe: features and effects of primary job quality', *Transfer: European Review of Labour and Research*, 27(2): 181–99.

Prassl, J. (2018) *Humans as a Service: The Promise and Perils of Work in the Gig Economy*, Oxford: Oxford University Press.

Pulignano, V. (2019) 'Work in deregulated labour markets: a research agenda for precariousness', ETUI, working paper no. 2019.03. Available from: www.etui.org/sites/default/files/WP-2019-03-labour%20markets-pulignano-WEB.pdf [Accessed 29 March 2022].

Pulignano, V., Piasna, A., Domecka, M., Muszyński, K. and Vermeerbergen, L. (2021) 'Does it pay to work? Unpaid labour in the platform economy', ETUI, policy brief no. 2021.15. Available from: https://etui.org/sites/default/files/2021-11/Does%20it%20pay%20to%20work.%20Unpaid%20labour%20in%20the%20platform%20economy_2021.pdf [Accessed 29 March 2022].

Rahman, K.S. and Thelen, K. (2019) 'The rise of the platform business model and the transformation of twenty-first-century capitalism', *Politics & Society*, 47(2): 177–204.

Rani, U. and Furrer, M. (2021) 'Digital labour platforms and new forms of flexible work in developing countries: algorithmic management of work and workers', *Competition & Change*, 25(2): 212–36.

Rosenblat, A. and Stark, L. (2016) 'Algorithmic labor and information asymmetries: a case study of Uber's drivers', *International Journal of Communication*, 10: 3758–84.

Rubery, J. (2015) 'Change at work: feminisation, flexibilisation, fragmentation and financialisation', *Employee Relations*, 37(6): 633–44.

Rubery, J. and Piasna, A. (2016) 'Labour market segmentation and the EU reform agenda: developing alternatives to the mainstream', ETUI, working paper no. 2016.10. Available from: www.etui.org/sites/default/files/web%20version-WP%202016.10.pdf [Accessed 29 March 2022].

Rubery, J., Grimshaw, D., Keizer, A. and Johnson, M. (2018) 'Challenges and contradictions in the "normalising" of precarious work', *Work, Employment & Society*, 32(3): 509–27.

Scholz, T. (2016) *Uberworked and Underpaid: How Workers Are Disrupting the Digital Economy*, Cambridge: Polity.

Schor, J.B., Attwood-Charles, W., Cansoy, M., Ladegaard, I. and Wengronowitz, R. (2020) 'Dependence and precarity in the platform economy', *Theory & Society*, 49: 833–61.

Shanahan, G. and Smith, M. (2021) 'Fair's fair: psychological contracts and power in platform work', *International Journal of Human Resource Management*, 32(19): 4078–109.

Shapiro, A. (2018) 'Between autonomy and control: strategies of arbitrage in the "on-demand" economy', *New Media & Society*, 20(8): 2954–71.

Snyder, B.H. (2016) *The Disrupted Workplace: Time and the Moral Order of Flexible Capitalism*, Oxford: Oxford University Press.

Stone, K. and Arthurs, H. (2013) *Rethinking Workplace Regulation: Beyond the Standard Contract of Employment*, New York: Russell Sage Foundation.

Sundararajan, A. (2016) *The Sharing Economy: The End of Employment and the Rise of Crowd-Based Capitalism*, Cambridge, MA: MIT Press.

Tassinari, A. and Maccarrone, V. (2017) 'The mobilisation of gig economy couriers in Italy: some lessons for the trade union movement', *Transfer: European Review of Labour and Research*, 23(3): 353–7.

Urzí Brancati, M.C., Pesole, A. and Férnandéz-Macías, E. (2020) 'New Evidence on Platform Workers in Europe. Results from the Second COLLEEM Survey', Publications Office of the European Union. Available from: https://publications.jrc.ec.europa.eu/repository/bitstream/JRC118 570/jrc118570_jrc118570_final.pdf [Accessed 29 March 2022].

Vallas, S. and Schor, J.B. (2020) 'What do platforms do? Understanding the gig economy', *Annual Review of Sociology*, 46: 273–94.

Vandaele, K., Piasna, A. and Drahokoupil, J. (2019) '"Algorithm breakers" are not a different "species": attitudes towards trade unions of Deliveroo riders in Belgium', ETUI, working paper no. 2019.06. Available from: www.etui.org/sites/default/files/WP-2019-06-web.pdf [Accessed 29 March 2022].

van Doorn, N. (2017) 'Platform labor: on the gendered and racialized exploitation of low-income service work in the "on-demand" economy', *Information, Communication & Society*, 20(6): 898–914. Weil, D. (2019) 'Understanding the present and future of work in the fissured workplace context', *RSF: the Russell Sage Foundation Journal of the Social Sciences*, 5(5): 147–65.

Wood, A.J. (2016) 'Flexible scheduling, degradation of job quality and barriers to collective voice', *Human Relations*, 69(10): 1989–2010.

Wood, A.J., Graham, M., Lehdonvirta, V. and Hjorth, I. (2019a) 'Good gig, bad gig: autonomy and algorithmic control in the global gig economy', *Work, Employment & Society*, 33(1): 56–75.

Wood, A.J., Graham, M., Lehdonvirta, V. and Hjorth, I. (2019b) 'Networked but commodified: the (dis)embeddedness of digital labour in the gig economy', *Sociology*, 53(5): 931–50.

Wu, Z., Baimbridge, M. and Zhu, Y. (2009) 'Multiple job holding in the United Kingdom: evidence from the British Household Panel Survey', *Applied Economics*, 41(21): 2751–66.

10

A Pandemic-related Turning Point: Precarious Work, Platforms and Utopian Energies

Patrick Cingolani

The pandemic and outsourcing

The COVID-19 crisis is a milestone in the digitalization of social life and work activities. Social distancing measures have led to a process that reduces social circles and makes sociability scarcer while also reconfiguring professional and domestic daily life through digital systems and platforms. A rescaling of economic activity has been possible, restructuring the relationships between work and home, particularly in service industries, and conferring professional tools and concerns on the domestic space. The virtualization of companies, which until now was mainly characterized by a process of outsourcing, including sub-contracting and offshoring, has found a novel extension through teleworking and, more generally, through remote working. The domestic unit has, more than ever before, emerged as a segmented and insular production unit.

Only the power of the digitalization of socio-professional life could bring about such a shift. The tools hitherto available to platforms, whether for micro-tasks or professional work, have been extended to a wide range of managers and employees. In fact, these platforms, and in particular the large conglomerates (Amazon), have leveraged an opportunity presented by the pandemic to strengthen their power by adjusting as much as possible to the lockdown and the health-related restrictions through their distanced business model. They have strengthened their control over e-commerce, increased their market shares and extended their spheres of hegemony to new activities (such as Zoom Video Communications), receiving high praise from international financial markets. According to e-commerce watchdogs, online sales in France now account for almost 15 per cent of all retail trade (Bertrand, 2021). In addition to employing workers who are monitored, poorly paid, often hired on temporary contacts and in economically depressed areas in their warehouses, the major North American platforms have mobilized delivery agents in the streets who are subject to piecework and exposed to accidents. Amazon has been subject to criticism and lawsuits, to the extent that one of its vice-presidents, Tim Bray, resigned in protest. UberEats, Deliveroo and other home delivery platforms, which employ micro-entrepreneurs at the mercy of the fluctuations of a pandemic-hit economy, have extended their sphere of influence over urban areas and have taken advantage of the new competition between delivery drivers and the available workforce of the jobless to cut the rate for deliveries, which are increasingly paid as piecework. The challenge of this widespread presence of platforms is less, in our view, about a return to a 'domestic system' (Acquier, 2017) and more about the continuation and extension of a work deregulation process already achieved by precarious work, which has been established through intermediation systems, of which sub-contracting and temporary work have, to varying degrees, been models.

In this chapter, we will demonstrate how the platforms of the 21st century continue the insecure forms of work of the second half of the 20th century, and we will consider their implications in the pandemic. We will conclude by seeking to identify avenues for alternative energies from recent protests by platform workers and their local and activist roots in some working-class districts.

Digitalization, platforms and precarious work

For nearly 20 years now in France, our publications have emphasized the epistemological and political importance of the polysemy of the term *precarious* and we have put forward three major meanings of this word: precarious work (*travail précaire*), the precarious (*précaires*) and precariousness (*précarité*) – each of which refers to a specific moment in history dating from approximately the second half of the 20th century (Cingolani, 2017 [2005]).

(1) In the case of *precarious work*, it is the multiple and differentiating functionality of a discontinuity of work and employment that we find significant. This includes the wide range of intermittencies, for a duration of one or more months (temping and fixed-term contracts) or a few hours a day during the week (part-time work), and the segmentation of companies by outsourcing some of the workers, increasing the number of legal statuses and resulting in a specific system of working conditions and times. The functions of adjustment, availability and

circumvention of regulations are the focus of systems that result in job insecurity for the worker, in some cases to the extent of informal and illegal work.

(2) The word *precarious* implies both a certain historical system of subjectivation (the emergence of the precarious movement, the self-styling of some groups as 'precarious') together with some uses of intermittency (consecutive or simultaneous multi-activity, avoidance tactics regarding work constraints and social allocations of employment). Through their practices and movements, people in precarious situations have criticized morphological, space- and time-related standards established on the basis of Fordism. They supported the historic push to oppose bureaucratic organizations along the lines of multi-activity and a diversification of work times (Gorz, 1980, 1997).

(3) *Precariousness* emerges as one of the latest major inflections of the word 'precarious' in the 20th century. It does this against the backdrop of *new poverties* around the mid-1980s in France. Related to forms of unemployment, precarious work and their repercussions in terms of risks, precariousness is at the crossroads between several forms of insecurity, in particular, family crises and their after-effects, a lack of cultural and qualification levels and, as a result, inequalities regarding education and the degradation of local areas and so on (Wresinski, 1987).

We will consider each of these major meanings in order to address the relationships between precarious work and platform capitalism, to discuss the current situation regarding insecurity during the COVID-19 crisis and to conclude by outlining the emerging alternative energies.

While precarious or insecure work (particularly temporary work and short-term contracts) was a specific means of outsourcing workers to enable companies to form an available 'workforce safeguard' (Bellon, 1975), platforms are emerging as a new form of outsourcing system through their intermediation. They are restructuring the legal status of this workforce, on the basis of the micro-entrepreneur and self-employed worker status, and of an on-demand labour economy. The adjective *precarious*, which was hitherto related to an atypical job or workforce, has shifted to describe some self-employed workers and to trivialize the status of insecure micro-entrepreneurs, which admittedly account for a minority of workers in France when compared to their counterparts in the UK. The conditions of subordination through algorithmic controls and GPS data undermine the conventional construction of the worker employee. One of these undermining elements is related to the way in which platforms, for which the model stretches much further beyond the famous GAFAM companies (Google, Apple, Facebook, Amazon, Microsoft) , are altering the gains that can be made by professionals and professionalism by recreating spaces for informal work, which includes the promotion of amateurs as a key feature (Leadbeater and Miller, 2004; Flichy, 2017).

The fragmentation of tasks and the international competition between professionals and, on a local level, between professionals and amateurs are undermining employment criteria. The intrusive nature of digital technology in our private and daily lives increases the potential for extended work times: late in the evening, in a waiting room, while shopping. The confiscation of creative and communicative digital resources means that these creative or recreational activities become commercial and are becoming professionalized through self-entrepreneurship (YouTube). As the enthusiasm and encouragements of stock prices appear to indicate, platforms are the armed wing of a new hegemony that quietly enforces the market and its laws as a model for new social relationships. Implicitly, they normalize a social model that is characterized by piecework, uncertainty, last-minute actions and algorithms that instantly call on workers and then terminate their services without notice. It is clear that these are the very characteristics that have been the criteria of precarious work as an instrument of a more flexible labour market for the past 50 years. The concept of the 'gig economy' is the euphemism for this new system of insecurity, which also affects other craft activities (YoupiJob, NeedHelp, TaskRabbit, and so on), and which recently seized part of the 'knowledge worker' market on a global scale (Freelancer.com, Upwork.com, Malt.fr, and so on). This model of capitalism appears to be relatively constrained at present, yet, due to its malleability, it can go viral and expand its commercial colonization to spheres of activity that were not thought to be subject to transactions or compensation (Cingolani, 2021). The case of Click and Walk, an application through which customers check prices and analyze product visibility, is a prime example of platforms' power to penetrate areas of experience that were, up to now, neglected by capitalism, as well as of their social informalization capacity.

The strength of the blurring of spatial and temporal labour boundaries, and the permeability of times and places brought about by platforms, operate as instruments that deregulate the employee model, erode employment and, relatively, debase the workforce. The digital processing of the workforce is based on informal labour situations and one of the repercussions of this is the major reduction in rights and social safeguards that almost appear to be illegitimate.

While telework is focused more on professionals and appears to have no direct effect on job insecurity, it must nevertheless be considered in relation to remote working, as the latter reconfigures employment and work conditions more extensively and more incisively, particularly in the cultural and knowledge work sectors. In the 20th century, working from home was the ultimate manifestation of an activity that combined employment and precarious work. It displayed most of the criteria that define the latter: irregular quantities of work and schedules, porous temporal separations between work and non-work, poor relationships with the workers of the sub-contracting company, irregular pay, and payments for piecework or services provided (Lallement, 1990). Telework may not have the same consequences as working from home or remotely, but it does reconfigure the relationship to time and space to an equal degree. 'Always on' technologies, which are constantly plugged in or connected, result in availability by encouraging an infringement of the markers of domestic life. They grab time and attention and result in random overwork. While leaving the employee isolated and with greater uncertainty regarding information and organization, they allow remote disciplinary checks (Walker, 2021) and diagnostics on his/her state of health using biopolitical systems that control concentration, irritability and even exhaustion (Alloa, 2021).

The halo of precariousness around digital technology

This reconfiguration of precarious work has repercussions for the condition of insecurity. In his analysis of the 'anthropological crisis of the workforce', Robert Castel insisted on the continuities between the most extreme forms of poverty and companies' mechanisms of making the workforce more flexible or outsourcing work. The pandemic does not invalidate this movement, which he defined according to the concept of a 'destabilization of stables' (Castel, 2011: 429) and which expressed the link between precarious work and precariousness, between the labour crisis and endemic forms of poverty (Cingolani, 2017 [2005]). Rather, platform capitalism opens up new avenues to this link, less from a relationship of continuity, as defined by Castel, but more from an acentric and plural trend that weakens the established structures of employment and workers' rights and gradually undoes regulations. Due to its ability to penetrate all the societal interstices, there is a virality of platform capitalism that was not present in corporate strategy in the second half of the 20th century.

Throughout the 'destabilization of stables' process, the vagueness of the unemployment category identified at the turn of the century has expanded (Demazière, 2003). While the time and status of the unemployed were limited in the past, these criteria lose their clarity due to the multiplication of forms of unemployment and their long-lasting and recurring nature. Self-entrepreneurship only gives rise to unemployment benefits in rare cases. An available workforce, characterized by short-term contracts, casual work and unreliable pay, survives alongside employees in ongoing employment. Yet while, as we have just observed, platform capitalism increases these forms of atypical and short-term jobs, changes to the unemployment benefit system in recent years have called into question the rights of employees with discontinuous jobs, furthering a long-term trend that alienates these types of workers. The coming reforms in France will reduce the amount of benefits they receive, thereby increasing the halo of insecurity around the condition (Grégoire et al, 2020).

The pandemic has had a direct impact on these workers, who, more often than not, belong to the working classes or to the more vulnerable groups of the middle classes. Short-term contracts were the first not to be renewed, and for this very reason these workers were ineligible for the short-time work schemes, which enabled others to mitigate the effects of the crisis, and were unable to shift to telework – predominantly concerning services and IT activities. In the peripheral areas of major cities or those in periurban areas known for the Yellow Vest (*Gilet Jaune*) movement, the consequences of unemployment have heightened the process of impoverishing the poorest. The endemic problems in districts and local areas, namely over-crowded housing, scarcity of public services, a lack of accessible medical care and the digital divide, have been exacerbated by the pandemic. In the working-class suburbs, where a large number of frontline workers – cashiers, delivery people, healthcare workers – live, people were the most exposed to COVID-19 and often had to deal with increased risk levels, particularly due to commute times. High population density, poor housing conditions and multi-generational cohabitations favoured the transmission of the virus. The mortality rate for workers of immigrant origin and those with careers in high-risk occupational sectors was greater, while almost all the structures responding to the health crisis lacked the means and resources required (Brun and Simon, 2020).

As regards endemic forms of poverty and insecurity, conventional demands are not enough. Trade union structures concern and advocate more for workers with open-ended employment contracts who have hegemonic lifestyles rather than for precarious workers who are often located in peripheral areas and have less socially standardized lifestyles. The latter includes single people, single mothers who have to do part-time or irregular work, young people starting out on the labour market, for whom short-term contracts often go hand-in-hand with reduced employer contributions, and so on. The local nature of poverty does not lend itself to the type of action traditionally built up from within the company. The pandemic has been an opportunity for social practices and experiments that suggest potential alternatives. While the idea here is clearly not to deal exhaustively with this question, we will strive to outline a few methods adopted by the working classes to tackle insecurity. It is in relation to this last point that we see the specific social characteristics of the precarious.

New precarious subjectivations

Beyond institutional decisions to reclassify drivers of private hire vehicles in various countries across the world, platform capitalism has come up against a significant basis of dissent in recent years, starting directly at the grassroots level with delivery agent movements. From 2016, protests by delivery riders have spread like wildfire across Europe: first in England, against Deliveroo; in Italy, against Foodora; then in Germany and Spain, against Deliveroo; and, finally, in France, sporadically and insistently from 2016 to today. Working-class actions, launched by delivery agents deprived of severance pay when Take Eat Easy was forced into liquidation, have subsequently been reflected in recurring resistance, particularly against Deliveroo.

The main reason for the protests has been the promotion of piecework by the delivery platforms as a means of managing the workforce. The intensity and viral nature of these protests in the different countries, and the creation of a Transnational Federation of Couriers, reflect a social basis specific to the movement. This includes young people with no qualifications, students, workers holding down several jobs due to specific needs (for instance, single parents) and immigrants, some of whom are undocumented. During the strike in Brighton, Deliveroo ignored the trade union that the delivery agents had created. Like the bosses of the 19th century, the management dared to tell the riders who were demanding a collective bargaining system that it only had to listen to each worker's concerns individually (Cant, 2019: 9). Yet riders, despite being inexperienced in protest, turned this denial of acknowledgement and rights into new methods of action by making their ability to communicate and their spontaneity a means of launching strikes without notice, paralyzing the entire network of restaurants that make up the platform's clientele (Cant, 2019: 114). They have re-engaged with the tone of the struggles of the precarious as a subjectivation of an experience of intermittencies and uncertainties.

The platform business model opens up an area of conflict in which the specific and pernicious effect of triangulation (software, customer and worker) can be reciprocated by workers themselves, throwing algocratic management into crisis. Workers' effective autonomy leaves the platform in a relationship of dependence due to this blind spot. The system's malleability can be used by the delivery agents themselves. This has led to various local cooperative experiments that replace the micro-entrepreneur system with an employed workforce and offer other tempos of work and other relationships. Given the fact that 'free work' culminates in a dead-end situation, subject to the asymmetry of capitalist platforms and of piecework, alternative practices have emerged from the platform system, making it a means of acquiring greater autonomy and reconfiguring its socio-economic significance.

For example, the CoopCycle federation, founded in 2017, brings together around 40 bicycle delivery cooperatives in France. Some local structures are working with this federation, pooling their delivery software programmes, mobile applications and sales services, and in doing so, shifting the platform's operation from an asymmetrical to a reciprocal instrument.

The pandemic has also been the context for a change in function, and, as a result, in the meaning of delivery platforms. Against the neo-domesticity aspect, which is emerging increasingly clearly in a delivery economy exclusively aimed at private individuals, delivery agents working for cooperatives have turned to associations such as the Secours Populaire and to municipal councils. They have organized the delivery of food parcels to elderly or isolated persons and have leveraged their experience of the city and its geography to meet the needs of insecure social groups for whom the COVID-19 crisis has further heightened their poverty. The cooperative structure in this specific case creates an ad hoc common foundation in which the intermediation characteristic of the platform no longer acts as a broker between individuals through the market, but instead, brings together groups with common interests and solidarity. Just as digital technology's capacity to disconnect becomes a means of isolating and fragmenting workers, the cooperative platform is becoming a means of bringing workers together and pooling resources.

Against the backdrop of the pandemic, this revitalization of structures of solidarity, information and protest, aimed at those suffering from insecurity, leads to utopian energies, or at least to alternatives in underprivileged districts. Following on from popular protests against everyday poverty and unemployment, and also from efforts to resist evictions, some districts in major cities have organized themselves in a drive based on conflict and solidarity. Local stakeholders have attempted to combat poverty and loneliness by reoccupying the urban territory and by supporting solidarity and protest initiatives, or by requisitioning restaurants with a history symbolic of local life. In places that welcome the jobless, to support them with their administrative formalities, to defend their rights and to protest against the termination of benefit payments, there are now also solidarity initiatives to tackle poverty through the organization of various precarious populations within a single urban area. Food aid and the need to feed part of the local insecure population have become a major challenge in the pandemic, linking social and environmental issues. Protests have called for places of socialization and redistribution to offer basic necessities at prices adjusted to the incomes of customers in these districts and, in some cases, second-hand items in a barter economy. In a deprived area of Marseille, a fast-food chain was taken over by the people, thereby combining job creation and the distribution of food parcels. Faced with territorial inequalities and isolation that have been heightened by the pandemic, daily life in the district has changed. This drive for action, inspired by the popular moral economy, is built upon practices rolled out through the creation of exchange networks between districts and rural activities. As the drop in food prices is closely related to the relocation of production and short food circuits, cooperative platforms have been used to organize online orders and to pool logistics in order to streamline transportation and the sale of farm produce to a certain number of markets or consumers.

In these repossessions of the use of platforms, and in this break from the asymmetry and opacity of the algorithm, novel types of relationship emerge that may be exemplary of the experiences of the precarious and experiences of precariousness. The two distinct figures of a social relation, with intermittency on one side and poverty on the other, have converged in unique and significant ways. In these popular practices, and in this creativity from the bottom-up, we see less a 'vitalist pragmatics', a term used by Veronica Gago in reference to popular protests in Argentina's informal economy (Gago, 2015), and more of a well thought out alternative activity that is openly in tension with the market economy. While the COVID-19 crisis has opened up opportunities for platform capitalism and has shed light on inequalities and insecure living conditions, the hybrid reaction (young precarious people and deprived populations) within this subjectivation trend results in expressions of non-consent and of alternatives. A daily life is recreated that leverages new relations to tackle adversity. While, as we have seen, platforms have completed the movement launched by various systems of insecure work, an alternative is emerging in the organization of solidarity on the basis of the intermediated relationship. Thus, local commons are bringing together consumer and producer communities seeking fairer transactions and a specific socialization system. While the sharing economy has been, to some extent, the gimmick of platform capitalism and of a business model of exceptional brutality and cynicism at the start of the 21st century, this concept can be understood and employed in multiple ways. The collective action of those in precarious situations results in either a state-led or cooperative repossession of platforms, as they are increasingly the intermediaries of our daily lives: they organize our social interactions (Facebook), our play (Twitch), our creative and critical experiences (YouTube and blogs), our intellectual and inventive work (Freelancer, Upwork), our extremely segmented tasks (AMT), our housing conditions (Airbnb), our travel and our walks. The time has come for this apparatus, captured by a few engineers and CEOs, to be subject to reappropriation and a real sharing community.

A precarious world?

It will doubtless be argued that these social experiments are insignificant given the historic turning point due to the pandemic and the monopolistic power of certain platforms. They do, however, belong to a school of thought regarding experimental social systems that is part of the utopian heritage of the workers' movement in England and France, which was particularly active at the turn of the 19th century. Since Fourier's utopian projects (Fourier, 1822), the cooperative movement in France has constantly applied itself, with ups and downs, throughout the 19th and 20th centuries. Today, the renewal of cooperatives on both a local and national level, whether they organize self-employed workers (Coopaname) or relations between consumers and producers, is emerging as a key aspect of resistance to increases in insecurity, particularly by enabling ad hoc structures that can provide security to the self-employed by making them employees (Corsani, 2021). This ambition, to pool the social welfare of workers, takes on new meaning against the backdrop of emerging platforms, as the cooperatives of young delivery agents, which are rooted in local solidarity (districts or municipalities), are signs of a broader movement combining struggles and a trend for the emancipation of the commons. Faced with the looting of data, the manipulation of self-employed workers through algorithms and the ever-increasing subjugation of daily life to merchandise (Cingolani, 2021), the collective appropriation of these platforms turns the situation around and results in exchanges that respect the axiological challenges of equity and solidarity, and in forms of common control by platform users.

Yet the neoliberal state has remained in a generally weak position compared to the major global monopolies (GAFAM), and has even encouraged, in various ways, the creation of work platforms that thrive off de-salarization by hampering any opportunities for reclassification. The task now is to demand that the state regulates labour relations (European Commission, 2021) and supports the popular appropriation of platforms. The need for regulation and to control practices that are sometimes on the edge of criminality, in terms of the gathering and screening of data (Zuboff, 2019) or of lies and bluster in the case of the promotion of independent and flexible work (Kalanick, 2015), includes a legislative and legal arsenal that, without ignoring multi-activity, regulates and even prohibits the intrusive power of platforms in our daily lives, and their extension in the sphere of the informal.

The COVID-19 pandemic is an opportunity to reconsider the term 'precarious' in its broadest sense. Taking into account a point of view in which this word conveys a 'catch-all' concept that is conceptually inconsistent, we remain convinced that it is its polysemy that makes it so rich against a backdrop in which the challenges related to it are constantly being updated. On the basis of its Latin root, the term *precarity* (*précarité* in French) has been used in relation to issues concerning care (Butler, 2015; Lorey, 2015) and the environment (Tsing, 2017). Indeed, precarity must no longer be viewed as an adjacent exteriority but our environment as affected by the complex nature of the intersections between the erosion of a guaranteed social model based on work and employment, a rise in inequality and, now, the decline in environmental living conditions. On a daily basis, we hear this terminology used to describe our social life as much as the state of the planet. We believe that this type of precarious situation is the basis from which meaning can once again be given to the conflicts and struggles within capitalism.

References

Acquier, A. (2017) 'Retour vers le futur: quand le capitalisme de plate-forme nous "renvoie au domestic system" préindustriel', *The Conversation*, 3 September. Available from : https://theconversation.com/retour-vers-le-futur-quand-le-capitalisme-de-plate-forme-nous-renvoie-au-domestic-sys tem-preindustriel-72917 [Accessed 1 April 2022].

Alloa, E. (2021) 'Une si puissante fatigue', *Esprit*, 473 (June). Available from: https://esprit.presse.fr/article/emmanuel-alloa/une-si-puissante-fati gue-43390 [Accessed 1 April 2022].

Bellon, B. (1975) *Le volant de main d'œuvre*, Paris: Seuil.

Bertrand, P. (2021) 'La vente en ligne pèsera bientôt 15% du commerce de détail', Les échos, 4 February. Available from : www.lesechos.fr/industrie-services/conso-distribution/la-vente-en-ligne-pesera-bientot-15-du-commerce-de-detail-1287350 [Accessed 1 April 2022].

Brun, S. and Simon, P. (2020) 'L'invisibilité des minorités dans les chiffres du Coronavirus: le détour par la Seine-Saint-Denis', *De facto*, May.

Butler, J. (2015) *Notes Toward a Performative Theory of Assembly*, Cambridge, MA: Harvard University Press.

Cant, C. (2019) *Riding for Deliveroo: Resistance in the New Economy*, Cambridge: Polity.

Castel, R. (2011) 'Au-delà du salariat ou en deçà de l'emploi? L'institutionnalisation du précariat', in S. Paugam (ed) *Repenser la solidarité*, Paris: Presses Universitaires de France, pp 415–33.

Cingolani, P. (2017 [2005]) *La précarité*, Paris: Presses Universitaires de France.

Cingolani, P. (2021) *La colonisation du quotidien*, Paris: Éditions Amsterdam.

Corsani, A. (2021) *Les chemins de la liberté*, Vulaines sur Seine: Editions du Croquant.

Demazière, D. (2003) *Le chômage – comment peut-on être chômeur?*, Paris: Belin.

European Commission (2021) 'Proposal for a Directive of the European Parliament and of the Council on Improving Working Conditions in Platform Work, Brussels', 2021/0414 (COD). Available from: https://ec.europa.eu/social/BlobServlet?docId=24992&langId=en [Accessed 4 April 2022].

Flichy, P. (2017) *Les nouvelles frontières du travail à l'ère numérique*, Paris: Seuil.

Fourier, C. (1822) *Traité de l'association domestique-agricole*, Paris: Bossange.

Gago, V. (2015) *La razón neoliberal*, Buenos Aires: Tinta Limón.

Gorz, A. (1980) *Adieux au prolétariat*, Paris: Galilée.

Gorz, A. (1997) *Misère du présent, richesse du possible*, Paris: Galilée.

Grégoire, M., Vivès, C. and Deyris, J. (2020) 'Quelle évolution des droits à l'assurance chômage? (1979–2020)', report for the CGT, IRES. Available from: www.ires.fr/index.php/etudes-recherches-ouvrages/etudes-des-organisations-syndicales/item/6177-quelle-evolution-des-droits-a-l-assurance-chomage-1979-2020 [Accessed 4 April 2022].

Kalanick, T. (2015) 'The future of work: independence and flexibility', Pacific Standard, 15 October. Available from: https://psmag.com/economics/the-future-of-work-independence-and-flexibility [Accessed 4 April 2022].

Lallement, M. (1990) *Des PME en chambre: Travail et travailleurs à domicile d'hier et d'aujourd'hui*, Paris: L'harmattan.

Leadbeater, C. and Miller, P. (2004) *The Pro-Am Revolution: How Enthusiasts are Changing our Economy and Society*, London: Demos.

Lorey, I. (2015) *State of Insecurity: Government of the Precarious*, London and New York: Verso.

Tsing, A. (2017) *Le champignon de la fin du monde – Sur les possibilités de vivre dans les ruines du capitalisme*, Paris: La Découverte.

Walker, P. (2021) 'Call centre staff to be monitored via webcam for home-working "infractions"', The Guardian, 26 March. Available from: www.theguardian.com/business/2021/mar/26/teleperformance-call-centre-staff-monitored-via-webcam-home-working-infractions [Accessed 4 April 2022].

Wresinski, J. (1987) *Grande pauvreté et précarité économique et sociale*, Conseil économique et social, 4074.

Zuboff, S. (2019) *The Age of Surveillance Capitalism*, New York: Public Affairs.

PART III

Experiences, Concretizations and Struggles

11

The Embodiment
of Insecurity: How Precarious
Labour Market Trajectories Affect
Young Workers' Health and
Wellbeing in Catalonia (Spain)

Mireia Bolíbar, Francesc X. Belvis and Mariana Gutiérrez-Zamora

Introduction

Social epidemiology has revealed that health and disease occur socially and historically.[1] Beyond biological and lifestyle factors, the vast number of social, environmental and economic factors that arise from the structure of each society and social group play a decisive role in determining collective health (Krieger, 2001; Benach and Muntaner, 2005). Power relations, along with macro-social institutions such as the provision of welfare, labour rights and neoliberal regulations and discourse, lead to the social production of health inequalities. In other words, structural factors, or the 'causes of the causes', shape the patterns of health, disease and health inequalities (Marmot and Wilkinson, 2005; Navarro, 2008).

In this context, epidemiological research has established, albeit not always unequivocally and subject to variations, that precarious employment conditions[2] are usually associated with various negative outcomes, such as greater perceived insecurity at work (Keim et al, 2014); a higher rate of occupational accidents (Benavides et al, 2006); worse working conditions (Clarke et al, 2007); and less investment in training (Draca and Green, 2004); as well as several health indicators, such as worse self-perceived and mental health, and specific diseases, which are manifested in the form of increased morbidity and mortality and greater inequality in their distribution among the population (Benach et al, 2014).

However, there is not so much research available that has examined the health impact of precarity in the working trajectories of young people. In line with the hegemonic view of health that emphasizes lifestyles and risk factors from an individualized, decontextualized standpoint, research and health promotion interventions among young people have focused on cultural and attitudinal issues and are aimed at preventing risky behaviours (see Furlong, 2009). However, the fact that young people are an especially vulnerable social group in the labour market is often overlooked.

Indeed, over the past 30 years, young adults have been socially unprotected and more exposed to precarious, insecure or temporary employment. Macro-structural changes linked to economic globalization, labour market deregulation and the trend towards individualization have exerted a profound influence on the processes of the emancipation of young individuals in post-Fordist societies (Mínguez et al, 2012). The overall process of the destandardization of labour markets has resulted in a destandardization of the transition to work (Harkko, 2018). Consequently, rather than a single event or transition, the transition from school to work is increasingly perceived as a complex, fragmented, non-linear process (O'Reilly et al, 2019). Young people's career paths include periods of unemployment, inactivity, entrapment in temporary employment (Verd et al, 2019), underemployment, changes in type of contract and in level of studies, inconsistency between the level of education and type of employment (McGuinness et al, 2018), constant mobility in the labour market through odd jobs and various employers (Vancea and Utzet, 2017), and even non-standardized varieties of work, such as scholarships, paid internships or bogus self-employment. These factors all affect young people's career paths, including among the most qualified (Benedicto et al, 2014). However, this does not prevent destandardization from having a greater impact on the most vulnerable young people, as social stratification factors such as class background, gender, place of origin or parents' educational level significantly influence the level of education and subsequent career path of their children (O'Reilly et al, 2019).

Although these processes affect all western countries, in the European Union (EU), the difficulties of entering the job market and the precarious employment experiences faced by young people are particularly marked in the countries of Mediterranean Europe: Greece, Spain, Portugal and Italy (Marshall and Butler, 2015). Several causes have been pointed to in order to explain this, including poorly embedded vocational education and training systems; high levels of labour market segmentation, which particularly affects young people; differences in labour market institutions (including collective bargaining, wage-setting mechanisms and labour market regulation); and these countries' interactions with demand shocks (see O'Reilly et al, 2019).

As a result, in the Spanish and Catalan labour market, unemployment rates and general contractual temporariness are well above the average for the EU (Banyuls and Recio, 2017), and acquire dramatic overtones in the under-25s age group.

In fact, although many factors may influence the phenomenon, the increased prevalence of mental health problems among young people since the 1990s has, in some countries, been associated with this toughening of labour market conditions (Lager and Bremberg, 2009). Thus, in Finland, the proportion of young people taking sick leave and receiving disability pensions almost doubled between 1995 and 2012, mainly due to mental illness. Achieving the expected level of education and having a successful transition to the working world has positive effects on mental health, while the loss of employment and episodes of unemployment harm it (Paul and Moser, 2009). The review of 44 articles by Vancea and Utzet (2017) concluded that both unemployment and precarious employment worsened the health of young people, taking into account a wide range of indicators, such as mental disorders, risky behaviour, poor quality of life and occupational accidents.

By looking further into this background, this research aims to fill a gap in the existing literature, studying the relationship between employment *history* and health in young people, as well as the specific mechanisms through which precarity in the former affects the latter. Given that youth is itself a period of transition to adulthood (Furlong and Cartmel, 2007), for the study of youth employment precarity and its effects on health it is crucial to adopt a longitudinal perspective that does not look statically at job precarity but, instead, bears in mind the sequence of events throughout the career path that shape both the transition from study to employment and the quality of employability and consolidation in the labour market. To this end, we draft and characterize a typology of youth labour market trajectories for later use as a predictor of self-perceived health and risky behaviour indicators. Finally, we seek to look further into the experience of youth precarity, using qualitative methods, to identify causal pathways and mechanisms that explain the impact of job precarity on the health dimensions analyzed.

Methodology

This study combines quantitative and qualitative methods used sequentially so that the qualitative information provides explanations for the previously identified statistical relationships. In the quantitative phase, and prior to descriptive analysis, the retrospective labour market trajectories were reconstructed of a sub-sample of n=1,247 young people interviewed in the Catalan Youth Survey of 2017 (EJC-2017). At the time of the survey, the recruited subjects were aged between 20 and 34 years and had completed their initial training at least five years before. The issue of the different lengths of trajectories was resolved by attributing an arbitrary number of time units (251) to all, but which were of different real duration for each individual. The statuses considered concerning the labour market were: (1) studies (return to); (2) work in the household; (3) childcare; (4) other situations of inactivity; (5) unemployment; (6) informal work; (7) temporary contract; (8) self-employment; (9) permanent contract; and (10) does not know/does not answer (DK/DA). The resulting sequences were grouped according to type of youth labour market trajectories (hereinafter YLMT) using the non-parametric cluster analysis technique, calculating the distance between sequences by means of optimal matching. Median dates for each cluster and time unit were also calculated in order to provide a sense of the clusters' evolution in real chronological time over the observation period. The cases were weighted by post-stratification weights, which were provided by the EJC-2017.

Then, the association of the type of YLMT with a series of subjective health indicators (poor self-perceived health, levels of dissatisfaction with life, and the use of drugs)[3] was studied and adjusted for sex, age at the time of transition to work, foreign nationality and social class of origin using ordinary least squares (OLS) and logistic regression models. In the qualitative phase, semi-structured interviews of approximately 50 to 80 minutes were conducted on a sub-sample (n=13) of participants in the EJC-2017, distributed according to their type of YLMT and additional criteria concerning sex and nationality.[4] The interviewees were asked to reconstruct and comment on their working life, assessing its possible relationship with their health status and the adoption of risky behaviours. The interviews were recorded, transcribed and subjected to thematic analysis. Categories were created abductively, combining prior theoretical orientations and concepts arising in the narratives. The analyses were performed using TraMineR and Atlas.ti software.

Results

Diversity of youth labour market trajectories and implications for health

The retrospective labour market trajectories analyzed have a duration of between five and 20 years before the survey (2017), with an average of 11.1 (SD 3.7) years. The aggregate distribution of statuses, considered as a whole, shows that the percentage of individuals in employment remains more or less constant (at around 75 per cent) throughout the period of observation, instead of showing a trend towards greater labour market participation. What changes, though, is the quality of employment: the percentages of temporary and informal situations decrease in favour of permanent contracts and self-employment. This redistribution is quicker at the beginning of the period and then practically stabilizes (data not shown).

Inspection of the dendrogram and the elbow method diagram, as well as the silhouette method, strongly suggest a solution of k=3 clusters. The aggregate distribution of statuses during the period of observation for the three types of YLMT can be seen in Figure 11.1, and it is characterized as follows. The first cluster, which we call 'permanent' trajectories (PT), corresponds to trajectories with a predominance of employment with permanent or open-ended contractual arrangements. Among PT, this state is the most prevalent one from the beginning and grows proportionately until a point of inflection, when episodes of unemployment, temporary employment and, particularly, self-employment then slightly increase. The PT group encompasses 38.5 per cent of trajectories.

The second cluster, which we call 'temporary' trajectories (TT), is characterized by a high predominance of episodes of temporary contracts, which lose some ground in favour of permanent hiring, although most individuals with this type of trajectory remain in temporary employment. In general, situations of informal employment and non-employment are somewhat more prevalent in TT than in PT. This group encompasses 29.0 per cent of trajectories.

The last cluster we call 'discontinuous' trajectories (DT), and it is essentially defined by the prevalence of situations of non-employment and informal work. Unlike the other two, DT indicate a weak link with the labour market. Although there are some variations, no clear progress in formal employment is observed from the beginning to the end of the observation period. This group encompasses 32.5 per cent of trajectories. The DT cluster is more heterogeneous than the other two and almost certainly mixes profiles. In particular, it involves people oriented towards household care and housework, and others oriented towards employment but encountering difficulties in joining the labour market, plus those who work for themselves.

The types of trajectories have a certain relationship with the major axes of inequality. In general, one can speak of a gradient in which PT are more prevalent in the most favoured category and DT are more so in the least favoured one, while TT are in an intermediate situation. Such a gradient occurs with nationality, studies, and a whole range of variables related to self-determination, including independence from the family of origin, emancipation from the family unit, the risk of poverty and individual income (Table 11.1). In contrast, and against expectations, the relationship of trajectories with family class background is apparently weak, as is the relationship with the occupational category of those working at the time they are surveyed. Differences by sex and age are also of scarce magnitude. Regarding the relationship between labour market trajectory and health indicators, TT (OR 1.90; p<0.01) and DT (OR 2.22; p<0.001) represent a significant risk of poor self-perceived health when compared to PT.

Figure 11.1: Evolution of labour market status (%) over the observation period, by cluster

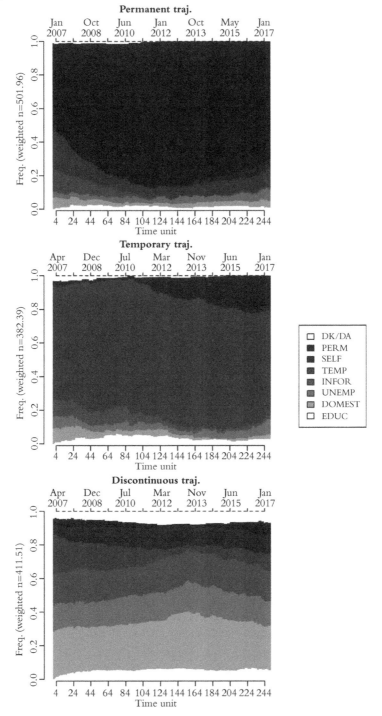

Table 11.1: Social characteristics of young people in each labour market trajectory

Variables	Trajectories				(per cent lost values)
	Permanent (n=480)	Temporary (n=362)	Discontinuous (n=405)	All (n=1,247)	
Sex					
Female	48.8	49.5	52.7	50.2	0.0
Nationality					
Non-Spanish	19.9	21.2	35.9	25.3	0.1
Highest level of education					
Compulsory	37.7	41.8	47.8	42.1	0.0
Voc. training	24.4	24.5	19.4	22.8	
Non-compulsory secondary	10.4	6.0	11.9	9.6	
Higher	27.5	27.7	20.9	25.5	
Living arrangement					
Emancipated	79.3	71.2	55.3	69.3	4.4
Parents' Socioeconomic Status					
Directors and managers	5.3	5.0	4.0	4.8	9.5
Technicians and professionals	23.1	23.4	20.7	22.5	
Skilled occup.	55.5	53.2	51.6	53.6	

(continued)

Table 11.1: Social characteristics of young people in each labour market trajectory (continued)

Variables	Trajectories			All (n=1,247)	(per cent lost values)
	Permanent (n=480)	Temporary (n=362)	Discontinuous (n=405)		
Elementary occup.	6.7	7.2	5.7	6.6	
DK/DA/Others	9.5	11.1	18.1	12.5	
Risk of poverty					
Yes	25.8	28.2	49.2	33.0	27.2
Age upon completion of initial training (mean/ sd, in years)	19.8 (3.4)	19.2 (3.3)	19.1 (3.4)	19.4 (3.4)	0.0
Individual monthly income (mean/sd, in €/ mth)[1]	1,300.8 (799.8)	1,071.9 (533.1)	976.4 (694.4)	1,140.8 (709.4)	23.1
Company size[2]					
1 person	7.3	8.0	24.4	11.4	8.4
From 2 to 10 people	18.4	23.0	32.5	23.1	
From 11 to 19 people	10.9	6.6	9.1	9.1	
From 20 to 49 people	10.4	18.1	11.5	13.1	
From 50 to 249 people	15.8	16.7	7.2	14.1	
250 or more people	37.1	27.5	15.3	29.2	

[1] Includes imputations

[2] Corresponding to young people who are working at the time of the interview, n=956

Table 11.2: Adjusted regression coefficients/odds ratios (OR) and 95% confidence interval (CI) of self-perceived health, life (dis)satisfaction and frequency in the consumption of several drugs, according to labour market trajectory (estimated with Permanent Trajectories as reference)

	Labour market trajectory		
	Permanent	Temporary	Discontinuous
Self-perceived health (Bad)	Ref.	1.896** (1,207; 2,980)	2.219*** (1,430; 3,438)
Life (dis)satisfaction	Ref.	0.204 (−0.042; 0.450)	0.277* (0.027; 0.528)
Smoking	Ref.	0.111 (−0.104; 0.326)	−0.011 (−0.228; 0.206)
Alcohol	Ref.	0.030 (−0.078; 0.139)	0.123* (0.014; 0.233)
Cannabis	Ref.	0.032 (−0.073; 0.137)	0.134* (0.028; 0.240)
Cocaine	Ref.	−0.012 (−0.044; 0.020)	0.051** (0.018; 0.083)

Note: *$p<0.05$; **$p<0.01$; ***$p<0.001$

OLS and logistic regression adjusted for sex, age at completion of studies, non-Spanish nationality and social class of origin

In addition, DT also display a significant risk of greater dissatisfaction with life (coeff. 0.277; $p<0.05$) and more frequent use of drugs like alcohol (coeff. 0.123; $p<0.05$), cannabis (coeff. 0.134; $p<0.05$) or cocaine (coeff. 0.051; $p<0:01$), always when compared to PT (Table 11.2). The labour market trajectory does not, however, condition significant differences with regard to smoking. These results remain stable if people with long-term illness or incapacity (n=6) are excluded from the analyses.

Explaining the relationship between precarity and young people's health

In the qualitative phase of this study, we identified three major channels or causal pathways through which the labour market trajectory can have an impact on health perception and which, therefore, explain the results shown by the quantitative part of the study. These channels include the resources available to young people; their capacity for agency in the construction of temporal horizons; and their exposure to physical and, especially, psychosocial risks at work. These three major factors generate a series of mechanisms that contribute to protecting the health and quality of life of young people with stable trajectories, while they tend to trigger or exacerbate problems of physical and mental health and may increase the risk of falling into frequent consumption of drugs by young people with temporary or discontinuous trajectories.

Stable trajectories

The narratives of individuals with Permanent Trajectories reveals, first, the idea that their employment has fulfilled the function of providing them with financial resources and, therefore, independence, which gives them the opportunity to emancipate themselves from the parental home and achieve *economic independence*. This allows the possibility of achieving relatively early emancipation and acquiring autonomy and security to pursue linear trajectories that follow an order regarded as 'standard' in the collective imaginary (work, find a partner, become independent, have children, and so on). In addition, their trajectories enable them to acquire resources and earn a good living, which gives them satisfaction, security and recognition.

Second, in relation to the ability of young people to think and act on an idea for the future and make plans or life projects, the young people interviewed with stable trajectories are seen to be quite capable of planning scenarios beyond the moment in which they are currently living. They are also confident regarding what the future holds as a result of good past experiences and experience that they consider proves them as workers. In this sense, having spent years in a stable employment scenario is regarded as being proof of future employability. As one of the interviewees puts it, "you gradually gain experience and that experience also has a market value" (Ferran, DT). This set of resources and the imaginary concerning their value can act to protect good mental health, as they offer self-esteem and self-confidence, as well as a perception of certainty and security, that reasonably leads to a sense of tranquillity regarding the future:

> 'Now, for the time being, I'm permanent, I'm a bit scared of changing and that it might not work out but anyway, if it doesn't you go on the dole and I reckon I'm worthy as a shop assistant and I'll always find something, it's been many years and Figueres [the town] knows me, 11 years in [anonymized shop] of Figueres well … I think that when people see a CV where the person has only been in four jobs over so many years and one of them is one in the same company where they had already been before, I suppose it means something.' (Julia, PT)

Similarly, the interviews have shown how the *ability to choose* – having the power to decide about their own career path – can become a protective factor against anxiety or stress. This capacity for agency, especially typical of stable trajectories, provides the choice to work in jobs free from stress and demands, which interviewees tend to value positively as they entail a certain degree of satisfaction and external recognition and appreciation, and in which they have the capacity to control their own time, so they can switch off and enjoy leisure time – aspects that can act as protectors of mental health and provide wellbeing and quality of life. Also, it is particularly important that (the perception of) the ability to choose enables them to *avoid employment situations in working conditions that may be potentially harmful to mental health*:

> 'This world of programming is a good crack and chilled, it's not at all stressful, I reckon if I had a stressful job I'd leave 'cos it wouldn't fit in with my way of life … if I don't like them, I go to something else, I'm not going to suffer in something I don't like.' (Cristian, TP)

Precarious trajectories

As we have identified many common elements in the experiences of young people with TT and DT, in this section we present jointly the mechanisms that explain the health implications of insecurity on trajectories, whether such insecurity is structured as a concatenation of temporary employment (TT) or clearer forms of exclusion from the labour market (DT). However, we have also observed two kinds of differences between these trajectories: the first is of degree, which cuts across all we set out in this section, in the sense that the intensity of the suffering and the extent of the negative perceptions and experiences among young people with DT tend to be higher than among young people with TT. And the second, which is specified when applicable, is related to the fact that some of the specific mechanisms triggering ill-health outcomes are produced especially by the unemployment and informality that are intrinsic to DT (while residual in TT).

First, in the interviews conducted with young people both with TT and DT, as already noted in the quantitative data, their precarious trajectories imply that young individuals have fewer resources and are at greater risk of poverty, either because of a continuous or intermittent lack of work (and, therefore, the absence of a salary), underemployment in terms of part-time working days, informal employment (which allows situations that are poorly remunerated, below the established minimum wage) and/or just low wages. Lack of resources has a clear pathogenic impact and is a major threat to the physical and mental wellbeing of young people. This impact has been widely studied (see Marmot and Wilkinson, 2005), and is also observed among precarious young people in Catalonia. It occurs through different mechanisms and is manifested in a multitude of health-related dimensions, from *difficulties in meeting basic needs* (such as healthy eating) and other needs when caring for oneself, to the psychological and emotional unrest caused by having problems in covering the costs of decent housing or transport and making ends meet:

> 'I felt really bad, you feel despair and powerlessness … not just 'cos you can't buy a loaf of bread, it's the fact that it's not one day, it's not

one week and it's not one month, it's month after month and on top you go to work and they pay you peanuts, in addition they walk all over you … it's a horrible feeling, I think anyone turns to drink or throws in the towel, it's a really horrible feeling, … it's a feeling inside that gnaws away at you, a despair of not knowing what to do, who to turn to.' (Maria, TT)

In addition, the lack of resources hampers emancipation, which can lead to frustration and a sense of life blockage, failure and uncertainty towards the future, and can bring about situations of *dependence* that result in feelings of shame, humiliation and a lack of personal accomplishment, and thus undermine autonomy and self-esteem: "My parents kept giving me money, but at some point you take it but it hurts" (Gustavo, TT).

Second, regarding the construction of temporal horizons, in the case of the most precarious trajectories, whether TT or DT, problems are identified arising from the *inability to plan and the lack of control over the future*. This inability, often associated with states of uncertainty, fear and frustration, can lead to the onset of negative effects on the mental health of employees, worsening it over time: "You were always afraid, saying: right, OK, today I've got this job, I'll get a call, but when and for what." (Gustavo, TT).

In this respect, the experience of unemployment among young people with DT is especially harmful. It tends to foster and aggravate situations of material deprivation, economic dependence and uncertainty, as well as the associated health and quality of life problems described previously. Moreover, when extended over time, unemployment can lead to traumatic experiences related to a feeling of entrapment and life blockage that increases anxiety, fear and the lack of confidence in one's own ability to control the future, which reinforces the (perceived) loss of agency and disempowerment of young people in the field of employment:

Interviewee: I feel awful because if I work things go well, not having many problems at home and we could make ends meet, but I don't have work and it's a problem, we're in a bad way.

Interviewer: Do you feel trapped?

Interviewee: Yes and there's no way out, whatever [door] I knock on it's closed, the door I knock on is closed, everything's closed.

Interviewer: These situations you've experienced, do you think they've affected your health?

Interviewee: At night I dream I've got work, I get up and nothing and I feel worse or that day I'm in a really bad mood, my husband takes the kids out, he tells them, "Today your mum's not well". (Beza, DT)

In addition, the experience of being unemployed tends to be accompanied by a strong *stigmatizing* and *guilt-inducing* symbolic burden that affects self-image and the social appraisal of oneself, and entails a *destructuring* of the tempos and rhythms of the everyday that puts young workers in a position of disconcertion, with few daily routines and few milestones to structure the day – a de-routinization of life that can contribute or lead to the consumption of drugs, such as cigarettes or cannabis:

Interviewee: When I'm stressed or overwhelmed, I smoke more.
Interviewer: More joints or cigarettes?
Interviewee: Joints. ... I went for a long time without smoking in Granollers. I got used to being there, with work, I came and went, I didn't have time for anything and I didn't ... didn't smoke. I can also tell you that when I am working I only smoke after work. I don't smoke either before or during work, not one bit, and normally when I am working and I get home I smoke once I've finished doing everything I've got to do. ... But if I don't [work], I do smoke all day, otherwise I don't ... I fancy it ... all day, you know? ... If you've got lots of free time you'll smoke more. (Yolanda, DT)

Finally, we have identified that the lack of decision-making capacity and control over the trajectory, which we have observed for both young people with TT and DT – although to a greater degree in the latter – leads them to work in jobs with worse working conditions. Thus, it shows how the perception of a lack of alternatives, the threat of unemployment and lack of job opportunities in general, in addition to being a risk factor in itself, acts as a disciplinary measure to accept poor working conditions:

'The truth is that I've never really had problems to find work, I've had shit jobs, if you'll excuse me, but it was that or nothing so ... there I had to take the first thing, which was cleaning, ugh, horrid. ... I don't like what I've done but as I need the money because nowadays without money you can't do anything and that's the way it is ... all day bitter, tired, not in the mood ... to have to go to work and you haven't gone in and you think that tomorrow you've got to go in again, it distressed me, not resting at night, I dreamt of work, a loop.' (Renata, TT)

The literature on public health has demonstrated in great depth the harmful effects on health posed by adverse working conditions (Theorell, 2000). In our study, we have identified some such aspects. The quantitative demands, that is, for example, a very intense workload, both insofar as the hours worked and the physical and/or mental demands, involve clear mental and physical exhaustion. Heavy workloads can cause extended moments of tension, emotional stress, fatigue and anxiety, as well as difficulties in switching off from work at times of rest. The pressure to fulfil tasks quickly can sometimes expose workers to risk their physical integrity or even push them into taking drugs to endure the fatigue or to cushion the emotional distress associated with work:

Interviewee: The worst moments were there, I do remember leaving work stressed, nervous and taking the car on the motorway and I came down the whole coastal motorway that comes from there from all that and I remember coming down really fast, with the sunroof open, the windows down, loud music, and screaming, crying, shouting and tears pouring, crying, I couldn't stay there any longer. ... I was bad, I was bad ... with tachycardia and crying, hysterical. ... The weekend suffering about what I'd have to do on Monday. It wasn't living, no way.

Interviewer: What did you do to feel better?

Interviewee: Nothing, I couldn't do anything, at least at that time if I smoked a spliff or something to relax. (Gustavo, TT)

We have also observed that young people with Discontinuous and Temporary Trajectories enter into employment relations with a clearly disadvantageous power relationship, hence in their interviews emerges a narrative alluding to their *vulnerability* in the face of authoritarian treatment and abuse by employers. Informal employees with DT, and to a lesser extent with TT, are particularly exposed to it. Entrapment in this situation can lead to various health problems, such as presenteeism (going to work despite being ill or recovering); the inability to demand occupational safety and health measures; and exposure to sexual harassment or other forms of abuse that may undermine an individual's health and physical integrity, as well as the recognition and self-appreciation of them.

It is noted that a sort of vicious circle exists that reinforces the exposure of these young people to health risk factors: the risks associated to the working conditions of precarious jobs are frequently assumed to avoid the risks linked to out-of-employment spells, which are, in turn, facilitated by insecure contractual arrangements.

Conclusion

In broad terms, this chapter highlights the implications of the precarization of the labour market on the physical and mental health of young people in Catalonia as a challenge for public health. The erosion of the standard employment relationship; the associated problems of unemployment and temporariness, and the consequent difficulties in entering the labour market; the delays and difficulties in achieving stable employment; and all the changes that have contributed to breaking the linearity and standardization of youth labour market trajectories (Furlong and Cartmel, 2007) are characteristic structural factors of the current socio-economic organization, established as social determinants of health and health inequalities (Benach et al, 2014, 2018). Through the shaping of more or less precarious labour market trajectories, such structural factors end up, to varying degrees, affecting the wellbeing, quality of life, and even health, of the young population.

In this chapter, we first identified a variety of youth labour market trajectories, marked by security in the employment conditions experienced throughout their career paths. The results show a clear structuring of youth employment experiences, especially regarding whether they have achieved certain employment stability (Permanent Trajectories), whether they have been greatly marked by temporality (Temporary Trajectories), or whether they have experienced a degree of exclusion from the labour market – in a host of different situations, characterized, above all, by experiencing unemployment, informal employment and inactivity (Discontinuous Trajectories).

The evidence provided, moreover, would suggest that these different types of trajectories, structured according to security in employment, have very important implications for life, being associated with differences in the perception of health, life satisfaction and drug use. Specifically, a certain gradient is observed in the health implications of precarity in labour market trajectories, in such a way that they affect both TT and DT, though the latter more strongly and in a greater variety of outcomes. The qualitative data provided delves further into the consequences of precarious employment upon health.

Second, we have identified the mechanisms that explain how the security/ insecurity that define these different forms of transitioning into and through the labour market cause such an impact on young people's health. Among these mechanisms we should highlight the major impact arising from problems of material deprivation and economic dependence, which are noted across the board but are mainly present among TT and, especially, DT. These results show that in-work poverty, as an emerging phenomenon in Spain that is unfortunately characteristic of the post-2008 great recession period (Fundación FOESSA, 2017), reinforces young people's economic dependence on the family, which, despite being considered a factor of social protection in societies with Mediterranean welfare states lacking other redistribution mechanisms and guarantees of security, is a clear generator of mental health disorders and psychosocial tensions (Espluga, 2001). In this context, furthermore, despite not having been able to delve further into this aspect in this chapter, the study has identified the overlapping of different axes of inequality, such as family social class, gender and ethnic origin, that intersect with the experience of precarity. Such overlapping makes the vulnerability resulting from a precarious trajectory particularly marked and harmful for young people in a weaker position in these axes of inequality.

Another issue to note is the fact that the young people interviewed who have experienced precarious trajectories, with a high degree of temporality and unemployment, tend to perceive far less agency or decision-making capacity and control over their trajectory. While employment experience tends to be seen by young people as a resource that increases their employability and, therefore, as insurance conferring optimism for the future, unwanted unemployment in the context of a precarious trajectory is rather associated with a strong stigma that generates frustration and a sense of failure, and is conceived as a disabling phenomenon that limits the chances of finding a way out. These experiences highlight the toxicity of the neoliberal dynamics of the criminalization and individualization of problems arising from the flexibility and precarization of the contemporary labour market (Jódar and Guiu, 2018). Furthermore, the perception of a lack of opportunities and alternatives, as well as the threat of unemployment and economic needs, in addition to being mental health risk factors in themselves, act as a disciplinary measure that forces young people to resign themselves to abusive labour relations and accept clearly pathological working conditions. In the words of Bourdieu (1998), through the generalization of objective and subjective insecurity, precarity acts as a new means of domination – it creates submissive dispositions and constrains workers to the acceptance of exploitation. It is a form of growing commodification and growing relevance of the market's influence upon individuals' lives, which, we note, has clearly harmful implications on the quality of life and health of the young working population. In short, the weakness in power relationships in the labour market implied by employment precarity shapes a (unequally distributed) pathogenic eco-social environment affecting young individuals' health and wellbeing. As Lorey (2015) states, by way of uncertainty and exposure to danger, precarity embraces the whole of existence, the body and modes of subjectivation.

Notes

[1] Funding: this work has been supported by the Catalan Youth Agency of the Catalan Government and by the Spanish Ministry of Science, Innovation and Universities under

grant agreement No. CSO2017-89719-R (AEI/FEDER, UE). In addition, Mireia Bolíbar holds a Serra Hunter fellowship.

[2] That is, the series of obligations, rights, rewards and expectations (formal and informal) under which individuals agree to carry out their work, and include issues such as salary, contract length, number of working hours and their structuring, and existing labour rights, as well as the actual ability to exercise them (Benach et al, 2010).

[3] The use of drugs is measured by means of a five-point Likert scale ranging from 'never' to 'very frequently'.

[4] In addition, we looked at the characteristics of the interviewee's labour trajectory in order to ensure that their experiences represented those of their YLMT type, considering having had open-ended contracts, temporary employment and unemployment as inclusion criteria for Permanent Trajectories (PT), Temporary trajectories (TT) and Discontinuous Trajectories (DT) cases, respectively.

References

Banyuls, J. and Recio, A. (2017) 'Labour segmentation and precariousness in Spain: theories and evidence', in D. Grimshaw, F. Colette, G. Hebson and I. Tavora (eds) *Making Work More Equal: A New Labour Market Segmentation Approach*, Manchester: Manchester University Press, pp 129–49.

Benach, J. and Muntaner, C. (2005) *Aprender a Mirar La Salud ¿Cómo La Desigualdad Social Daña Nuestra Salud?*, Maracay: Instituto de Altos Estudios en Salud Pública.

Benach, J., Muntaner, C. Solar, O. Santana, V. and Quinlan. M. (2010) *Empleo, trabajo y desigualdades en salud: una visión global*. Barcelona: Icària.

Benach, J., Vives, A., Amable, M., Vanroelen, C., Tarafa, G. and Muntaner, C. (2014) 'Precarious employment: understanding an emerging social determinant of health', *Annual Review Public Health*, 35: 229–53.

Benach, J., Julià, M., Bolíbar, M., Amable, M. and Vives, A. (2018) 'Precarious employment, health, and quality of life: context, analysis, and impacts', in R.J. Burke and C.L. Cooper (eds) *Violence and Abuse in and around Organisations*, New York: Routledge, pp 292–314.

Benavides, F.G., Benach, J., Muntaner, C., Delclos, G.L., Catot, N. and Amable, M. (2006) 'Associations between temporary employment and occupational injury: what are the mechanisms?', *Occupational and Environmental Medicine*, 63(6): 416–21.

Benedicto, J., Fernández de Mosteyrín, L., Gutiérrez Sastre, M., Martín-Pérez, A., Martín-Coppola, E. and Morán, M.L. (2014) *Transitar a la intemperie: jóvenes en busca de integración*, Madrid: INJUVE.

Bourdieu, P. (1998) 'Job insecurity is everywhere now', in *Acts of Resistance. Against the New Myths of Our Time*, Cambridge: Polity, pp 81–7.

Clarke, M., Lewchuk, W., de Wolff, A. and King, A. (2007) '"This just isn't sustainable": precarious employment, stress and workers' health', *International Journal of Law and Psychiatry*, 30(4–5): 311–26.

Draca, M. and Green, C. (2004) 'The incidence and intensity of employer funded training: Australian evidence on the impact of flexible work', *Scottish Journal of Political Economy*, 51(5): 609–25.

Espluga, J. (2001) 'Atur juvenil, salut i exclusió social', *Revista Catalana de Sociologia*, 15: 41–67.

Fundación FOESSA (2017) 'Desprotección social y estrategias familiares'. Available from: http://www.pensamientocritico.org/foessa1017.pdf [Accessed 20 July 2021].

Furlong, A. (ed) (2009) *Handbook of Youth and Young Adulthood: New Perspectives and Agendas*. London: Routledge.

Furlong, A. and Cartmel, F. (2007) *Young People and Social Change: New Perspectives*, Maidenhead: McGraw-Hill.

Harkko, J. (2018) 'Transitions to adulthood among Finnish young people: a mixed-methods study based on longitudinal register data and interviews with street-level professionals' (doctoral dissertation). University of Helsinki, Faculty of Social Sciences, Finland. Available from: https://helda.helsinki.fi/handle/10138/256018 [Accessed 1 April 2022].

Jódar, P. and Guiu, J. (2018) Parados en movimiento (1st edition), Barcelona: Icària.

Keim, A.C., Landis, R.S., Pierce, C.A. and Earnest, D.R. (2014) 'Why do employees worry about their jobs? A meta-analytic review of predictors of job insecurity', *Journal of Occupational Health Psychology*, 19(3): 269–90.

Krieger, N. (2001) 'Glossary of social epidemiology', *Journal of Epidemiology and Community Health*, 55: 693–700.

Lager, A.C. and Bremberg, S.G. (2009) 'Association between labour market trends and trends in young people's mental health in ten European countries 1983–2005', *BMC Public Health*, 9(325).

Lorey, I. (2015) *State of Insecurity: Government of the Precarious*, London: Verso.

Marmot, M. and Wilkinson, R. (2005) *Social Determinants of Health*, Oxford: Oxford University Press.

Marshall, E.A. and Butler, K. (2015) 'School-to-work transitions in emerging adulthood', in J.J. Arnett (ed) *The Oxford Handbook of Emerging Adulthood*, New York: Oxford University Press.

McGuinness, S., Bergin, A. and Whelan, A. (2018) 'Overeducation in Europe: trends, convergence, and drivers', *Oxford Economic Papers*, 70(4): 994–1015.

Mínguez, A.M., Peláez, A.L. and Sánchez-Cabezudo, S.S. (2012) *La transición de los jóvenes a la vida adulta: crisis económica y emancipación tardía*, Barcelona: Obra Social 'La Caixa'.

Navarro, V. (2008) 'Neoliberalism and its consequences: the world health situation since Alma Ata', *Global Social Policy*, 8(2): 152–5.

O'Reilly, J., Leschke, J., Ortlieb, R., Seeleib-Kaiser, M. and Villa, P. (eds) (2019) *Youth Labor in Transition: Inequalities, Mobility, and Policies in Europe*, New York: Oxford University Press.

Paul, K.I. and Moser, K. (2009) 'Unemployment impairs mental health: meta-analyses', *Journal of Vocational Behavior*, 74(3): 264–82.

Theorell, T. (2000) 'Working conditions and health', in L. Berkman and I. Kawachi (eds) *Social Epidemiology*, Oxford: Oxford University Press, pp 95–117.

Vancea, M. and Utzet, M. (2017) 'How unemployment and precarious employment affect the health of young people: a scoping study on social determinants', *Scandinavian Journal of Public Health*, 45(1): 73–84.

Verd, J.M., Barranco, O. and Bolíbar, M. (2019) 'Youth unemployment and employment trajectories in Spain during the great recession: what are the determinants?', *Journal for Labour Market Research*, 53(1): 4.

12

Precarity and Migration: Thai Wild Berry Pickers in Sweden

Charlotta Hedberg

Introduction

'The "migrant" is the quintessential incarnation of precarity.' This expression, from Schierup and Jørgensen (2016: 949), captures the idea that the study of international migrants and their status in the labour market, and beyond, enhances our understanding of precarity. Migrants are particularly exposed to social inequalities and reveal the causes and consequences of precarity. The concept of precarity has been adopted in migration studies, reflecting the need for a language to express the multidimensional inequalities experienced by migrants (Strauss, 2018). As suggested by Strauss and McGrath (2017), precarious migrant work should be analyzed together with unfree labour relations and precarious legal status. Precarious conditions in the labour market are linked to 'a "continuum" of unfreedom', ranging from forced labour and trafficking, to workers in disempowered positions in relation to their employers (Fudge and Strauss, 2014). The legal status adds to the precarious arrangements of migrants, such as the conditional legal status of asylum seekers (van Kooy and Bowman, 2019), the informal status of irregular migrants (Ahmad, 2008) and the temporary stay of labour migrants (Strauss and McGrath, 2017). Temporary migration is often found in rural food production industries and is characterized by 'a "race to the bottom" in terms of pay and working conditions' (Rye and Scott, 2018: 936). Notably, though, the precarity of migrants does not end with poor working conditions but also permeates the whole situation of migrants' 'precarious lives' (Pye et al, 2012). During the COVID-19 pandemic, precarity has further increased due to the extreme risks taken by migrant workers (Suhardiman et al, 2021).

Taking the multidimensionality of precarity one step further, migration scholars have argued that precarious work is situated in the dynamics between structuring societal tendencies and migrant agency. Although based on structures of unfree labour, precarious work is still mediated by migrant agency (Strauss and McGrath, 2017). Individual migrants themselves act to migrate, due to the prospect of short-term gains and long-term empowerment. In this way, migrant precarity is characterized by ambiguity and tensions between exploitative situations and the hope for improved livelihoods (Tappe and Nguyen, 2019). Without neglecting the structural constraints faced by migrants, such as the neoliberal political economy in need of a 'globally mobile reserve army of labour' (Schierup and Jørgensen, 2016: 948), this perspective highlights the activities of migrants participating in, and enforcing, precarious structures.

This chapter discusses precarity, in all its complexity, in the interplay between structures and agency, exemplified by the empirical case of Thai wild berry pickers in Sweden. Thai farmers migrate temporarily to pick wild berries in Swedish forests, in a process characterized by high circularity and extremely short seasons (Hedberg et al, 2019). The process is structured by a globalized and neoliberal labour market, performed within one of the worlds' most deregulated migration schemes (Hedberg and Olofsson, 2022). Transnational employment relations subject Thai berry pickers to high risks, an absence of safety nets and exploitative work conditions (Axelsson and Hedberg, 2018). However, the individual migrants are voluntarily returning on an annual basis, attracted by the possibilities for socio-economic improvement of the household (Hedberg, 2021). In this way, migrant agency contributes to sustaining precarious labour migration. The chapter also analyzes the changing structural conditions that appeared during the COVID-19 pandemic, which further illuminate the precarious arrangements of migrant workers.

The chapter rests on previously published results from the author, which are based on research performed from 2012 to 2021, consisting of multi-sited fieldwork in rural Thailand and rural Sweden, including interviews with migrant workers, companies and institutions. Information about the seasons in 2020 and 2021 is based on secondary sources, mainly conversations with, and a paper written by, the journalist and expert Mats Wingborg (2020; 2021), who performed fieldwork in rural Sweden during this period, but also a series of articles published in the major Swedish newspaper *Dagens Nyheter* (Fröberg, 2020). Information about the process of COVID-19 testing on migrant workers is based on email conversations with a researcher active at a Swedish testing lab and a phone interview with the person responsible at the Thai embassy in Sweden. A phone interview was also performed in 2021 with an infection control physician responsible for the prohibition of the spread of COVID-19 in a region hosting many region berry pickers.

Migration and precarity: structure, agency and time

This chapter takes the view that precarity is a multidimensional concept, embedded in both the economic and social relations of the worker and the surrounding structures (Strauss, 2018). As such, rather than being focused on employment relations only, it encompasses all aspects of life, including work–life balance and socio-legal aspects. Alberti et al (2018: 494) ask for a more nuanced view on precarization, as a process which is 'inherent to all labour-capital relationships, to varying degrees', but also something that workers experience in their daily life. In relation to platform economies, and the new forms of 'open' employment relations, Schor et al (2020) identify heterogeneity and diverse 'levels of precarity', which boil down to the workers' differing degrees of dependency on the income. 'Varieties of precarity' are also stressed by Schierup and Jørgensen (2016) in relation to migrant workers, comprised of work relations, lived life and citizenship. Migrants' 'precarious lives' (Pye et al, 2012) are characterized by vulnerability in relation to legal statuses, political contexts, insecure and discriminatory conditions at work, and in other areas of life (Paret and Gleeson, 2016).

Many scholars identify neoliberal structures as the main driver for precarious work. As noted by Bourdieu (1998), neoliberal and deregulated labour markets create '*precarious arrangements* that produce insecurity' (emphasis in original). Kalleberg (2009) sees precarious work as a combined result of macro-economic and demographic changes, entailing detached relationships to employers, long-term unemployment, job insecurity, non-standard work arrangements and contingent work, and a shift in risk-taking from employer to employee. Among other consequences, precarious work results in economic inequality, insecurity and instability. Following the neoliberal 'economic miracle' of many Asian states, Cruz-Del Rosario and Rigg (2019) argue for an 'age of precarity in 21st century Asia', affecting groups such as transnational migrants and farmers. The critical political perspective of Schierup and Jørgensen (2016) brings more explanatory value to the role of workers, and migrants in particular, in the production of precarity. They identify a shift in the conceptualization of precarity, from a view of social exclusion as a problem that can be corrected through policy, towards a view of precarious workers as a group serving a purpose since they are 'open to exploitation' in neoliberal globalization. Simply put, precarious migrant workers enable companies in the global economy to maximize their profits (see also Colombini, 2020). Fudge and Strauss (2014) explore the linkages between unfree work and exploitative work conditions, finding that unfree labour at the bottom of the labour market is characterized by, for instance, insecurity, low pay or withheld wages, lack of control, few social benefits, immobility, and immigration statuses tied to the employment relationship.

To this critical perspective, however, migration scholars with a multidimensional view on precarity add a conceptual discussion about the interplay between structure and agency. Contemporary migration theory argues for structuration theory as a way to grasp the full complexity of international migration processes (O'Reilly, 2012; O'Reilly and Rye, 2020), and to incorporate the interplay between aspirations and capabilities of migrants (de Haas, 2021). Arguably, migration is structured by globalized, neoliberal and nationalist tendencies in states and labour markets, but simultaneously, it is deeply intertwined with the performance and agency of individual migrants and their life courses. Strauss and McGrath (2017) emphasize that the labour relations of precarious migrants are unfree, where intersections of gender, nationality, class, legal status and racialization co-produce subordinated positions of migrants. However, although structures are 'actively produced by employers and the state', they are also 'negotiated by workers' (Strauss and McGrath, 2017: 200). According to Tappe and Nguyen (2019), this can be explained by the ambiguous nature of labour migration: situations are both exploitative and, at the same time, empowering, contributing to improved livelihoods and local resilience.

The importance of incorporating agency in relation to broader structures has further been highlighted in labour geographies (Coe and Jordhus-Lier, 2011) and the idea that workers are able to (re)shape socio-economic structures (Grenzdörffer, 2021). A shift is identified from the collective agency of workers, in unions, towards the agency of individuals, families and communities to improve their situation (Martin, 2021). In contemporary studies on precarious work, labour agency has been investigated in relation to the 'platform economy', and the temporary and 'just-in-place' employment relations that are evolving through digital platforms (Wells et al, 2021). Research elaborates on how workers in digital economies are able to act within 'structurally vulnerable positions' (Sun and Chen, 2021). Only limited agency was found among workers, from both an individual point of view (Veen et al, 2020) and in the form of collective worker agency (Wells et al, 2021). In relation to migration studies, Paret and Gleeson (2016) highlight the struggle of individual migrants when they 'navigate structures of power' in order to either improve their own lives or contribute to social change for broader groups of migrants.

The emphasis on labour agency also brings novel spatiotemporal dimensions to the fore (Coe and Jordhus-Lier, 2011). Migrant agency can be intentional as a long-term plan, even for temporary migrants (Buckley et al, 2017). Axelsson et al (2017) explore how temporary Chinese restaurant workers accept precarious work conditions in order to receive permanent residency in Sweden. Yeoh et al (2017) and Hedberg (2021) discuss how transnational simultaneity can explain the continuation of precarious labour migration processes. Migrants endure precarious work in receiving societies as they imagine prosperous future lives for themselves and their families. Crucially, this biographical simultaneity is both temporal, looking at future promises, and spatial, placing expectations of a good life in a separate space to their homeland. Taken together, these accounts show the limitations of single workers in changing structures, but that individuals are, nonetheless, acting in order to change their individual lives.

Precarity of Thai wild berry pickers in Sweden

Precarious structures

The case of Thai wild berry pickers in Sweden illustrates well the complex relation between structure and agency in precarious labour migration. Labour migration to Sweden takes place within an extremely neoliberal and deregulated labour migration scheme, which has been directly influenced by actors in the wild berry industry (Hedberg and Olofsson, 2022). The industry is structured around imported, low-wage workers, based on the argument that access to cheap labour is necessary in order to be competitive in the world market (Svensk bärnäring, 2020). Swedish wild berries are picked by imported workers, frozen and exported for refinement in, among others, food and health industries in China and Finland. Accordingly, rural Sweden is mainly providing raw material, through the import of migrant workers, which is then processed abroad, enabling high profits for a few companies. The majority of the workers are imported from Thailand, complemented by a smaller number of European workers. The official migration scheme, inviting non-European workers, offers flexibility to the industry, which can choose to import the required number of workers for each season, fluctuating between 3,000 and 6,000 Thai workers each year. European workers are from Ukraine and Bulgaria, travelling within the free mobility scheme of the European Union. They are semi-organized, often brokered by informal groups in their home countries to informal hosts in Sweden, and as such are particularly exposed to precarious work (Vogiazides and Hedberg, 2013).

Much research has focused on Thai workers. They are brought to Sweden through Thai staffing agencies, which serve as the formal employers, while the Swedish berry companies are the 'hosts' for the workers (Axelsson and Hedberg, 2018). This arrangement enables Swedish companies to circumvent Swedish regulations, particularly payroll taxes, and to avoid the rights stated in the workers' Swedish collective agreement, such as minimum wages, prevention of excessive work hours and the right to paid transport. In a study on workers' earnings, it was found that one third received lower earnings than was stated in their collective agreement (Hedberg et al, 2019). This results from a gap between the formal wage, stipulated in the collective agreement, and the traditional custom in the industry of paying on a piecework basis, per kilogramme of berries picked. After the introduction of a collective agreement, a general practice in the industry was to continue offering the piecework salary while officially granting the workers incomes not lower than the agreement stipulated. However, our result is that Thai berry pickers are subject to 'subordinated exclusion' in Sweden, where their formal rights are not granted in practice (Tollefsen et al, 2020). At times, our fieldwork has shown that the workers are asked by Thai staffing agencies to choose between fixed wage and piecework salary. According to the 'Swedish model' of labour relations, the terms stated in the collective agreement are given and should not be negotiable between workers and employers. In Thailand, however, lacking a tradition of trade unions, the migration industry has been able to circumvent the Swedish collective agreement.

A major complaint among Thai berry pickers regarding the work in Sweden relates to the price they receive for berries in the piecework version of their salary. This price is uniform among companies in Sweden, set in an oligopolistic manner by Swedish wholesalers, and tends to be low and fluctuating within and between seasons. Piecework salaries not only give the workers low and/or insecure earnings but also transfer the risks to the workers, rather than the companies, and encourage excessive work hours. Work days are often interrupted by only a short night's sleep.

Taken together, it is easy to agree that neoliberal structures, and the interests of firms in creating an infrastructure to maximize profits, form the basis for the Swedish wild berry industry (Krifors, 2021). Although the state and trade unions have attempted to improve the situation, precarious arrangements and the import of migrant workers are fundamental in providing a group of workers that is 'open to exploitation' (Schierup and Jørgensen, 2016).

Precarious agency

Despite these exploitative conditions, however, individual migrants continually arrive for work in Sweden, showing that the process is characterized by strong agency among Thai workers. A survey of 165 Thai berry pickers revealed considerable circularity of return migration among the migrants (Hedberg et al, 2019). While the average worker had returned seven times, there were also a handful of cases with exceptionally high return rates, with the most frequent worker having been to Sweden 27 times. These figures indicate that a culture of migration has evolved in several Thai villages, and among many households, where villagers find strong motivation to continue their migration to Sweden, despite the precarious nature of the work.

A deeper explanation as to the dynamics behind Thai berry pickers' motivations to return to Sweden centres on a sense of transnational simultaneity and how the workers perform their work in Sweden while living their 'real life' in Thailand (Hedberg, 2021). This relates, first, to *rural livelihood diversification* (Ellis, 2000). The majority of wild berry pickers in Sweden are small-scale rice farmers coming from the rural, densely populated areas in north-eastern Thailand. The profile of the berry pickers is homogeneous; they tend to be middle aged, low-educated men, with a family remaining in the home village (Hedberg et al, 2019). Due to the agricultural transition in the area, most small-scale farmers have adopted strategies of livelihood diversification in addition to farm work (Buch-Hansen, 2001). Since alternative jobs are precarious, Thai villagers retain farm work as a safety net (Rigg et al, 2018). Many off-farm jobs involve internal migration within Thailand, for instance construction work in the capital region. Other migrants, though, take part in overseas labour migration, encouraged by the Thai government, particularly directed to other Asian countries, such as Taiwan, Singapore or South Korea.

Besides this, there are geographical pockets of labour migration directed towards the wild berry industry in Sweden (Hedberg et al, 2019). A particular feature of this livelihood diversification is the seasonal compatibility between the annual cycles of rice farming in Thailand and the harvesting of berries in Sweden (Hedberg, 2021). The timely synchronization of seasons provides an illustrative example of transnational simultaneity, where the migrants can perform their work in Sweden while the rice is literally growing in the fields in their home village. The migrants are co-arranging their lives in multi-sited space, simultaneously working in Sweden while they are 'doing' their work on the fields in Thailand.

The second explanation of transnational simultaneity is built on a *biographical* understanding of migration and the idea that not only present work conditions but also the future plans of the family are a major concern of the migrants (see also Yeoh et al, 2017). Thai migrant workers endure hard work in the Swedish forests as they are imagining a better future for their children (Hedberg, 2021). The survey revealed that most households with children of an appropriate age were using at least some of their earnings from berry picking for their children's education, in order to give them a more prosperous life than farm work in the villages can offer (Hedberg et al, 2019). The short season (70 days) that the migrants work in Sweden also makes the social costs for working in Sweden relatively low compared to other cases of international labour migration. This compensates for the fact that the earnings from piecework in Sweden are, in fact, often substantially lower than the workers expect.

Taken together, the rural livelihood diversification and the biographical motivations for work constitute spatiotemporal practices of simultaneity that are closely connected to precarity (Hedberg, 2021; see also Yeoh et al, 2017). They lower migrants' thresholds for tolerating precarious work conditions and create social inequalities in Sweden between groups of workers. Thai migrant workers are motivated to work as hard as possible in Sweden since their 'real' place of work and of living is in Thailand, and since they imagine a better future for their families. In this way, migrant agency in transnational social fields contributes to sustain precarious migration processes.

Precarity during COVID-19

COVID-19 and the wild berry industry

The COVID-19 pandemic has further illuminated the precarity of migrant workers (Suhardiman et al, 2021), and migrant workers in the wild berry industry are no exception. In springtime of 2020, closed borders showed the dependency of the industries on foreign workers. In Sweden, the interest organization the Federation of Swedish Farmers (LRF) expressed alarm at a shortage of agricultural workers, particularly within the fruit and vegetable industries where they feared that 8,000 workers would be missing, not including wild berry pickers (LRF, 2020). Their lobbying may have contributed to the Swedish government removing travel restrictions for migrant workers in food industries.

Thai staffing agencies had initiated the recruitment of berry pickers for Sweden before the outbreak of the pandemic. Due to the global escalation of the pandemic in the springtime, it was, until the day of arrival in Sweden, unclear if any berry pickers would arrive in Sweden. The Thai government opposed migrant work, and kept the borders closed. This caused major insecurity for Swedish berry companies. After intense lobbying of the Department of Employment (DOE) in Thailand, however, it was possible for 2,900 delayed Thai workers to arrive in Sweden in 2020, together with around 1,500 European workers (Wingborg, 2020). The entry of the Thai workers came with several restrictions: host companies should pay €1,000 extra per worker to the Thai government; negative PCR-tests should be provided 72 hours before workers returned to Thailand; and, on their return to Thailand, the workers had to stay in quarantine for two weeks. For the European berry pickers travelling by car or bus within the borders of the EU, there were no such restrictions. However, the Polish borders were closed, and it was difficult and time consuming for workers to reach Sweden.

Many Thai workers expressed doubts over whether they would travel to Sweden for work during the season, due to fear of COVID-19. However, the agricultural season in Thailand had been poor, characterized by drought that had caused severe economic crises in rural Thailand, so attracting farmers to work in Sweden despite the pandemic. Nonetheless, the 2,900 workers who finally arrived in Sweden was only half the number that the industry had planned to import for the 2020 season.

After the delays by the Thai government in opening the borders for migrant workers, Swedish companies were obliged to follow the general regulations of the COVID-19 pandemic in Sweden, such as enabling the workers to socially distance. The Swedish companies arranged their work facilities accordingly, implying that there should be fewer workers per accommodation. Also, workers were told that they should not shop in grocery stores or otherwise involve themselves in Swedish society.

For the Thai berry pickers, the actual results from the 2020 season can be summed up in positive terms thanks to an exceptionally good year for berries (Wingborg, 2020). In a normal year, workers can pick 60–65 kg of berries per day. In the 2020 season, however, they could often pick double this amount. Also, there were no major outbreaks of COVID-19 in the camps. Only two Thai berry pickers were infected, as was discovered after their return to Thailand. A number of workers had to be taken to hospital, but this was due to two serious road traffic accidents. The incidents occurred due to the enormous volumes of berries that the mini-buses were transporting back to the camps, which made the buses sag under the heavy weight of berries.

In the 2021 season, however, the situation was completely altered. Some 5,000 Thai berry pickers arrived in Sweden after having been tested and vaccinated once against COVID-19 (Wingborg, 2021). Due to the fast spread of the Delta variant of the virus, hundreds of workers ended up infected with COVID-19, and several camps in Sweden were severely affected. According to an infection control physician, the workers were probably infected during their travel to the camp in Sweden. Once in Sweden, the situation was favourable for stopping the disease as the workers worked and lived together in small groups of seven people, and some companies practiced quarantine accommodation for infected workers. Living isolated from the Swedish society, there was no risk of the workers spreading COVID-19 to the rest of society. After a few weeks, the infection was under control among the Thai berry pickers.

Precarious conditions

The COVID-19 pandemic directly highlights several points of concern regarding the precarity of berry pickers in Sweden. The most obvious issue is regarding the outbreak of the disease in 2021. Here, the industry failed to meet the requirements set out by the Swedish state, which could have prevented the spread of the disease. First, the workers had received only one shot of vaccine, instead of the two required, and, second, they were not tested according to the regulations. The workers should have been tested directly on arrival and then again five days later. The infection physician, however, remarked that the industry claimed to have received no information, which the physician labels 'naïve' on the part of the industry in not seeking out information about their duties during a pandemic. Infected workers continued working soon after infection in order to avoid losing income due to the piece rate salary. The physician explained that 'for most workers, a Covid infection is not much worse than an influenza infection, and I assume that they had worked with influenza before'. The precarious conditions hence implied that the workers would continue working.

Whereas the situation for Thai berry pickers was relatively regulated and adjusted to let the workers maintain social distance, for the European workers, the risks of infection were even higher. Their accommodations were not formally regulated and, as an example, it was exposed in the Swedish media that a group of 100 Roma migrant workers from Bulgaria were residing in an abandoned apartment building without electricity or water.

The payment of additional fees of €1,000 for Thai workers is alarming as it is unclear which actors actually paid them. Officially, the fee was paid by the Swedish companies, who transferred them through Thai staffing agencies to the DOE in Thailand. However, there is concern that at least part of these costs were passed on to the workers. Previous studies have shown that there are major problems with transparency regarding the already excessive fees of berry pickers (Hedberg et al, 2019). The fees of around €2,200 are suspected to include high service fees to the Thai staffing agencies. In general, the transnational construction of the employment relations between Thai staffing agencies as employers and Swedish berry companies as hosts also implies problems with recognizing responsibility between actors (Axelsson and Hedberg, 2018). There are signs that the general fees for the workers increased during the pandemic, which might be associated with the payment of the fee for COVID-19.

Lastly, in 2020, the practical arrangements for PCR testing caused major problems. According to the Thai embassy in Sweden, the analysis of tests in labs was arranged beforehand for only half of the workers. For the other half, it was uncertain until the workers should return to Thailand how the testing would be achieved. At that moment in time, in September, there was a general lack in lab capacity in Sweden for analyzing PCR tests, and migrant workers were not prioritized. The person responsible at the Thai embassy in Sweden believed that Swedish companies had been too eager to get the workers to Sweden and that they had suspected that the pandemic would be over by the time of return in early October. Shortly before the workers' return, the Thai government accepted quick tests, which could be taken at the airport, which resolved the issue. Nonetheless, this shows the fine line that the companies were walking while importing workers during the pandemic, and the difficulty in foreseeing problems. Arguably, bringing migrant workers to Sweden during the pandemic exposed the workers to a structural element of uncertainty and insecurity.

Conclusion

Aspects of precarity have been prominent in social science throughout the 2000s. In migration studies, migrant precarity has emerged as a conceptual framework to facilitate the analysis of inequalities and injustices that exist in relation to migration caused by societal structures and historical processes. As Strauss (2018: 625) points out, precarity adds an important ingredient to the analysis of international migration, since 'life is inherently precarious, but human societies and economies are organized in ways that render some lives more precarious than others, often but not exclusively through the capitalist wage relation and the division of paid and unpaid labour'. Although perhaps needless to point out, social inequalities and the distribution of resources in societies are often stratified along lines of ethnicity and migrant's legal statuses. In other words, migrants tend to be precarious.

This chapter shares the view of contemporary scholars in migration studies that migration processes are fruitfully explored through the intersection between structure and agency (O'Reilly, 2012; de Haas, 2021). In a general sense, social structures are crucial in constructing migration processes; however, just as important is the individual agency of the migrant, which contributes to creating and recreating migrant structures. In the literature on migration and precarity, this interplay between structure and agency contributes to explanations of why precarious migration processes are sustained. Research on precarious labour migration possesses an awareness that international migration is structured around global divisions of labour and neoliberal migration regimes, while at the same time incorporating the aspirations of individual migrants, their prospects for earnings, and hopes for creating a new and better life.

The case of Thai berry pickers in Sweden illustrates how global divisions of labour, neoliberal migration regimes and subordinated exclusion provide precarious structures for migrant workers. It shows how the wild berry industry, in order to compete and profit in the world market, is constructed as dependent on cheap, flexible labour from low-wage countries, particularly Thailand. The import of migrant workers is fully integrated into the system, which is why not even a pandemic such as COVID-19 could stop it. The pandemic throws further light on the precarious nature of the work while illuminating that, instead of pausing the import of workers, risks caused by the pandemic were transferred onto the workers. During the pandemic, states prioritized the interests of industry before the safety and integrity of workers. For the 2021 season, this resulted in a major outbreak of the virus among Thai wild berry pickers in Sweden.

Despite these precarious conditions, the case of Thai berry pickers in Sweden also shows how migrant agency sustains these structures. The migration process is characterized by circularity and high return rates among the migrant workers, who express a personal willingness to return. A biographical, future-casting view on migration explains how the workers imagine a better life for themselves and their families in their home villages in Thailand while performing their work in Sweden. This lowers the migrants' thresholds for performing precarious work, even at exceptional times such as the COVID-19 pandemic. This chapter shows that, in 2021, workers continued working despite being infected with the virus, in order to keep their earnings up. It illustrates the precarious nature of work based on piecework salaries.

When researching Thai wild berry pickers, one is often confronted with the view that the high circularity of individual migrants, the fact that they frequently and voluntarily return, mitigates the fact that they are doing precarious work and living precarious lives. By using a structuration perspective, I have sought to confront this argument, showing that the workers are both experiencing precarious structures and also, through their agency, contributing to sustaining such structures. The COVID-19 pandemic showed that the structures are rigid but that the workers supported them, both travelling long-distances to work and then working while being infected. Accordingly, the emphasis on agency is not intending to downplay the role of precarious structures but rather to highlight that migrants perform voluntary acts of migration repeatedly within neoliberal migration regimes. These acts, in turn, also recreate precarious structures.

References

Ahmad, A.N. (2008) 'Dead men working: time and space in London's ("illegal") migrant economy', *Work, Employment & Society*, 22(2): 301–18.

Alberti, G., Bessa, I., Hardy, K., Trappmann, V. and Umney, C. (2018) 'In, against and beyond precarity: work in insecure times', *Work, Employment & Society*, 32(3): 447–57.

Axelsson, L. and Hedberg, C. (2018) 'Emerging topologies of transnational employment: "posting" Thai workers in Sweden's wild berry industry beyond regulatory reach', *Geoforum*, 89: 1–10.

Axelsson, L., Malmberg, B. and Zhang, Q. (2017) 'On waiting, work-time and imagined futures: theorising temporal precariousness among Chinese chefs in Sweden's restaurant industry', *Geoforum*, 78: 169–78.

Bourdieu, P. (1998) 'The essence of neoliberalism', *Le Monde Diplomatique*. Available from: mondediplo.com/1998/12/08bourdieu [Accessed 24 June 2020].

Buch-Hansen, M. (2001) 'Is sustainable agriculture in Thailand feasible?', *Journal of Sustainable Agriculture*, 18: 137–60.

Buckley, M., McPhee, S. and Rogaly, B. (2017) 'Labour geographies on the move: migration, migrant status and work in the 21st century', *Geoforum*, 78: 153–8.

Coe, N.M. and Jordhus-Lier, D.C. (2011) 'Constrained agency? Re-evaluating the geographies of labour', *Progress in Human Geography*, 35(2): 211–33.

Colombini, I. (2020) 'Form and essence of precarization by work: from alienation to the industrial reserve army at the turn of the twenty-first century', *Review of Radical Political Economics*, 52(3): 409–26.

Cruz-Del Rosario, T. and Rigg, J. (2019) 'Living in an age of precarity in 21st century Asia', *Journal of Contemporary Asia*, 49(4): 517–27.

de Haas, H. (2021) 'A theory of migration: the aspirations-capabilities framework', *Comparative Migration Studies*, 9(8): 1–35.

Ellis, F. (2000) 'The determinants of rural livelihood diversification in developing countries', *Journal of Agricultural Economics*, 51(2): 289–302.

Fröberg, J. (2020) 'Så blev skogens guld till blodsbär i coronakrisens spår', Dagens Nyheter, [online] 30 August. Available from: www.dn.se/ekonomi/sa-blev-skogens-guld-till-blodsbar-i-coronakrisens-spar/ [Accessed 23 March 2021].

Fudge, J. and Strauss, K. (2014) *Temporary Work, Agencies and Unfree Labour: Insecurity in the New World of Work*. London: Routledge.

Grenzdörffer, S.M. (2021) 'Transformative perspectives on labour geographies – the role of labour agency in processes of socioecological transformations', *Geography Compass*, 15(6), e12565. https://doi.org/10.1111/gec3.12565.

Hedberg, C. (2021) 'Entwined ruralities: seasonality, simultaneity and precarity among transnational migrant workers in the wild berry industry', *Journal of Rural Studies*, 88, 510–17.

Hedberg, C. and Olofsson, I. (2022) 'Negotiating the Wild West: variegated neoliberalisation of the Swedish labour migration regime and the wild berry migration industry', *Environment and Planning A*, 54(1): 33–49.

Hedberg, C., Axelsson, L. and Abella, M. (2019) 'Thai berry pickers in Sweden: a migration corridor to a low-wage sector', Delegation for Swedish Migration Studies, Stockholm, Report 2019: 3. Available from: www.delmi.se/en/publications/report-and-policy-brief-2019-3-thai-berry-pickers-in-sweden-a-migration-corridor-to-a-low-wage-sector/ [Accessed: 31 March 2022].

Kalleberg, A.L. (2009) 'Precarious work, insecure workers: employment relations in transition', *American Sociological Review*, 74(1): 1–22.

Krifors, K. (2021) 'Logistics of migrant labour: rethinking how workers "fit" transnational economies', *Journal of Ethnic and Migration Studies*, 47(1): 148–65.

LRF (2020) 'Bristen på säsongsarbetare störst inom trädgårdsnäringen', The Federation of Swedish Farmers (LRF), [online] 4 July. Available from: www.lrf.se [Accessed 3 February 2021].

Martin, H.E. (2021) 'Local spaces of labour control or platforms for agency? The North East Durham Coalfield, 1820–1890', *Geoforum*, 119: 72–82.

O'Reilly, K. (2012) *International Migration and Social Theory*, Basingstoke: Palgrave.

O'Reilly, K. and Rye, J.F. (2020) 'The (re)production of the exploitative nature of rural migrant labour in Europe', in J.F. Rye and K. O'Reilly (eds) *International Labour Migration to Europe's Rural Regions*, London: Routledge, pp 228–45.

Paret, M. and Gleeson, S. (2016) 'Precarity and agency through a migration lens', *Citizenship Studies*, 20(3–4): 277–94.

Pye, O., Daud, R., Harmono, Y. and Tatat, S. (2012) 'Precarious lives: transnational biographies of migrant oil palm workers', *Asia Pacific Viewpoint*, 53(3): 330–42.

Rigg, J., Salamanca, A., Phongsiri, M. and Sripun, M. (2018) 'More farmers, less farming? Understanding the truncated agrarian transition in Thailand', *World Development*, 107: 327–37.

Rye, J.F. and Scott, S. (2018) 'International labour migration and food production in rural Europe: a review of the evidence', *Sociologia Ruralis*, 58(4), 928–52.

Schierup, C.U. and Jørgensen, M.B. (2016) 'An introduction to the special issue. Politics of precarity: migrant conditions, struggles and experiences', *Critical Sociology*, 42(7–8): 947–58.

Schor, J.B., Attwood-Charles, W., Cansoy, M., Ladegaard, I. and Wengronowitz, R. (2020) 'Dependence and precarity in the platform economy', *Theoretical Sociology*, 49: 833–61.

Strauss, K. (2018) 'Labour geography 1: towards a geography of precarity?', *Progress in Human Geography*, 42(4): 622–30.

Strauss, K. and McGrath, S. (2017) 'Temporary migration, precarious employment and unfree labour relations: exploring the "continuum of exploitation" in Canada's Temporary Foreign Worker Program', *Geoforum*, 78: 199–208.

Suhardiman, D., Rigg, J., Bandur, M., Marschke, M., Miller, M.A., Pheuangsavanh, N., Sayatham, M. and Taylor, D. (2021) 'On the coattails of globalization: migration, migrants and COVID-19 in Asia', *Journal of Ethnic and Migration Studies*, 47(1): 88–109.

Sun, P. and Chen, J.Y. (2021) 'Platform labour and contingent agency in China', *China Perspectives*, 1: 19–27.

Svensk bärnäring (2020) *Bärkraft med socialt ansvar: Skatteregler för hållbar bärplockning*, Stockholm: Westander.

Tappe, O. and Nguyen, M.T.N. (2019) 'Southeast Asian trajectories of labour mobility: precarity, translocality, and resilience', *TRaNS: Trans-Regional and -National Studies of Southeast Asia*, 7(1): 1–18.

Tollefsen, A., Hedberg, C., Eriksson, M. and Axelsson, L. (2020) 'Changing labour standards and "subordinated inclusion": Thai migrant workers in the Swedish forest berry industry', in J.F. Rye and K. O'Reilly (eds) *International Labour Migration to Europe's Rural Regions*, London: Routledge, pp 121–38.

van Kooy, J. and Bowman, D. (2019) '"Surrounded with so much uncertainty": asylum seekers and manufactured precarity in Australia', *Journal of Ethnic and Migration Studies*, 45(5): 693–710.

Veen, A., Barratt, T. and Goods, C. (2020) 'Platform-capital's "app-etite" for control: a labour process analysis of food-delivery work in Australia', *Work Employment & Society*, 34(3): 388–406.

Vogiazides, L. and Hedberg, C. (2013) 'Trafficking for forced labour and labour exploitation in Sweden', in N. Ollus, A. Jokinen and M. Joutsen (eds) *Exploitation of Migrant Workers in Finland, Sweden, Estonia and Lithuania*, Helsinki: European Institute for Crime Prevention and Control, affiliated with the United Nations, pp 171–237.

Wells, K.J., Attoh, K. and Cullen, D. (2021) '"Just-in-place" labor: driver organizing in the Uber workplace', *Environment and Planning A*, 53(2): 315–31.

Wingborg, M. (2020) 'När marken färgas blå', *Dagens Arena*, [online] 19 August. Available from: www.dagensarena.se/innehall/nar-marken-fargas-bla/ [Accessed 23 March 2021].

Wingborg, M. (2021) 'När covid-19 kom till skogen', *Dagens Arena*, [online] 22 August. Available from: https://www.dagensarena.se/innehall/nar-covid-19-kom-till-skogen/ [Accessed 12 November 2021].

Yeoh, B.S.A., Platt, M., Khoo, C.Y., Lam, T. and Baey, G. (2017) 'Indonesian domestic workers and the (un)making of transnational livelihoods and provisional futures', *Social & Cultural Geography*, 18(3): 415–34.

13

Revisiting the Concept of Precarious Work in Times of COVID-19

Barbora Holubová and Marta Kahancová

Introduction

Over the past two decades, increasing demands for labour market flexibility and internationalization fuelled the emergence of atypical, often precarious, forms of work. Precarious work is insecure and uncertain, providing limited economic and social benefits; it offers only limited statutory entitlements through labour laws, regulatory protection and labour rights (Kalleberg, 2018: 15). While the existing literature has studied the concept of precarious work both in times of economic downturn and prosperity, the COVID-19 pandemic that began in 2020 presents yet another set of challenges to our understanding of precarious work (Aust and Holst, 2007; Keller and Seifert, 2013; Kalleberg, 2018; Kahancová et al, 2020; Trif et al, 2021). Therefore, this chapter revisits the multidimensional concept of precarious work in the light of the recent COVID-19 pandemic. It argues that the pandemic facilitates a broader and deeper understanding of the dimensions of precarious work, which have not yet been systematically addressed in the available literature. The chapter attempts to elaborate on those dimensions of precarious work amplified by the pandemic or insufficiently captured in previous conceptualizations of precarious work. These refer, in particular, to health and safety at work, to precarity within telework and to precarity as a gendered phenomenon.

A multidimensional approach to precarity

Precarious jobs do not secure decent economic and social rights, career opportunities, or access to benefits and legal entitlements when compared to full-time and stable employment (Dörre, 2005; Aust and Holst, 2007). The available literature acknowledges precarious work as a multidimensional concept affecting pay, working time and job security (Wood, 2016; Doellgast et al, 2018; Keune and Pedaci, 2020).

First, income-related precarity emerges due to a higher incidence of low pay in precarious work, identified as income below two thirds of median gross hourly wages (Keller and Seifert, 2013; Kahancová et al, 2020). Second, working time precarity rises with unpredictable working hours and overall weekly working time, often involving excessive and/or unpaid overtime. Third, precarity often relates to job stability, such as lower job security as a result of flexible work arrangements, seasonal fluctuations in work, or work that formally does not fall under an employment relationship protected by relevant labour legislation, and thus, granting economic and social rights. Fourth, precarity relates to limited or absent social security entitlements, that is, constrained collective benefit entitlements and paid leave, depending on particular flexible work arrangements (for example, small contracts, zero hours, self-employment and so on). Fifth, precarious work may also demonstrate itself beyond formal contractual arrangements. Regarding discretion and autonomy at work, precarious work lacks features associated with decent working conditions, such as access to training, skill development and career opportunities. It generates high exposure to work-related stress and lack of autonomy over employees' work. Finally, precarious work demonstrates a lack of interest in workers' collective representation. Traditional trade unions often lack the capacities required to organize precarious workers (Doellgast et al, 2018; Trif et al, 2021), or precarious workers themselves are not able to demand interest representation (Kahancová et al, 2020).

Evidence supports the contention that precarious work, expressed through the aforementioned dimensions, was on the rise before the COVID-19 pandemic. There was an increase in the number of workers who involuntarily earned low wages (Grimshaw et al, 2018), worked irregular or unpredictable working hours (Wood, 2016), faced high levels of job insecurity (Benassi and Dorigatti, 2015; Doellgast et al, 2018) and lacked access to union representation (Keune and Pedaci, 2020; Trif et al, 2021). But how has the pandemic influenced trends in precarious work and the multidimensional concept of precarity?

The COVID-19 pandemic brought about widespread social adaptations and structural market changes. While the emphasis on self-protection and reluctance to apply precautionary principles was present also in pre-pandemic times (Nichols and Walters, 2014), during the pandemic, the issue of workers' health acquired a new scope amid changing working conditions. Precarity demonstrates itself through various new features, which emerge in an environment with an increased risk of infection accompanied by a lack of knowledge on the mechanisms of disease transmission and without clear instructions on prevention. These changes, reflected in widespread public discourse, call for a revisiting of the concept of precarious work and the dimensions presented earlier. Therefore, the remainder of this chapter seeks to address two questions: first, how have the dimensions of precarity, as identified in the literature, transformed during the COVID-19 pandemic; and, second, what new dimensions of precarious work, not systematically analyzed in earlier literature, have emerged or been amplified in direct response to the pandemic.

Revisiting precarity in times of COVID-19

From the perspective of precarity, public discourses related to work during the pandemic have centred mostly around three important trends. First, health and safety at work were placed in the spotlight as the COVID-19 pandemic led to greater demand for detailed health and safety rules at the workplace. This was especially the case for individuals working directly in high-risk areas. Second, the pandemic saw a massive increase in teleworking, facilitated by digital technologies. While teleworking might have saved jobs and guaranteed job stability, it may also potentially have been a source of precarity due to lack of regulation in working hours. Third, changes in work patterns due to the pandemic, including telework, not only blurred the boundaries between work, parenting and free time, but also intensified overtime work. These changes in work patterns played out differently among men and women, suggesting a need to scrutinize precarity during the COVID-19 pandemic as a gendered phenomenon.

Health and safety at work

The COVID-19 pandemic has not only augmented the importance of safety and health at work but has also fuelled questions regarding precarity at work from the perspective of health and safety, which comprises a set of standards and preventative measures that should assure the wellbeing of the employee. The existing literature highlights the link between job insecurity and individual health deterioration (Domenighetti et al, 2000; Kalleberg, 2009; Caroli and Godard, 2016), with the link between health and working conditions within the literature on precarious work being relatively recent (Becker and Engel, 2018). The pandemic not only affected workers' health and safety but also raised awareness about the relevance thereof. The demands in terms of health and safety standards of people working in contaminated or high-risk environments have increased in sectors such as healthcare, social care, retail and public transport. The full range of how their expectations and the actual health and safety measures in place changed is not yet known, yet a plenitude of manifestations of precarity, via (a lack of) health and safety measures, has been documented.

The shortage of personal protective equipment (PPE) is one of the most profound signs of work precarity during the COVID-19 pandemic. The lack of face masks or their low quality; shortages of gloves and germicidal solutions, clothing or face shields; and the inaccessibility of tests or vaccinations during the pandemic for women and men working in the red zones confirmed the unpreparedness of employers and state institutions for this situation. Due to the lack of protective equipment, women and men from essential services were forced to work without proper protection (Schneider and Harknett, 2020; Pelling, 2021) or were forced to utilize unprofessional, often homemade, aids (Atzori et al, 2020; Livingston et al, 2020; Measuria et al, 2021). Surveys by the Finnish Nurse Association found that health workers used raincoats for improvised protection and face masks made out of tissue paper (Pelling, 2021). Even when the supply of the protective aids improved, later in the course of the pandemic, the risk of being infected could never be entirely eliminated.

Evidence of the number of frontline workers infected or dead due to exposure to COVID-19 at work is still incomplete. The latest global estimate shows that at least 17,000 health workers died from COVID-19 over the past year (Amnesty International, 2021). Similarly, essential long-term care workers found themselves on the frontline of the COVID-19 pandemic, caring for the elderly and aiding the most vulnerable and, in turn, becoming vulnerable themselves. In the United States alone, nearly 500,000 long-term care workers have been infected. So far, in the countries studied, at least 1,385 long-term care workers have died in the US, 469 in the UK and 25 in Canada (UNI Global Union, 2021). The interrelation between the insufficient supply of PPE and the deaths of healthcare professionals and social workers will probably never be fully investigated.

Additional phenomenon contributing to the health and safety precarity is the violation of the statutory minimum staffing standards in the time of the pandemic. In occupations with intensive personal work, such as healthcare and long-term social care, the minimum number of nurses per bed aims to assure the quality of the service provided. Less attention is paid to the fact that the staffing standards of the number of nurses per bed also protect the employees from unmanageable workloads and burnout. The health crisis exacerbates the lack of staff, leading to gross violations of the mandatory staffing standards. To illustrate the impact of this violation of the minimum staffing standards, let us focus on evidence from Slovakia. The standard here is approximately one nurse per two beds. During the most severe crisis periods, we observed situations in an intensive care unit when five patients needed urgent care at the same time. The only nurse on duty had to take care of them simultaneously. In another hospital, the nurse had 14 patients in dire situations with different diagnoses. In another instance, a single doctor was found caring for 48 patients (Katuška, 2021). Such situations reveal that the statutory minimum number of doctors and nurses per bed were definitely not observed during the pandemic. The shortage of nurses is a long-term problem in Slovakia and the data shows that the number of nurses is significantly lower than the EU average: 5.7 versus 8.5 per 1,000 citizens (European Commission, 2020), with the mean age of nurses being 48 years. In 2020, the number of retiring nurses was the highest it had been in the past three years (Katuška, 2021). This will likely lead to repeated violations of the minimum staffing standards and result in unbearable workload and exhaustion of the healthcare workforce.

The health and safety dimension thus adds to the already precarious working conditions of specific occupations and multiplies the effects of precarity for various professions. For example, social care staff working on temporary agency contracts, with an indecent income level and in facilities with low staff-to-bed ratios, have faced additional hardship. In Slovakia, due to the lack of PPE and enormous pressure to protect high-risk elderly people from infection and death, long-term care workers have been exposed to extraordinarily humiliating conditions. They have been forced to stay in facilities in which they are crammed into a small room and have to sleep on the floor, and, most importantly, are isolated from their families for several weeks (see, for example, Heilová, 2020). Care workers have been praised for their self-sacrifice and devotion, yet have been forced to work irrespective of their fears and exposure to risky health conditions, not to mention the dread of job loss and income at a time of likely deterioration in employment.

Moreover, COVID-19 intensified the effects of precarity on mental health to a new degree, reminiscent of the effects of wartime service. The link between precarious work and mental health is well documented beyond the COVID-19 pandemic (for example, Stansfeld and Candy, 2006; Blake et al, 2021). In general, workers' mental health is endangered by non-standard employment, which often includes shift work, part-time assignments and temporary work (OECD, 2020). The pandemic exaggerated the adverse effects of precarious working conditions on mental health for many professions, most especially for those in healthcare. Although health professionals might be trained to cope with stressful situations and to deal with death, records reveal an unmanageable amount of uncertainty and stress during the COVID-19 pandemic (Khanal et al, 2020; Neto et al, 2020). Many health workers show symptoms similar to soldiers from war zones, including post-traumatic stress disorder (PTSD). Health professionals have been forced to determine whom to save and whom to leave to die in cases where there was a lack of breathing equipment. Their exhaustion and diminished interest in continuing their professional careers forces them to consider whether to resign in order to preserve their own mental health (Katuška, 2021).

A significant component of precarity related to health and safety during COVID-19 is essential workers' limited control and powerlessness. In many countries, including Czechia and Slovakia, the requirement to continue to work regardless of the risk to one's own health integrity has been ensured by declaring a state of emergency or special regulations. In essential services, the state of emergency erased workers' free choice to refuse to take up employment, even if the employer did not provide PPE. The pandemic showed that becoming infected by the virus at the workplace was not the responsibility of employers. There was virtually no legal enforceability for damage to health during employment. The provision of essential services for the general population was often ensured to the detriment of the health and safety of many employees (Amnesty International, 2020; Loustaunau et al, 2021).

To sum up, the concept of precarious work needs to acknowledge the dimension of health and safety to a greater extent. The following elements of work are perceived as precarious from the health and safety perspective: (1) increased threats to bodily integrity due to exposure to high-risk situations accompanied by the lack of PPE; (2) the absence or unprecedented violation of the minimum staff–patient ratios in healthcare; and (3) unmanageable mental stress resulting in PTSD and other mental illness. All these elements occurred in the background of a lack of autonomy at work and exposure to hazardous working conditions in some occupations, with employers' refusal to bear responsibility for the state's failure to meet regulations for personal protection at workplaces.

Telework as a flexible work arrangement

Telework can be defined as work performed using information communication technology outside the employer's premises. Before the pandemic, telework was perceived as a result of modernization and digitalization of work. Telework has been promoted as a flexible work arrangement with a range of benefits. Employees could expect increased work autonomy, better reconciliation of work, private and family life, and reduced commuting time. Employers benefit from decreased costs for premises, energy and facility services, as well as an increase of work effectiveness and performance of employees working from their homes.

However, teleworking also demonstrates adverse effects. The challenges of telework were already recognized before the pandemic, with the interrelation of work flexibility and precarity having been presented as a flexibility trap (Pedaci, 2010) or a threat to job security contributing to the precarity of work (Kahancová et al, 2020). In addition, telework gained new and often highly contested attributes during the pandemic. From a family-friendly work arrangement, teleworking became a necessity, and in some cases was even mandatory after the outbreak of the pandemic. As a result, the share of people working purely from their homes has risen to an estimated 33.7 per cent, from the less than 5 per cent share before the pandemic (Eurofound, 2020a). This shift has been enormous, spreading to all professional levels and occupations that allow it.

Nevertheless, telework is not accessible to everyone and its share depends on the structure of the economy (Eurostat, 2021). On average, the proportion of people typically teleworking in the EU reached only 5.7 per cent of all employed people aged 15–64 in 2020 (Eurostat, 2021). The lowest shares have been reported from Bulgaria (1.2 per cent), Romania (2.5 per cent), Croatia (3.1 per cent) and Hungary (3.6 per cent). In comparison, teleworking in Finland, Luxembourg and Ireland reached approximately 20–25 per cent in the same year.

Electronic equipment, Internet connectivity and security systems, and an ergonomic work setting are preconditions for teleworking. The question emerged as to whether all workers who were suddenly placed on mandatory teleworking had access to these conditions, and who would bear the related costs. For example, how many employers have acknowledged additional electricity and heating/cooling costs and reflected this in higher wages? Employees might accept implicitly the expectation that there are no extra costs involved with teleworking, however, teleworking may create explicit precarity when the increased costs for utilities and other needs are carried by the employee.

Even before the pandemic, fixed telework arrangements were disputed (Eurofound and ILO, 2017). The pressure to stay electronically connected and reachable outside the regular working hours initiated the legislation on the right to disconnect from work (for example, in France, Code du travail – Article L2242-17) (EurWork, 2019). Studies addressing this problem due to teleworking during the pandemic reveal the growth and normalization of the 24/7 work culture and the complete collapse of the frontiers between professional and family life, which is exaggerated by the surveillance of telework (Manokha, 2020). The right to disconnect needs to be anchored in legislation, however, it also needs to be applied without any hidden penalties to teleworkers, such as withdrawal from access to information and a decrease in performance assessment.

Another side effect of telework during the pandemic has been the rise in the use of monitoring and surveillance software. While these tools were widely used prior to the pandemic, the crisis gave impetus to their rise and allowed the increased monitoring of people while working. Building a board of faces with the photos of teleworkers that is updated via laptop camera every five minutes to track the teleworkers' activity without their awareness is just one extreme example (Cushing, 2020).

As telework theoretically enables employees to adapt the workplace and working time to their preferences, many studies confirm a positive impact on work–life balance (for example, Chung and van der Horst, 2018). Telework should help reconcile work- and home-related tasks, allowing mothers to maintain their working hours after giving birth and thus remain in human capital intensive jobs (Fuller and Hirsh, 2019). These positives of telework for work–life balance were already contested before the pandemic and indicate that working at home may not lead to a more gender-balanced distribution of care and household responsibilities but, instead, may reinforce traditional gender roles (Wellington, 2006; Lott and Chung, 2016; Giovanis, 2018).

Studies on the impact of telework during the pandemic on gender roles indicate ambiguous trends (Hupkau and Petrongolo, 2020). On the one hand, an increase in women's care work stemmed from the lack of available public childcare. Thus, pre-existing gender disparities have intensified to the detriment of women. However, on the other hand, the necessary redistribution of domestic tasks during lockdown may have contributed to a fairer distribution of parental and other care responsibilities between women and men (Eurofound, 2020b). However, in countries where the gender roles are strictly defined, such a redistribution of care and domestic work due to telework might not occur. In contrast, due to the persistence of rigid gender roles in households, telework likely turned into precarious telework, especially for women.

To conclude, with teleworking having been on the rise during the pandemic, it can, on the one hand, provide job stability, but on the other, increase precarity by exposing workers to additional costs, intensified controls and increased working hours. Adverse external conditions thus accelerate multiple risks to workers' wellbeing. We identified the following elements contributing to precarity due to telework during the pandemic: (1) inaccessibility of telework because of the type of work; (2) inaccessibility of telework due to the lack of adequate information and telecommunication devices; (3) extreme surveillance practices by employers to control teleworkers; and (4) additional costs of telework assumed by workers without reimbursement. These elements are closely related to autonomy at work and working time arrangements as dimensions in precarious work, which were acknowledged in the multidimensional conceptualization of precarity even before the COVID-19 pandemic.

Precarity as a gendered phenomenon

The gendered stratification of society implies imbalances in societal power, freedom of choice and value, influencing social phenomena occurring both inside and outside the labour market. In the light of some summary indicators, such as the Gender Equality Index's score (67.4 points out of 100 for EU-27 in 2020) or the overall gender earnings gap (39.6 per cent for EU-28 in 2014), it is evident that gendered stratification is to the detriment of women (Eurostat, 2021). The link between gender and precarity is well documented in numerous studies (Bonfiglioli, 2014; Ivancheva et al, 2019). Nevertheless, this link needs to be incorporated into the multidimensional conceptualization of precarious work more explicitly. The unequal gendered settings create a path dependency phenomenon, increasing the probability that women's work will be more precarious along certain dimensions in comparison to men's. Path dependency can be defined as a tendency of institutions to develop with highly predictable features, resulting from the initial structural settings, beliefs and values (see, for example, Mahoney, 2006).

The following tendencies illustrate the path dependency phenomenon in terms of precarious gendered work. Women are socialized to be primary caregivers, rhetorically praised for self-sacrifice and devotion to family and other dependents (Giddens, 1997; Lindsey, 2015). At the same time, caring and nurturing is perceived as an inborn female ability, not necessitating a qualification, and is therefore undervalued, underpaid or unpaid (Cancian et al, 2000). These rigid beliefs about women's inherit care abilities have multiple adverse consequences for their lives. Women's employability in the formal, paid, labour market will be limited and likely in sectors complying with their supposedly inborn abilities. Sectors in which female employment predominates will be undervalued due to a presumed lack of need for any qualification and the unpaid work performed by women already in private circumstances.

As a result of the previously described gendered settings, we have observed that the number of women in precarious work has increased over the past decade. This is partly due to cutbacks in the public sector in the aftermath of the economic crisis of 2008–9. This pushed women out of good quality employment into precarious work, resulting in 26.5 per cent of female and 15.1 per cent of male employees aged 15–64 in the EU working in precarious work (EIGE, 2017).[1] The main factor behind this development was the disproportionate amount of time women spend in caregiving roles. The unequal care time distribution interrelated with the shift away from standard employment contracts to more atypical forms of employment – notably, part-time work (in the EU in 2019, 73.8 per cent of part-time contracts belong to women) and zero-hour contracts (Buckingham et al, 2020).

The unequal structural settings in the labour markets have contributed to women's vulnerabilities during the COVID-19 pandemic. Women are more likely to have either lost their jobs or quit since the start of the pandemic (Buckingham et al, 2020). This shows that, more often than men, women readjust working and caring capacities during crises. This is partially due to the higher opportunity cost for men in terms of quitting their jobs compared to women, interrelated with women's lower pay and involuntary part-time work, consigning them to appointments with inferior pay and career progression. Another gendered effect of the COVID-19 pandemic is that many people struggle to access the financial support measures put in place by governments due to their limited access to social protection, for example, payment of parental leave in an even more precarious situation. Alongside of the health crisis, the pandemic of intimate partner violence erupted, resulting from lockdowns and lack of emergency services for gender-based violence survivors. The above-mentioned gender inequalities contribute to lowering women's economic autonomy and exposing women to the risks of increasing precarity and uncertainty of continued employment in paid and unpaid work (Buckingham et al, 2020).

Women's greater exposure to precarious work can be traced through all the dimensions of precarity mentioned earlier. It derived from a lack of health and safety arrangements in some jobs, and teleworking in others. The probability of precarity due to lack of health and safety regulations during the pandemic was higher in frontline services such as healthcare, social care, education and retail, all of which are female dominated. Precarity through telework tended to impact women more than men, at least in terms of the increased care and household work. Some evidence could be drawn from surveys on working from home during the pandemic (Eurofound 2020a, 2021). The share of women working from home and with children under 12 who declared themselves to be 'too tired after work to do household jobs' was higher than the share of men in similar situations (39 per cent for women versus 24 per cent for men with children under 12) (Eurofound, 2021).

In sum, conceptualizing precarious work as a gendered phenomenon, we argue that the gendered stratification of society creates and reproduces unequal labour market conditions for women by exposing them to a higher risk of precarity during the COVID-19 pandemic. The pandemic has served as a catalyst for gendered work precarity. The gendered nature of precarity strikes across all dimensions of precarious work and operates as a multiplier of these dimensions.

Conclusion

While the concept of precarious work has been studied and fine-tuned both in times of economic downturn and prosperity, the COVID-19 pandemic presents yet another set of challenges to the understanding and conceptualization of precarious work. This chapter captures several phenomena observed during the COVID-19 crisis, which feed into the revision of the concept of precarious work in a multidimensional perspective. First, precarity intensified from the perspective of health and safety at work due to threats to bodily integrity, unmanageable mental stress and a lack of autonomy to refuse exposure to hazardous working conditions, which was exacerbated by the lack of PPE. Second, as a kind of flexible work arrangement, telework turned into a mandatory work arrangement during the pandemic and yielded multiple risks of precarity. Elements such as ICT inaccessibility, extra hidden costs or extreme surveillance practices are only a few examples. Third, theorizing precarity as a gendered phenomenon, the chapter highlights that a gendered stratification of the labour market intensified the work–life imbalance during the COVID-19 crisis.

We argue that the phenomena described built additional layers to the dimensions of precarious work already known before the pandemic. In other words, changes to working conditions during the pandemic do not constitute precarity as such but are likely to trigger the emergence of precarity from new sources. A health crisis could be seen as an experimental circumstance allowing us to revisit the concept of precarious work.

The structuring of precarity into particular dimensions serves to understand the concept better and observe manifestations and effects of its particular layers. It also allows considerations of precarity in two or more dimensions simultaneously. This conclusion, then, opens a range of questions for future endeavours attempting to further reconsider the concept of precarity with supporting empirical evidence. Will the cumulative impact of labour market changes create new dimensions of precarity or only extend the ones already known? How do the concepts of intersectionality and multidimensionality interact in the attempt to conceptualize work precarity? How would it be possible to operationalize the dimensions to precarity and constitute indicators from an empirical underpinning of their existence? Complex social phenomena are usually measured via composite indexes – would this be the way in which to improve the current, relatively narrow, measurement of precarity? These are only a few of the questions to be explored in future research now that the COVID-19 pandemic has opened up new areas for investigation in conceptual and empirical terms.

Note

[1] Calculation based on the European Institute for Gender Equality's (EIGE) typology of precarious work, namely a job with either one or a combination of the following factors: very low pay, very short working hours or low job security.

References

Amnesty International (2020) *Exposed, Silenced, Attacked: Failures to Protect Health and Essential Workers during the Covid-19 Pandemic*, London: Peter Benenson House.

Amnesty International (2021) 'Covid-19: health worker death toll rises to at least 17000 as organisations call for rapid vaccine rollout', Amnesty International, [online] 5 March. Available from: https://www.amnesty. org/en/latest/news/2021/03/covid19-health-worker-death-toll-rises-to-at-least-17000-as-organizations-call-for-rapid-vaccine-rollout/ [Accessed 15 May 2021].

Atzori, L., Ferreli, C., Atzori, M.G. and Rongioletti, F. (2020) 'Covid-19 and impact of personal protective equipment use: from occupational to generalized skin care need', *Dermatologic Therapy*, 33(4): e13598.

Aust, A. and Holst, H. (2007) 'Von der Ignoranz zur Organisierung? Gewerkschaftliche Strategien im Umgang mit atypisch Beschäftigten am Beispiel von Callcentern und Leiharbeit', *Industrielle Beziehungen*, 13(4): 291.

Becker, K. and Engel, T. (2018) 'Temporary workforce under pressure. Poor occupational safety and health (OSH) as a dimension of precarity?', *Management Revue*, 29(1): 32–54.

Benassi, C. and Dorigatti, L. (2015) 'Straight to the core – explaining union responses to the casualization of work: the IG Metall campaign for agency workers', *British Journal of Industrial Relations*, 53(3): 533–55.

Blake, A.A., Kelsey, L.A. and Wilkins, K.G. (2021) 'Precarious work in the 21st century: a psychological perspective', *Journal of Vocational Behavior*, 126(2): 103491.

Bonfiglioli, C. (2014) 'Gender, labour and precarity in the south east European periphery: the case of textile workers in Štip', *Contemporary Southeastern Europe*, 1(2): 7–23.

Buckingham, S., Fiadzo, C., Dalla Pozza, V., Todaro, L., Dupont, C. and Hadjivassiliou, K. (2020) 'Precarious work from a gender and intersectionality perspective, and ways to combat it', FEEM Committee – European Parliament, European Union. Available from: www.europarl.europa.eu/ RegData/etudes/STUD/2020/662491/IPOL_STU(2020)662491_EN.pdf [Accessed 29 March 2022].

Cancian, M. F., Stacey, J. and Oliker, S. (2000) *Caring and Gender*, Lanham: Rowman & Littlefield.

Caroli, E. and Godard, M. (2016) 'Does job insecurity deteriorate health?', *Health Economics*, 25(2): 131–47.

Chung, H. and van der Horst, M. (2018) 'Women's employment patterns after childbirth and the perceived access to and use of flexitime and teleworking', *Human Relations*, 71(1): 47–72.

Cushing, T. (2020) 'Another coronavirus side effect: in-home surveillance by remote workers' employers', *Techdirt*, [online] 8 April. Available from: https://www.techdirt.com/articles/20200401/14133144215/another-coronavirus-side-effect-in-home-surveillance-remote-workers-employers.shtml [Accessed 16 May 2021].

Doellgast, V., Lillie, N. and Pulignano, V. (eds) (2018) *Reconstructing Solidarity: Labour Unions, Precarious Work, and the Politics of Institutional Change in Europe*, Oxford: Oxford University Press.

Domenighetti, G., D'Avanzo, B. and Bisig, B. (2000) 'Health effects of job insecurity among employees in the Swiss general population', *International Journal of Health Services*, 30(3): 477–90.

Dörre, K. (2005) 'Die Zone der Verwundbarkeit. Unsichere Beschäftigungsverhältnisse, Prekarisierung und die Gewerkschaften', in M. Sommer, K. Dörre and U. Schneidewind (eds) *Die Zukunft war vorgestern: der Wandel der Arbeitsverhältnisse: Unsicherheit statt Normalarbeitsverhältnis?*, Oldenburg: Bibliotheks- und Informationssystem der Universität, pp 19–55.

EIGE (2017) 'Gender, skills and precarious work in the EU', research note, Vilnius: European Institute for Gender Equality. Available from: https://eige.europa.eu/sites/default/files/documents/ti_pubpdf_mh0217250enn_pdfweb_20170503163908.pdf [Accessed 4 April 2022].

Eurofound (2020a) 'Living, Working and Covid-19 First Findings', April, Luxembourg: Publications Office of the European Union.

Eurofound (2020b) 'Telework and ICT-Based Mobile Work: Flexible Working in the Digital Age', Luxembourg: Publications Office of the European Union.

Eurofound (2021) 'Living, Working and Covid-19 (Update April 2021): Mental Health and Trust Decline across EU as Pandemic enters another Year', Luxembourg: Publications Office of the European Union.

Eurofound and the International Labour Office (2017) 'Working Anytime, Anywhere: The Effects on the World of Work', Luxemburg/Geneva: Publications Office of the European Union/The International Labour Office.

European Commission (2020) 'Country Report Slovakia 2020, European Commission', [online] 26 February. Available from: https://eur-lex.europa.eu/legal-content/EN/TXT/?qid=1584543810241&uri=CELEX%3A52020SC0524 [Accessed 20 May 2021].

Eurostat (2021) 'Gender overall earnings gap [online data code: teqges01]', *Eurostat*, [online] 7 June. Available from: https://ec.europa.eu/eurostat/databrowser/view/teqges01/default/table?lang=en [Accessed 30 June 2021].

Eurostat (2021) 'How usual is it to work from home?', *Eurostat*, [online] 17 May. Available from: https://ec.europa.eu/eurostat/web/products-eurostat-news/-/edn-20210517-2 [Accessed 19 June 2021].

EurWork (2019) 'Right to disconnect', *Eurofound*, [online] 22 October. Available from: https://www.eurofound.europa.eu/observatories/eurwork/industrial-relations-dictionary/right-to-disconnect [Accessed 2 July 2021].

Fuller, S. and Hirsh, C.E. (2019) '"Family-friendly"jobs and motherhood pay penalties: the impact of flexible work arrangements across the educational spectrum', *Work and Occupations*, 46(1): 3–44.

Giddens, A. (1997) *Sociology*, Cambridge: Polity.

Giovanis, E. (2018) 'Are women happier when their spouse is teleworker?', *Journal of Happiness Studies*, 19(3): 719–54.

Grimshaw, D., Marino, S., Anxo, D., Gautié, J., Neumann, L. and Weinkopf, C. (2018) 'Negotiating better conditions for workers during austerity in Europe: unions' local strategies towards low pay and outsourcing in local government', in V. Doellgast, N. Lillie and V. Pulignano (eds) *Reconstructing Solidarity: Labour Unions, Precarious Work, and the Politics of Institutional Change in Europe*, Oxford: Oxford University Press, pp 42–67.

Heilová, L. (2020) 'Zamestnancom v sociálnych službách vyplatil PSK odmeny', *Prešovský samosprávny kraj* [press release] 11 December. Available from: https://www.po-kraj.sk/sk/samosprava/media/tlacove-spravy/tlac ove-spravy-2020/koronavirus/zamestnancom-socialnych-sluzbach-vypla til-psk-odmeny.html [Accessed 28 May 2021].

Hupkau, C. and Petrongolo, B. (2020) 'Covid-19 and gender gaps: latest evidence and lessons from the UK', *VoxEU*, [online] 22 April. Available from: https://voxeu.org/article/covid-19-and-gender-gaps-latest-evide nce-and-lessons-uk [Accessed 6 July 2021].

Ivancheva, M., Lynch, K. and Keating, K. (2019) 'Precarity, gender and care in the neoliberal academy', *Gender, Work & Organisation*, 26(4): 448–62.

Kahancová, M., Meszmann, T. and Sedláková, M. (2020) 'Precarization via digitalization? Work arrangements in the on-demand platform economy in Hungary and Slovakia', *Frontiers in Sociology*, 5: 3.

Kalleberg, A. (2009) 'Precarious work, insecure workers: employment relations in transition', *American Sociological Review*, 74(1): 1–22.

Kalleberg, A. (2018) *Precarious Lives: Job Insecurity and Well-Being in Rich Democracies*, Cambridge: Polity.

Katuška, M. (2021) 'Pandémia bola poslednou kvapkou, zo zdravotníctva odchádzajú stovky sestier', SME Daily Paper, [online] 20 May. Available from: https://domov.sme.sk/c/22657266/slovensko-zdravotnictvo-sestry-odchody-covid-pandemia.html?ref=tit [Accessed 6 July 2021].

Keller, B. and Seifert, H. (2013) *Atypische Beschäftigung zwischen Prekarität und Normalität. Entwicklung, Strukturen und Bestimmungsgründe im Überblick*, Berlin: Edition Sigma.

Keune, M. and Pedaci, M. (2020) 'Trade union strategies against precarious work: common trends and sectoral divergence in the EU', *European Journal of Industrial Relations*, 26(2): 139–55.

Khanal, P., Devkova, N., Dahal, M., Padel, K. and Joshi, D. (2020) 'Mental health impacts among health workers during Covid-19 in a low resource setting: a cross-sectional survey from Nepal', *Global Health*, 16(89).

Lindsey, L.L. (2015) 'The sociology of gender theoretical perspectives and feminist frameworks', in L.L. Lindsay (ed.) *Gender Roles: A Sociological Perspective*, London: Routledge, pp 23–48.

Livingston, E., Desai, A. and Berkwits, M. (2020) 'Sourcing personal protective equipment during the COVID-19 pandemic', *JAMA*, 323(19): 1912–14.

Lott, Y. and Chung, H. (2016) 'Gender discrepancies in the outcomes of schedule control on overtime hours and income in Germany', *European Sociological Review*, 32(6): 752–65.

Loustaunau, L., Stepick, L, Scott, E., Petrucci, L. and Henifin, M. (2021) 'No choice but to be essential: expanding dimensions of precarity during Covid-19', *Sociological Perspectives*, advance online publication, https://doi.org/10.1177/07311214211005491.

Mahoney, J. (2006) 'Analyzing path dependence: lessons from the social sciences', in A. Wimmer and R. Kössler (eds) *Understanding Change*, London: Palgrave Macmillan, pp 129–39.

Manokha, I. (2020) 'Covid-19: teleworking, surveillance and 24/7 work. Some reflexions on the expected growth of remote work after the pandemic', *Political Anthropological Research on International Social Sciences (PARISS)*, 1(2): 273–87.

Measuria, H.D., Verman, Y.V., Kerstein, R. and Tucker, S. (2021) 'Modified full-face snorkel mask: answer to the PPE crisis?', *BMJ Innovations*, 7(2): 308–10.

Neto, M., Almeida, H.G., Esmeraldo, J.D., Nobre, C.B., Pinheiro, W.R., de Oliveira, C., Sousa, I., Lima, O., Lima, N., Moreira, M.M., Lima, C., Júnior, J.G. and da Silva, C. (2020), 'When health professionals look death in the eye: the mental health of professionals who deal daily with the 2019 coronavirus outbreak', *Psychiatry Research, Elsevier Public Health Emergency Collection*, 288(2020): 112972.

Nichols, T. and Walters, D. (2014) *Safety or Profit? International Studies in Governance, Change and the Work Environment*, London: Routledge.

OECD (2020) 'Workforce and safety in long-term care during the Covid-19 pandemic'. OECD, [online] 22 June. Available from: https://www.oecd.org/coronavirus/policy-responses/workforce-and-safety-in-long-term-care-during-the-covid-19-pandemic-43fc5d50/ [Accessed 15 May 2021].

Pedaci, M. (2010) 'The flexibility trap: temporary jobs and precarity as a disciplinary mechanism', *Journal of Labour and Society*, 13(2): 245–62.

Pelling, l. (2021) 'On the corona frontline. The experiences of care workers in nine European countries – summary report', Friedrich-Ebert-Stiftung – Politics for Europe. Available from: https://library.fes.de/pdf-files/bueros/stockholm/17490.pdf [Accessed 4 April, 2022].

Schneider, D. and Harknett, K. (2020) 'Essential and unprotected Covid-19-related health and safety procedures for service sector workers', research brief, *SHIFT Project*, [online] May. Available from: https://shift.hks.harv ard.edu/files/2020/05/Essential-and-Unprotected-COVID-19-Health-Saf ety.pdf [Accessed 30 June 2021].

Stansfeld, S. and Candy, B. (2006) 'Psychosocial work environment and mental health – a meta-analytic review', *Scandinavian Journal of Work, Environment and Health*, 32(6): 443–62.

Trif, A., Paolucci, V., Kahancová, M. and Koukiadaki, A. (2021) 'Power resources and successful trade union actions that address precarity in adverse contexts: the case of Central and Eastern Europe', *Human Relations*, advance online publication, https://doi.org/10.1177/00187267211020189.

UNI Global Union (2021) *The Most Dangerous Job. The Impact of Covid-19 on Long-Term Care Workers in the US, UK, Canada, Ireland, and Australia*, Nyon: UNI Global Union.

Wellington, A.J. (2006) 'Self-employment: the new solution for balancing family and career?', *Labour Economics*', 13(3): 357–86.

Wood, A.J. (2016) 'Flexible scheduling, degradation of job quality and barriers to collective voice', *Human Relations*', 69(10): 1989–2010.

14

Precarious Workers and Precarity through the Lens of Social Movement Studies

Alice Mattoni

Introduction

Precarious workers are relevant actors in processes of political participation, defined as the set of activities that citizens develop to select their political representatives or influence their political choices (Verba and Nie, 1987). In this regard, scholars considered precarious workers as an aggregate of individuals who participate in activities such as voting in elections. Starting from this definition of political participation, over the years, several authors have noted a steady decline in the level of political participation, especially in Western democracies (Grasso, 2016). However, despite the loss of centrality of the intermediate bodies of politics, other forms of political participation seek to influence the choices of political representatives. They do so through channels that lie outside institutional politics (Inglehart, 1990), thus also going so far as to partially modify the repertoire and objectives of political participation (Norris, 2002). Particularly relevant, among other political actors, are the so-called movement organizations that promote the development of a wide range of collective actions: from street demonstrations to the collection of signatures for a petition, citizens often organize autonomously from political parties to support various demands and, in so doing, try to produce change at a social and political level that they imagine as just and desirable. In doing so, they often give rise to social movements characterized by a close link with the sphere of politics. With their street mobilizations, citizen assemblies and political proposals, social movements today are also relevant for their ability to produce innovation within democratic political institutions (della Porta, 2020).

Social movements are social processes characterized by the presence of dense networks of relationships between different types of social and political actors who engage, together, in the organization of conflicting collective actions of a political nature (Diani and Bison, 2004; della Porta and Diani, 2020). From this perspective, social movements are social processes that strongly intersect with politics in their different forms. Indeed, movement organizations, protest participants, and allies of such protests relate to social change – either resisting or supporting it – thus becoming a part of political processes of different natures, from the transformation of political systems to the advancement of new public policies.

In the remainder of this chapter, I will address three relevant dimensions of social movements to uncover the challenges that precarious workers' movements and the related movement organizations must face: collective identities, organizational patterns and the repertoire of protest. Then, in the conclusion, I will share some reflections on how these three dimensions become relevant when considering an emerging and yet growing type of precarious worker: platform workers.

Looking for collective identities in precarious workers' movements

Movement organizations that promote social movements share beliefs, values and meanings that develop during the preparatory stages, which consist of public assemblies, organizational meetings and exchanges of views among those who participate in such organizations (Melucci, 1996). During moments of mobilization, this set of beliefs, values and meanings crystallizes into a collective identity that is publicly visible during demonstrations and other forms of protest. On these occasions, movement organizations present their identities to different publics, explaining who they are and what they want, advancing their claims, and demanding recognition as legitimate social and political actors who can relate to their opponents to achieve their goals. Often, when social movements make themselves visible through public protest, a tension emerges 'between a movement's definition of itself and the recognition it is accorded by the rest of society' (Melucci, 1996: 74). Not coincidentally, many social movements are involved precisely in 'conflicts of recognition', where the point at issue is the 'recognition of a distinct identity' (Pizzorno, 1993) concerning identities already present and accepted both in society at large and in the sphere of institutional politics more specifically.

Movement organizations that mobilize on precarity deal with various material conditions related to the existence of a broad range of working arrangements in the realm of precarity. The job market sector, the type of contract, and the kind of working relationship between workers and their employers might indeed vary to a great extent. Furthermore, these employment-related dimensions often combine with other demographic features of precarious workers, among which gender, age and nationality are significant. Consequently, the precarious workers' workforce is highly fragmented and difficult to mobilize around a common cause. The development of collective identities is never linear and often requires continuous adjustments and negotiations (Touraine, 1988). This also happens within social movements themselves, since conflicts do emerge within social movements about the interpretations that activists and protest participants attach to the means, the ends and the whole field of collective action (Melucci, 1995). Therefore, from a collective identity perspective, broad mobilizations of precarious workers seldom rely on a cohesive collective identity. Indeed, they can rarely unite various working and living conditions under the same shared belief about who precarious workers are and what they need to achieve to improve their condition and gain new rights. Past attempts of organizing large demonstrations of precarious workers often went hand in hand with activists' efforts to develop an inclusive understanding of precarious workers' collective identities. The mobilizations of precarious workers that developed in Italy from 2001 to 2006 are a telling example in this regard. Among others, the organization of the Mayday Parade on 1 May in the streets of Milan and other Italian cities aimed at reclaiming visibility for precarity and precarious workers in the public space while also seeking to develop a shared sense of belonging among precarious workers in the country (Mattoni, 2012).

Indeed, the call for actions related to the parade made an explicit reference to precarious workers as the new proletariat, hence referring to labour struggles of the past, in which workers were represented as a cohesive political subject. This reference to the proletariat signals activists' willingness to go beyond the differences that inevitably characterize precarious workers to develop a cohesive political subject. At the same time, the activists' attempt to construct a cohesive yet internally diversified political subject also renders apparent the fact that collective identities in precarious workers' movements are an evolving process rather than a static and reified quality of their mobilizations. This is, of course, more generally the case for collective identities in social movements, which continuously unfold across the tension between how protesters interpret who they are, how they represent themselves in public, and how others – including protest targets and potential allies – understand them (Melucci, 1996). However, the notion of collective identity as a process, best, then, understood as collective identification, seems particularly relevant in precarious workers mobilizations. They often go beyond the demand for material changes to include a work of signification related to the definition, depiction and recognition of precarious workers as a legitimate political subject, able to mobilize collectively to bring forward its claims, demands and aspirations.

The example of the precarious workers' parade refers to collective identities in large national demonstrations able to mobilize hundreds of thousands of precarious workers. However, the process of collective identification is also relevant in the case of small-scale mobilizations organized not just at the local level but within specific workplaces, production chains and job sectors. In this regard, back in the early 2000s, the struggles of call centre operators in the Atesia company, one of the biggest call centre businesses in Italy, also aimed at developing a sense of common belonging among precarious workers. With this aim, some precarious workers founded Precari Atesia, a political collective within the company and created a printed zine that was distributed among the call centre operators to sustain concrete connections beyond the different situations of each precarious worker in the company (Mattoni, 2012). The political collective sought to mobilize the call centre operators to reclaim their rights and improve their working conditions. However, to increase the chances of their success in recruiting protesters, activists knew that they also had to work at the more symbolic level of collective identification. Efforts to build a more cohesive collective identity also seem to be relevant in the case of more structured movement organizations, such as trade unions. For instance, Melanie Simms et al (2018) argue that effective union representation is strictly linked to the union's decisions to put its energies towards constructing a shared identity among young precarious workers, either work related or sector related.

Whether we are speaking about the organization of large, inclusive demonstrations or the unionization of specific workplaces, in the case of precarious workers, movement organizers have to deal with a significant challenge at the level of identification processes. Indeed, precarious workers are a highly individualized workforce for whom the recognition into a common identity, which also bears with it an empowering potential, is tough to achieve. Often, developing a cohesive collective identity around precarity is not the starting point from which movement organizations build their recruitment and mobilizing strategies. On the contrary, building collective identities goes hand in hand with generating a more effective capacity for mobilization. However, to do so, precarious workers and the movement organizations that work with them also need to find effective ways to organize their political work. The following section discusses some dilemmas related to the organizational features of precarious workers' movements.

The organizational features of precarious workers' movements

As noted earlier, social movements are not actors per se but social and political processes that activate thanks to different social and political actors. These actors are usually collective and are generally named movement organizations: understanding their characteristics is relevant to appreciate the varieties of ways in which precarious workers might come together to reclaim their rights at the collective level. Social movements can be supported by both structured movement organizations requiring formal membership and less articulated movement organizations, which are generally based on more informal participation by those who decide to join them (della Porta and Diani, 2020). Precarious workers might gather into collective actors that can take either of these two forms.

On the one hand, there are more structured associations of precarious workers, which represent their members' voices at the political level while at the same time providing some essential services. This is the case for those civil society organizations that include precarious workers who are somehow homogeneous in terms of at least one feature of their working relationship, like being employed in the same labour market sector. Professional associations of precarious workers active in the creative sector might be one of the many possible examples. Trade unions created around the issue of precarity offer another telling example. Since these types of movement organizations also offer services to their members, they are organized through specific hierarchical structures that allow them to allocate the resources at their disposal. In other words, they are professionalized, often rely on some paid staff and regulate their membership according to formal rules. Among other features, independent grassroots unions that value members' active participation have frequently been at the frontline of precarious workers' struggles by combining service provision with a strong inclination towards the use of public protest. This was the case with Greek independent grassroots unions organizing against precarity at the beginning of the 2000s, which often operated in workplaces where open-ended workers coexisted with temporary workers. In this case, trade unionists decided to employ the framework of the class struggle, countering the idea that only open-ended workers could be unionized and organizing campaigns within workplaces to increase their legitimization in the eyes of precarious workers. For instance, in the construction, engineering and telecommunications sectors, the Salaried Technicians' Union (SMT) organized 'surprise visits' to companies that employed non-unionized precarious workers, distributing leaflets and talking to employees to raise their awareness about precarity and its consequences for workers (Vogiatzoglou, 2010).

On the other hand, there are also movement organizations that are highly informal, with few resources and primarily based on the voluntary participation of precarious workers. An example is offered by grassroots political collectives that organize within and outside workplaces to defend the rights of precarious workers and demand improvements in their working and living conditions. Frequently, such informal movement organizations deal with issues other than precarity. For instance, in Italy in the early 2000s, a large number of university students' collectives began to address the issue of precarious workers from the perspective of 'workers in the making', forming alliances with the networks of precarious researchers who mobilized against the reform of Italian universities in 2005 (Mattoni, 2012), in 2008 (Caruso et al, 2010) and then again in 2010 (Commisso, 2013).

The two types of movement organizations – to simplify, the most formal ones versus the least formal ones – rely on different organizational structures and self-governing bodies to make everyday decisions and support their work at the political level. However, inter-organizational patterns among various types of movement organizations seem to be even more relevant for the ability of precarious workers to become visible at the political level, mainly when they aim at addressing national political arenas. In such cases, one movement organization can seldom support broad social movements independently from the contentious issue at stake. The literature on social movements cast light on various forms of collaboration among movement organizations when considering social movements and the mobilizations they can sustain, such as social movement networks or social movement coalitions (della Porta and Diani, 2020). While the former sees fluid forms of collaborations among movement organizations, the latter tend to be more structured forms of cooperation based on stable interactions that might last for a considerable amount of time. When considering precarious workers, inter-organizational dynamics within movement networks and coalitions might be particularly difficult to manage due to the existence of many forms of precarity and, hence, of many work and lived experiences of being a precarious worker.

However, intra-organizational dynamics might be even more difficult to sustain when we move to the transnational level of contention, where we find transnational movement networks and coalitions. In this regard, a telling example has been Italian activists' attempt to scale-shift the Mayday Parade to the European level, organizing a transnational day of struggle against precarity, significantly occurring on 1 May – labour day in Italy and in many other countries – in several cities across Europe. This process reached its peak from 2004 to 2006. Principally based on informal movement organizations, the intra-organizational infrastructure was somewhat fluid and based on the voluntary participation of many grassroots movement organizations that participated in the social movement network. A shared website, a mailing list and a series of transnational preparatory meetings held in various European cities functioned as the organizational backbones of the Euro Mayday Parade network (Mattoni, 2008b). The mailing list and the preparatory meetings were crucial in ensuring that movement organizations with different political backgrounds could coordinate their efforts based on a solid mutual understanding of the mobilization. However, various interpretations of what precarity was and how it affected precarious workers were, of course, present among activists, who came from various European cities that were sometimes highly diverse when it came to welfare state provisions for precarious workers. Therefore, the most critical organizational challenge was not so much to be found at the level of mere coordination of the actual parade on 1 May, but rather in promoting a shared understanding of the contentious issue at the centre of the Euro Mayday Parade. The work of political translation (Doerr, 2018) was vital to sustaining bonds between activists across national borders. Hence, the organizational features that characterized the Euro Mayday Parade also matched the need for movement organizations to develop a common ground for mobilization at the symbolic level of meaning-making and collective identities.

This telling example shows that when precarious workers' movements emerge around broad mobilizations, they seldom rely on a homogeneous movement organization network. On the contrary, the coexistence of different types of political and social actors might be both a richness for the mobilization and its organizational patterns and, at the same time, a challenge that activists need to take into serious consideration. The variety of precarious workers' lived experiences and working conditions leads to various types of movement organizations, each with its own internal organizational structure that also affects how activists make decisions and represent precarious workers' demands.

The reinvention of public protest in precarious workers mobilizations

A characteristic element of social movements is protest, both public and collective. Movement organizations engage in various forms of contentious action to communicate their goals and demands to different publics. Therefore, the various forms of protest have a powerful communicative dimension because they are public performances designed to be understood by the social and political actors with whom the movement actors confront (Tilly, 2004). Although forms of protest vary in time and space, social movements generally rely on specific repertoires of protest in which there is a stable definition and interpretation of the roles of movement actors and their opponents, as well as of the various forms of collective action through which the two are linked (Tilly and Tarrow, 2007: 16). For example, in the tradition of workers' movements, the repertoire of protest revolves around strikes, picket lines and other forms of collective action that connect workers and employers according to a specific communicative canon, which both the former and the latter are familiar with and know how to interpret.

However, many traditional forms of protest that characterize workers' struggles might not easily fit precarious workers. The reason is to be found, once again, in the high level of atomization and individualization that precarity brings with it: precarious workers are not a cohesive social group. Instead, they experience different working and contractual conditions, sometimes even when hired in the same workplace. Massive demonstrations, general strikes and picket lines that characterized past workers' struggles might be familiar to movement organizations that mobilize on precarity. However, they often decide not to employ them when protesting, opting for less common forms of protest in the realm of labour struggle and, in this way, innovating the repertoire of contention that is traditionally associated with workers' movements. As in the previous section, I illustrate this point through two examples taken from the wave of precarious workers mobilizations that hit Italy from 2001 to 2006. Instead of traditional street demonstrations, movement organizations in Milan decided to organize a colourful parade on the afternoon of 1 May – the Mayday Parade – to oppose themselves to the morning workers' demonstration usually organized by the Italian confederate trade unions (Mattoni, 2012). While in the morning workers would march side by side with the trade unions' banners and chant more traditional workers' slogans, in the afternoon, a diverse range of workers would dance side by side in a colourful parade equipped with sound systems. The idea was not just to become visible, have a voice and reclaim precarious workers' rights. They also wanted to develop a collective, yet internally diverse, discourse around precarity: to this end, the Mayday Parade organizers asked activist groups wishing to participate in the parade to build their floats to represent their vision of precarity. Similarly, in 2004, a series of direct actions by precarious workers groups in supermarkets, bookshops, theatres and other places of consumption were aimed at establishing a sense of shared belonging between, on the one hand, activists and customers, and, on the other, activists and workers (Mattoni, 2008a; Tarì and Vanni, 2005). Although activists, customers and workers have different roles in the context of such direct actions, these protest events underlined the everyday experience of precariousness, able to unite different figures, binding to the same destiny of uncertainty not only the workers of supermarkets, bookshops and so on, but also the customers who attended those same places of consumption.

In other cases, movement organizations and the precarious workers who participate in them might even decide to avoid public protest to develop other forms of collective action. Instead of making public claims, they prefer to cultivate solidarity networks to support precarious workers in their daily lives. This, for instance, happened in Italy and Greece after the economic crisis that began in 2008 hit the two countries, where the use of contentious collective actions was aimed at creating the resources that precarious workers needed to support themselves (Mattoni and Vogiatzoglou, 2014). The movement organizations in the two countries attempted to develop a range of services for precarious workers, often supporting them through direct actions, such as the occupation of buildings.

In Italy, one example is the wave of occupations of theatres in various Italian cities, starting with perhaps the most famous case: the occupation of the Teatro Valle, which occurred from 2011 to 2014 in Rome. On this occasion, a group of precarious workers in the performing arts employed a form of protest quite common in Italy – the squatting and recovery of abandoned buildings – to obtain a suitable physical space in which to continue working while at the same time trying to generate income for themselves and defend the Teatro Valle as a common good that was made available to the neighbourhood and citizenship. The experience of the Teatro Valle Occupato mixed protest and work-related practices, combining activism with artistic production in a rather creative manner (Borchi, 2017). Another relevant case in this sense is creating shared workspaces for precarious self-employed workers, and those who are temporarily unemployed, who do not even have an adequate workspace in the companies that employ them as self-employed workers. This is, for example, the objective of the Spazio Ufficio Condiviso in Milan, born from the collaboration between the Rete dei Redattori Precari and Piano Terra, an occupied space in the Isola district (Zambelli, 2014). Another interesting experience is Officine Zero in Rome. In this case, a factory closed in 2008 was occupied by 33 former workers. A group of neighbourhood activists assisted the workers in converting the factory into a multifunctional space that could provide services to the local community: a small self-managed student house; a co-working space for precarious and autonomous workers; and the Camera per il Lavoro Autonomo e Precario. Activists who manage these co-working spaces do this outside the logic of profit. Their objective is to create connections between precarious self-employed workers by recognizing the importance of sharing the same workspace to create mutual trust, exchange experiences and, eventually, decide to engage in collective action to improve working and living conditions.

Some reflections on platform labour

In the previous sections of this chapter, I discussed three relevant features that movement organizations working with precarious workers face when mobilizing. In this section, I will discuss some of the challenges that movement organizations face concerning collective identities, organizational patterns and repertoire of contention when dealing specifically with platform workers.

Precarious workers who work with the support of digital platforms are highly individualized, usually self-employed, and perform micro-tasks. Furthermore, their work relationship is highly mediated by technology. First, online platforms administer micro-tasks; second, algorithms that include customers' ratings and other variables evaluate workers, scoring the quality of the micro-tasks they performed (Howcroft and Bergvall-Kåreborn, 2019). Platform workers might work entirely online, like the Mechanical Turk workers whose micro-tasks are digital and often employed to sustain sociological research investigations (Shank, 2016). However, platform workers might also provide their services in the offline world, hence entering into contact with the final customers. Platform workers in the food delivery sector, for instance, became increasingly visible during the COVID-19 pandemic, when companies such as Foodora, Deliveroo and Glovo became centrally important to restaurants and their customers (Pirone et al, 2020).

The extreme individualization of platform workers poses some relevant challenges to collective actions aimed at improving their working and living conditions. While this is the case for precarious workers in general, as I have argued throughout, having a working experience that is highly technologically mediated and usually geographically dispersed renders the encounter among platform workers even more difficult. However, platform workers often create Facebook or WhatsApp groups to exchange information about their working conditions, creating a shared space to meet and chat despite not working together side by side (Tassinari and Maccarrone, 2020). At the same time, in the context of food delivery workers, physical locations where riders wait for the next delivery task are also important because they allow them to interact, exchange opinions and speak about their grievances (Tassinari and Maccarrone, 2020). Furthermore, collective identity development at the national level among Deliveroo workers in the UK was supported through a workers' bulletin that circulated information about working conditions and successful protest actions in different cities (Cant, 2020). Similar to the Precari Atesia collective, discussed previously, the creation of an 'alternative media' (Atton, 2002) empowered workers further, allowing them to nurture further a shared sense of belonging, going beyond the specificities of the different urban settings in which the riders worked and lived.

As for organizational patterns, platform workers' mobilizations seem to rely on more grassroots movement organizations that are frequently autonomous from unions, which might become relevant allies once the mobilization increases. For instance, Foodora riders in Turin began to organize as an autonomous collective, and only at the peak of their mobilizations did they build an instrumental alliance with the independent grassroots union Confederazione dei Comitati di Base (COBAS) (Tassinari and Maccarrone, 2017). This is in line with a more general, deep-rooted distrust between the autonomous collectives of precarious workers and the confederated trade unions in Italy. This was already evident in previous waves of mobilizations (Mattoni, 2012) and remains central today in grassroots organizations of platform workers in the delivery sector, where alliances between the two types of actors are rare (Borghi et al, 2021). Both in France (Borghi et al, 2021) and in the UK (Tassinari and Maccarrone, 2020) delivery workers also began their mobilization autonomously. However, they then developed a more solid alliance with either confederate trade unions or independent grassroots unions. Overall, in the case of platform workers, inter-organizational dynamics between different types of social and political actors are often challenging to sustain, partly due to the different interpretations related to the discursive identification of platform workers (Borghi et al, 2021).

Similar to what has been discussed earlier in the case of precarious workers, the repertoire of contention became a combination of traditional and innovative forms of protest in the case of platform workers. Furthermore, given the relevance of digital technologies in regulating their labour relationships, the repertoire of contention includes both offline and online forms of protest. In the Deliveroo workers' mobilization in London in 2016, platform workers resorted to pickets across the city to increase their visibility in the urban space. However, they also directly interacted with the platform, logging out from the app that distributed food delivery tasks to them, and attacked Deliveroo on social media through a naming and shaming campaign (Tassinari and Maccarrone, 2020). Something similar happened in Turin, where Italian Foodora riders also organized moving pickets across the city, distributing flyers in crowded squares and outside popular restaurants. The riders aimed to raise awareness among restaurant owners and their customers about the working conditions of the Foodora workers, asking them to boycott the Foodora app (Tassinari and Maccarrone, 2017). These forms of protest are partially traditional in their aims, since the riders want to damage the platforms for which they work while also increasing their visibility within the urban environment in which they perform their delivery tasks. At the same time, though, they are necessarily innovative because they enter into a direct relationship with digital technologies: the food delivery platforms become a protest target, and the social media platforms like Facebook might become allies to the extent that they help precarious workers' spread their messages, recruit new protest participants and extend their solidarity networks. In a sense, then, such forms of protest are inherently digital in their character.

Conclusion

In this chapter, I have discussed three significant dimensions that help us grasp the peculiar features of precarious workers' political engagement from the perspective of social movement studies. First, the effective development of collective identities or, at least, the recognition of the difficulties in recombining different working and living experiences into a broad, inclusive and shared identity related to precarity. Second, that various organizational forms go hand in hand with different strategies for the recruitment and mobilization of precarious workers. Third, the innovations at the level of the repertoire of contention, in which more traditional forms of protest somehow lose some of their potential and meaning. More specifically, I have illustrated how these three dimensions might be helpful in casting light on the mobilization dynamics that develop around various forms of precarity, including those that are linked to the most recent experiences of platform workers, whose performance is deeply tied to digital technologies.

Overall, these three dimensions are relevant when gaining an understanding of how people come together to mobilize through collective action, how they can efficiently coordinate their efforts and what the main choices they have to make are when selecting a suitable form of protest. These are all particularly relevant questions when dealing with mobilizations that involve vulnerable groups of people and dealing with contentious issues that are neither at the top of the political agenda nor the centre of the public debate. In the past decades, there has been a growing literature that deals with precarious workers. Nevertheless, precarious workers and precarity remain at the margin of policy-making activities, despite their increased, and still increasing, fragility due to the COVID-19 pandemic and its aftermath. For this reason, there are still some important aspects that precarious workers' grassroots collectives, independent grassroots trade unions, confederate trade unions and all the other labour actors interested in supporting precarious workers' movements need to take into consideration. These include, first, reflecting on how to develop a solid sense of belonging despite the individualization of precarious workers. Second, how to organize a highly fragmented workforce through innovative patterns of coordination and fruitful alliances with more traditional labour stakeholders. And third, how to invent innovative, effective and sustainable forms of protest.

References

Atton, C. (2002) *Alternative Media*, London: Sage.

Borchi, A. (2017) 'Teatro Valle Occupato: protesting, occupying and making art in contemporary Italy', *Research in Drama Education: The Journal of Applied Theatre and Performance*, 22(1): 126–9.

Borghi, P., Murgia, A., Mondon-Navazo, M. and Mezihorak, P. (2021) 'Mind the gap between discourses and practices: platform workers' representation in France and Italy', *European Journal of Industrial Relations*, advance online publication, https://doi.org/10.1177/09596801211004268.

Cant, C. (2020) *Riding for Deliveroo: Resistance in the New Economy*, Cambridge: Polity.

Caruso, L., Giorgi, A., Mattoni, A. and Piazza, G. (2010) *Alla Ricerca dell'Onda. I Nuovi Conflitti nell'Istruzione Superiore*, Milan: Franco Angeli.

Commisso, G. (2013) 'Governance and conflict in the university: the mobilisation of Italian researchers against neoliberal reform', *Journal of Education Policy*, 28(2): 157–77.

Diani, M. and Bison, I. (2004) 'Organisations, coalitions and movements', *Theory and Society*, 33(3–4): 281–309.

della Porta, D. (2020) *How Social Movements Can Save Democracy: Democratic Innovations from Below*, Cambridge: Polity.

della Porta, D. and Diani, M. (2020) *Social Movements: An Introduction*, Hoboken: John Wiley & Sons.

Doerr, N. (2018) *Political Translation: How Social Movement Democracies Survive*, Cambridge: Cambridge University Press.

Grasso, M.T. (2016) *Generations, Political Participation and Social Change in Western Europe*, London: Routledge.

Howcroft, D. and Bergvall-Kåreborn, B. (2019) 'A typology of crowdwork platforms', *Work, Employment & Society*, 33(1): 21–38.

Inglehart, R. (1990) *Culture Shift in Advanced Industrial Society*, Princeton: Princeton University Press.

Mattoni, A. (2008a) 'ICTs in national and transnational mobilizations', *tripleC: Communication, Capitalism & Critique. Open Access Journal for a Global Sustainable Information Society*, 6(2): 105–24.

Mattoni, A. (2008b) 'Serpica Naro and the others. The media sociali experience in Italian struggles against precarity', *PORTAL: Journal of Multidisciplinary International Studies*, 5(2). Available from: https://epress. lib.uts.edu.au/journals/index.php/portal/article/view/706 [Accessed 3 November 2021].

Mattoni, A. (2012) *Media Practices and Protest Politics: How Precarious Workers Mobilise*, Burlington: Ashgate.

Mattoni, A. and Vogiatzoglou, M. (2014) '"Today we are precarious: tomorrow, we will be unbeatable": early struggles of precarious workers in Italy and Greece', in D. Chabanet, D. and F. Royall (eds) *From Silence to Protest: International Perspectives on Weakly Resourced Groups*, Burlington: Ashgate, pp 67–82.

Melucci, A. (1995) 'The process of collective identity', in H. Johnston and B. Klandermans (eds) *Social Movements and Culture*, Minneapolis: University of Minnesota Press, pp 41–63.

Melucci, A. (1996) *Challenging Codes: Collective Action in the Information Age*, Cambridge: Cambridge University Press.

Norris, P. (2002) *Democratic Phoenix: Reinventing Political Activism*, Cambridge: Cambridge University Press.

Pirone, M., Frapporti, M., Chicchi, F. and Marrone, M. (2020) *Covid-19 Impact on Platform Economy. A Preliminary Outlook*, Bologna: AMSActa Research Repository. Available from: https://amsacta.unibo.it/6471/ [Accessed 17 May 2021].

Pizzorno, A. (1993) *Le radici della politica assoluta e altri saggi*, Milan: Feltrinelli.

Shank, D.B. (2016) 'Using crowdsourcing websites for sociological research: the case of Amazon Mechanical Turk', *The American Sociologist*, 47(1): 47–55.

Simms, M., Eversberg, D., Dupuy, C. and Hipp, L. (2018) 'Organising young workers under precarious conditions: what hinders or facilitates union success', *Work & Occupations*, 45(4): 420–50.

Tarì, M. and Vanni, I. (2005) 'On the life and deeds of San Precario, Patron Saint of precarious workers and lives', *The Fibreculture Journal*, 5. Available from: https://fibreculturejournal.org/fcj-023-on-the-life-and-deeds-of-san-precario-patron-saint-of-precarious-workers-and-lives/ [Accessed 1 April 2022].

Tassinari, A. and Maccarrone, V. (2017) 'The mobilisation of gig economy couriers in Italy: some lessons for the trade union movement', *Transfer: European Review of Labour and Research*, 23(3): 353–7.

Tassinari, A. and Maccarrone, V. (2020) 'Riders on the storm: workplace solidarity among gig economy couriers in Italy and the UK', *Work, Employment & Society*, 34(1): 35–54.

Tilly, C. (2004) *Social Movements, 1768–2004*, London and New York: Routledge.

Tilly, C. and Tarrow, S.G. (2007) *Contentious Politics*, Boulder, CO: Paradigm Publishers.

Touraine, A. (1988) *Return of the Actor: Social Theory in Postindustrial Society*, Minneapolis: University of Minnesota Press.

Verba, S. and Nie, N.H. (1987) *Participation in America: Political Democracy and Social Equality*, Chicago: University of Chicago Press.

Vogiatzoglou, M. (2010) 'Precarious Workers' Unions in the Greek Syndicalist Movement', thesis, University of Crete.

Zambelli, L. (2014) 'Spazi di socialità precaria: da internet all'ufficio condiviso', *Lo Squaderno*, 31: 29–31.

15

Organizing and Self-organized Precarious Workers: The Experience of Britain

Jane Hardy

Introduction

One narrative about precarious workers, in Britain and elsewhere, is that their growing numbers in the labour force have undermined the collectivity of the working class – its ability to organize in the workplace and engage in struggles. Guy Standing's (2011) book, *The Precariat: A Dangerous Class*, reignited debates about the changing nature of the working class across the broader sweep of the global economy. His contribution raises critical questions about work and class in contemporary society and about the capacity of the working class for resistance and self-emancipation under conditions of neoliberal capitalism. Standing (2011: 6) argues that there is a binary divide between those workers 'in long-term fixed hour jobs, with established routes of advancement, subject to unionisation and collective agreement' and a growing underclass of workers peripheral to mainstream work and disconnected from organized labour. This posits a pessimistic view of a fractured working class that is unable to organize against what is viewed as an inexorable drive towards insecurity. Taking Britain as a focus, this chapter argues that the notion of a growing army of precarious workers is not only overstated but also politically problematic. Coupled with amnesia about important historical struggles and a lack of attention to more recent industrial disputes, it encourages a defeatist mindset whereby the organization of precarious workers, either by trade unions or through self-organization, is seen as a formidable or even impossible task.

The chapter begins by setting the case studies in the context of the dimensions of precarious work in British neoliberal capitalism. This is followed by an outline of the strategies deployed by trade unions, and other social actors, to organize and mobilize precarious workers. The main part of the chapter draws on case studies in four sectors – care, cleaning, hospitality and warehousing – where precarious work predominates, but where workers have organized to achieve substantial victories in gaining better pay and conditions.

Dimensions of precarious work

The four sectors involved in the case studies reflect different dimensions of precarious work. First, while the mobility of capital has been seen as a major culprit of precarious work by some (see Hardt and Negri, 2000; Harvey, 2005), it is the range of fixed and immobile activities associated with producing the infrastructure (roads, airports, warehousing) and with social reproduction (the care sector, health and education) that are often sites for insecure employment. These areas of work are subject to costs being constantly driven down and working conditions attacked and casualized – a trend that has been intensified by the austerity that followed the 2008 financial crisis. As we shall see in the case study of women carers employed by local government, it was their low pay that was the source of their precariousness at work.

Second, and also related to the aftermath of the financial crisis, the idea of a 'salariat' (Standing, 2011: 12) that is a separate and privileged class characterized by permanent work, guaranteed hours and pensions does not fit with the reality of work. There have been accelerated attacks on pensions in the public sector and workers have experienced a new form of precariousness with stagnating wages and longer hours at work in order to maintain a basic standard of living (Clarke and Cominetti, 2019). In Britain, public sector workers report feeling more precarious. Their experience of work has been one of commodification and marketization, with an increase in stress and bullying underpinned by the imposition of 'targets' and 'metrics', and the intensification of work through technology (Upchurch, 2014; Moore and Hayes, 2017; Moth, 2020).

The third dimension of neoliberal capitalism that has impacted on the security of work has been the increase in privatization and outsourcing by successive governments since 1979 that is interlinked with financialization. From the perspective of workers, financially driven targets in the context of sluggish profits have led to the squeezing of labour costs and the intensification of work. Grady and Simms (2019: 497) go even further and present an apocalyptic vision of the impacts of financialization on organized labour, arguing that it 'not only pits workers against each other, it pulls workers in multiple directions and makes it more difficult to identify a single set of interests'. This dimension of precarious work has been a particular challenge for cleaners as contracts are bounced from one firm to another and workers in the same workplace are on a myriad of contracts. Cutting across these three dimensions is the fact that these sectors are dominated by women, migrant and young workers whose oppression or vulnerabilities make them particularly subject to exploitation.

Strategies of trade unions and social actors

There have been four broad strategies in British labour organizations in the new millennium that have engaged with precarious workers: community unionism, the 'organizing model', trade union strategies focused on migrant workers and the formation of new trade unions.

Community unionism has entered the lexicon of trade union strategies in Britain. However, there is no universal definition and the form and purpose of these types of organization varies enormously within and between countries. The idea of community unionism is most developed in the United States and is often focused on workers' centres. These developed because of the poor record of some sections of the union movement in organizing migrant workers and addressing both their problems at work and wider problems they face. However, these centres have often relied on broad campaigns rather than putting workplace organization at the centre of their politics. In her study, Janice Fine (2006: 257) notes, 'I was struck by how little workers' centres utilised the potential economic power of low wage immigrant workers themselves'.

There is no real equivalent of workers' centres in Britain, but there are examples of campaigns that carry some of the same politics. In 2001, The East London Citizens Organisation (TELCO), with 40 affiliated community and union organizations, persuaded some employers to pay the 'living wage' as opposed to the minimum wage.[1] This was followed by a campaign by the Transport and General Workers Union[2] in 2004, which recruited about 1,500 cleaners and obtained agreements with leading contractors in the Canary Wharf financial district in London. Winning improvements in the pay and working conditions for one of the most badly treated and poorly paid groups of workers was a significant achievement. There are, however, limitations to some models of community organizing, with it being argued that a 'wide diversity of actors with a multiplicity of interests' can operate in the place of workers' self-organization (Wills, 2008: 306). The issue of class is sidelined as ' "workers" issues have been recast as community-wide concerns and class interests read through the lens of community, immigration, and race and religion' (Wills, 2008: 309).

The organizing model has been used to recruit and mobilize precarious workers. While the servicing model relies on a professional trade union hierarchy that delivers collective and individual services to a passive membership, the organizing model, imported from the United States and, particularly, from the tactics used by the Service Employees International Union (SEIU), focuses on building an active membership. There is no one agreed model, but in Britain, Jane McAlevey's (2016) book, *No Shortcuts: Organising for Power*, and her seminars about the experience of organizing in the United States are highly influential and popular with many of the activists and union organizers interviewed for the case studies.

McAlevey talks about wresting power away from deal-making by professional trade union negotiators behind closed doors by expanding and involving the base of ordinary members who have never previously been involved in debate or activity. There are three strands to her argument. First, that organic leaders must be identified, that is those who have the respect of and the ability to win over other workers. Second, McAlevey (2016: 28) emphasizes the importance of community in winning a dispute; as she puts it, 'organic ties to the broader community form the potential strategic wedge needed … to leverage power'. The third strand is using structure tests to gauge how effectively an organic leader can win the majority on their shift or within their unit to taking 'high risk action' by testing the ground with, for example, getting the majority of workers to sign a petition.

Some have argued that effectively organizing precarious workers has been undermined by ignoring the specific status and experience of migrant workers (Alberti et al, 2013). On the contrary, although strategies between and within trade unions vary, there have been extensive debates in trade unions about recruiting and integrating migrant workers, particularly since 2004 when Britain opened its borders to workers from countries that had newly joined the European Union from Central and Eastern Europe. An estimated one million workers arrived in the first year to fill acute shortages in the labour market. They were concentrated in poorly unionized private sectors of the economy: warehousing, logistics and hospitality. The challenge this represented was evident in poor levels of trade union density in the private sector, which was 13 per cent in 2019, compared with around 52 per cent in the public sector.

In contrast to other European countries where labour organizations had opposed the opening of borders to these new workers, the responses at the top of British trade unions was relatively positive. This was particularly true of the large general unions – Unite and the GMB[3] – who saw new opportunities for recruiting in the private sector. The recruitment of migrant workers themselves as organizers opened up spaces for intensified activity at the base of the union, reflected in a plethora of wide-ranging initiatives on the ground (Fitzgerald and Hardy, 2010).

Finally, two new trade unions have been founded with an orientation on precarious workers in outsourced industries (for example cleaners) – often migrant workers – and those working in sectors that were previously unionized (the legal sector, games developers, sex workers). The Independent Workers of Great Britain (IWGB) and United Voices of the World (UVW), founded in 2013 and 2014 respectively, have a few thousand members between them but, as we shall see, have punched above their weight in terms of their achievements.[4]

Case studies of struggles

This section presents four brief outlines of some of the struggles faced by precarious workers.[5] These case studies are based on interviews conducted with activists and trade union organizers close to their members in the British cities of London, Birmingham, Glasgow and Sheffield.

Women carers: low pay, precarious livelihoods

In May 2019, 82 days of strike action over a two-year period by women care workers forced their employers – Birmingham City Council – to withdraw draconian proposals to cut their hours and incomes. This was a landmark struggle of women workers that hardly registered in the mainstream media. These women were not precarious workers measured in terms of the narrow legal definition – in fact, they had permanent contracts, full or part-time, with the council. The precarious nature of their work lay in their low incomes. Many women faced real financial hardship, and even meeting their most basic needs meant re-mortgaging their homes, depending on overdrafts and getting into debt.

In 2017 there were 460 Home Care Enablement Workers, nearly exclusively women, employed to care for people when they were discharged from hospital. Although 95 per cent of the women were in the giant Unison[6] public sector trade union, they had no history of or experience in taking strike action. In fact, Unison had previously treated them as a special case on the basis of their jobs to exempt them from taking action in previous industrial disputes. In April 2017, under a Labour Party-run council, employers attacked their working conditions by trying to introduce split-shift contracts that would have meant they worked 14 hours a day for eight hours' pay because of having to wait around between shifts and clients. Although the council backed down after a strike was threatened, they came back with a new tactic to wear down the women by embarking on a protracted period of interviews for voluntary redundancies – often without union representation – as a way of bullying women out of their jobs. The next move of Birmingham City Council, in June 2018, was to commission consultants at a cost of £12 million to review care and elderly services. In the worst kind of scientific management, these consultants proposed reducing all contracts to part-time: 14, 21 or 22.75 hours a week, which would have meant a large cut in workers' wages.

There were three parallel strands to prosecution of the workers' campaign. First and foremost, there was strike action. By the end of the dispute the women had been on strike for 82 days, starting with token two-hour strikes that escalated to five-day strikes. These were bolstered by rallies and demonstrations supported by Unison branches and other trade unions. The second strand of the campaign was to get public support and union solidarity. Nationally, Unison paid out £180,000 in strike pay, but an equal amount was raised through the donations of other trade unions and individuals. The third strand of the campaign, in the face of a war of attrition by management over a long period of time, was to keep the momentum of the dispute going. The branch did this by raising the political awareness of the women and placing their dispute in the context of wider politics and historical struggles through film screenings and linking up with other campaigns. Activities included organizing a trip to London to lobby members of parliament and visit the headquarters of their union, Unison. Women brought their daughters, many of whom had never left Birmingham before. In September 2018, the women lobbied the Labour Party conference; delegations also went to the anti-Trump demonstration in London in July 2018; the Stand Up to Racism conference[7]; and they led the protests at the Conservative Party conference in the same year.

The victory of these women in May 2019 was only a brief respite from struggle. As the COVID-19 pandemic erupted in March 2020 they were once again on the frontline. Unable to 'work from home' on Zoom, they were supporting vulnerable people in their homes. They drew on the combativeness and confidence they had gained from their dispute to fight for the protective personal equipment they so urgently needed.

Cleaners: the dirty work of neoliberalism

The cleaning industry is characterized by a bewildering merry-go-round of firms, with mergers, takeovers, changes of names, and contracts being ditched and passed on, with the result that cleaners are bounced from one contract and employer to another, like so much human cargo. This case study looks at the struggles of cleaners in the new millennium in the Unison branch at the School of Oriental and African Studies (SOAS), University of London. The challenge of trade union organization in this workplace was compounded by the fact that migrant workers, mainly from Latin America, dominated the workforce. However, after 11 years of struggle, they won the living wage, better terms and conditions, and services were taken back in house.

Their campaign started in 2007 and was built through public meetings, online petitions, a teach-in, a May Day march through central London and a lobby of the governing body, which was actively supported by the SOAS students' union. In June 2008, they won the London Living Wage, with the pay of the cleaners increasing by 34 per cent. The following year the cleaners won union recognition with the contractor ISS. But the employers had their revenge for being forced to make this concession. Only three days later, on 12 June 2009, ten cleaners were taken into detention and six of them deported within 24 hours. Cleaners were told to attend an 'emergency staff meeting' at 6.30 am. This was used as a false pretext to lure them into a closed space from which the immigration officers were hiding to arrest them. This did not have the desired effect of intimidating the workers. Union recruitment increased and spread to catering and security, and by 2013, there was 100 per cent membership, with seven trained representatives in Unison.

In 2014, the campaign for bringing these jobs in house was ratcheted up with a 48-hour strike in January that shut the whole campus. Trade union delegations came from all over London, and other union branches up and down the country sent workplace collections. Workers achieved an important win when sick pay and other conditions were harmonized with those of directly employed workers, including an extra ten days paid holiday. Their momentous and final victory came in August 2018 when employers agreed to bring cleaning and other services back in house. This meant that previously outsourced workers not only benefitted from full university pay and conditions but also opportunities for training and development that had previously been denied to them.

This struggle inspired confidence in other workers and brought about successful campaigns and strikes for better wages and conditions, and against outsourcing, in other London universities and government departments, as well as resulting in skirmishes of hospital workers with their employers up and down the country. This industrial action was mounted by both mainstream trade unions and the newly established IWGB and UVF. For example, in 2019, 25 cleaning and 17 catering staff, members of the Public and Commercial Services (PCS) trade union, working at the government department of Business, Energy and Industrial Strategy (BEIS) walked out on indefinite strike. After 12 weeks they won a massive victory, achieving the 'gold standard' in pay and terms and conditions. The deal they won included receiving the London Living Wage as a minimum; annual pay rises; occupational sick pay on full pay; and up to six extra days annual leave, as well as increases in the overtime rate. In Wigan, in north west England, in June 2018, after a series of strikes – a 48-hour strike followed by a five-day strike – hospital workers forced their National Health Service trust to drop all plans for outsourcing cleaning, catering and domestic services, which was a blow to the employer's plans for privatization.

In David and Goliath disputes, despite these organizational barriers, ruthless tactics from employers and, sometimes, disinterest from established trade unions, these cleaners – and other outsourced workers – have taken on giant service sector multinationals and powerful institutions in higher education and government and won stunning victories.

Inhospitable workplaces in the 'hospitality' sector

A feature of the landscape of struggle since 2015 has been that both mainstream and new trade unions have started organizing workers in jobs and sectors that, until now, have been largely untouched or neglected by labour organizations, often focusing on young workers in highly precarious work offered by the so-called hospitality sector. For example, although McDonald's workers on insecure contracts have been deemed to be unorganizable, since 2020 there have been three strikes, mainly organized by the small Bakers and Food Allied Workers Union (BFAWU, often known as the Bakers' Union).

In September 2017 history was made when McDonalds workers from two branches of the Bakers' Union – Cambridge and Crayford, South London – went on strike. As a result of the strike, in January 2018, McDonald's gave workers an above-inflation pay rise. On 12 November 2019, members of the Bakers' Union in six London branches went on strike as part of an international day of action for fast-food workers' rights. The demands were for a 'new deal', including £15 per hour, an end to lower youth rates of pay, the choice of guaranteed hours a week, notice of shifts four weeks in advance and union recognition.

There are other success stories in the hospitality sector. The Better than Zero (BTZ) campaign was embedded in large mainstream unions in Scotland. Initiated by bar workers who were members of the Unite trade union in 2015, it was given the stamp of approval by the Scottish Trade Unions Congress. Rather than the campaign being the property of one union, it spans Unite; the Public and Commercial Services Union (PCS); the Broadcasting, Entertainment, Communications and Theatre Union (BECTU); and the Bakers' Union, as well as including grassroots activists. Since its formation, BTZ has had some resounding wins. In 2017, following two years of direct action from BTZ and slow-but-steady organizing from Unite hospitality members on the inside, the G1 Group (Scotland's largest hospitality employer) was forced to abandon zero-hour contracts for its workers in the 2895 bar and club, replacing them with minimum-hour contracts of at least 12 hours per week. Furthermore, the workers were no longer required to pay for their uniforms and were promised a contract before they started working. According to the Unite union organizer, these campaigns have increased the number of young workers joining trade unions, with recruitment increasing by 38,000 members under the age of 30 between 2015 and 2018 in Unite alone.

The Bakers' Union, with far fewer resources and members than Unite,[8] has had to work with a much more transient group of workers, in what the organizer referred to as 'fluid regional structures', mobilizing support through 'community outrage'. An example of how this relatively small trade union worked in wider networks is illustrated by the 'Sheffield Needs a Pay Rise' initiative. Inspired by the 'Fight for $15' campaign in the US, and triggered by the publication of an academic report demonstrating that Sheffield had the lowest pay of all major cities in Britain, Sheffield Trades Council took the decision to make contact with and try to organize precarious workers. A turning point in the campaign in 2020 was the hiring of a young woman organizer, with 50 per cent of her salary funded by the Bakers' Union and the other half by contributions from other trade unions, Labour Party wards, local community groups and charities. She enlisted 20 volunteers and used 'summer patrols'[9] to go into workplaces, managing to get 79 per cent union membership in three pubs in the city. In addition, she also recruited to other unions and reinvigorated 'dead membership' workers. The campaign mobilized mainly, but not exclusively, young people in a more open model of trade unionism – geographically based and horizontally networked.

The Sports Direct warehouse: hyper-flexibility through agencies

Workers' accounts of notorious work practices at the Sports Direct distribution warehouse, exposed by the media through the Unite trade union, prompted a House of Commons Select Committee report (2016). This documented a litany of abuses in a culture of fear and bullying. A 'six strikes and you are out policy', for instance, meant a worker could get a strike for a minor misdemeanour such as taking too long in the toilet. Compulsory searches carried out after shifts had ended meant that workers were systematically paid below the minimum wage. A poor record of health and safety meant that a total of 110 ambulances or paramedic cars were dispatched to the warehouse's postcode between 2013 and 2016.

The Sports Direct warehouse is in Derbyshire, East Midlands, and was built on the site of a coal mine that had closed in 1993, leaving a legacy of high unemployment in the area. However, few local workers were employed, rather migrant workers, assumed to be cheaper and more compliant, were directly recruited from poor small towns and rural areas in Poland and, later, Romania. These workers faced the physical isolation of the workplace and often a lack of knowledge of their legal entitlements and the English language. There were only 200 employees on permanent contracts, with a reserve army of 4,000 other workers employed by two agencies who were, in effect, on zero-hour contracts.

From 2015 onwards, Unite mounted one of the most prominent examples of community unionism, in a high profile and lively campaign that engaged activists from local trade unions and the community, as well as members from its own Unite Community branches.[10] The campaign had two prongs: first, to name and shame Sports Direct on a national level and embarrass them into improving conditions and, second, to build links with and organize the workers from the warehouse. The campaign was highly successful in exposing poor conditions in the warehouse, leading to two television documentaries and protests, supported by the charity War on Want, outside Sports Direct shops in over 40 city centres. In January 2016, a banner smuggled into the stadium by the Newcastle United Football Supporters' Club (the football club owned by the CEO of Sports Direct) was unfurled with the words 'SportsDirectShame'. The second prong of the Unite campaign, and pivotal to forging links with workers at the warehouse, was a two-year English as a Second Language (ESOL) project set up by Unite in 2015, with a dedicated project officer and 14 teachers – all volunteers and mainly Unite Community members – trained by the union. After leaflets in four languages (Polish, Russian, Lithuanian and Latvian) were distributed outside the factory by members of Community Unite, 150 workers turned up for classes. Although this was only a small proportion of the workforce, it was an important gateway into the migrant communities.

As a result of the national and local 'name and shame' campaign, small improvements were made: the 'six strikes and you are out' policy was stopped, a nurse was employed on the premises and there were fewer searches. One well-publicized win was the agreement that Unite secured for workers to receive backdated pay to the tune of £1 million, given for unpaid, compulsory queuing while waiting to be searched after their shifts. However, although these gains were important for the workers, only a few hundred of them were given direct contracts with the firm. Other aspects of work have deteriorated significantly, for example, the introduction of mechanization after 2018 in the form of picking machinery has increased the amount of dust and raised temperatures to dangerously high levels.

By 2016, a functioning branch of Unite had been established with trained officers and representatives, and regular meetings were held in the local village and not the warehouse itself. Membership of the Sports Direct Unite branch at Shirebrook was far from including the majority of workers though, and although there was a recognition agreement between Unite and management, union representatives were 'fobbed off' when they tried to raise issues and complaints. By 2020, with key activists either ill, furloughed or having left the warehouse, the branch became semi-dormant.

The gains at Sports Direct appear disappointing, both in terms of winning better working conditions and union organization. One problem with the campaign against Sports Direct was a lack of consistency from Unite. In 2015, the first big push to systematically forge a relationship with the workers through ESOL resulted in building the membership, and external stunts meant that the campaign had a national profile. However, the ESOL project only lasted for two years, and winding down the campaign on the basis of the empty promises of the employer undermined the campaign and meant that the momentum was lost. Attempts to build an active branch at Sports Direct have to be understood in the wider politics of trade unions and their internal dynamics. Trade unions are not immune from metrics, and the Unite hierarchy wanted to know how resources translated into new membership. The commitment and diligence of two full-time Unite employees and the energy and persistence of individual Unite Community members who provided a link between the officialdom of Unite and workers in Sports Direct were no substitute for activism inside the warehouse. Industrial action was never on the agenda. The campaign at Sports Direct was a missed opportunity – a victory against a particularly pernicious employer would have been an inspiration to other workers in the poorly unionized warehouse sector.

Lessons and reflections

A feature of struggle in 21st-century Britain is that there are now no 'no-go' areas for trade unions. Precarious workers viewed as on the periphery of the labour market, and outside the scope of trade unions, have made impressive gains in bettering their terms and conditions. The importance of these struggles, often under the radar of the media, is not in the numbers involved but in the demonstration of the ability of workers to organize under difficult conditions, which acts as inspiration to others. It has been those workers deemed to be vulnerable or peripheral – women, migrant and young workers – who have been centre stage. Organization has been in the framework of, and with the support of, established trade unions – ranging from mega labour organizations such as Unison and Unite, to smaller energetic unions such as the Bakers' Union. New unions such as the IWGB and UVW have punched above their weight and made significant gains.

There is no magic bullet or tidy formula for the successful organization of precarious workers, and real-life disputes are not amenable to simple categorization that conforms to the community or organizing models. Well intentioned paper policies at the national level of trade unions do not provide an automatic recipe for success. Whether community unionism is a successful strategy for winning disputes depends on whether it relies on community resources to *substitute* for workers' struggles or whether it can be *mobilized* to support them.

The organizing model has been important for motivating and mobilizing precarious workers, particularly to win ballots for action in the context of highly restrictive trade union legislation in Britain. This approach codifies what committed activists have always done in the workplace instinctively – expressing and organizing around the grievances of rank-and-file workers. However, there is a danger of interpreting the organizing model in a prescriptive, linear and mechanical way. A strike by a small group of workers may be spontaneous and can gather momentum to involve a much wider group, as in the case of cleaning and catering workers taking action at BEIS. The case studies show that campaigning and taking action is more effective in building unions than recruitment in a vacuum. This was particularly evident with London cleaners and other support workers. When they saw that their grievances were being addressed and action being taken, they joined their local branches, got involved and gained confidence. Therefore, a dispute can trigger this process – even if it starts from quite a low base – bringing new activists and leaders to the fore. In the case of the hospitality sector, energetic organizers brought workers, particularly young workers, into union membership through activity that resulted in small workplace victories, setting off a virtuous cycle in building workplace union branches.

Positive and progressive policies on sexism, racism and xenophobia have been fought for in trade unions and are important in providing space and, sometimes, resources for activists on the ground. However, it was the recruitment, mobilization and involvement of workers at the base of the union, and their willingness to and zeal for taking strike action, that forced concessions from pressurized and embarrassed employers.

There is a history in Britain of periods when the trade union bureaucracy has kept a tight lid on strikes and action, and other periods in which rank-and-file workers have seized the offensive and dictated the militancy and tempo of disputes, in the early 1970s, for example. Although the case study disputes cannot be compared with the mass strikes driven by grassroots initiative in that era, the meaningful involvement of ordinary rank-and-file members has been key to winning disputes. Such involvement included democratic decision making, picketing and speaking in other workplaces to build the solidarity that is so important to the morale of the workers. Strike action and protest were central to success. Without 82 days of strike action by the women carers from Birmingham and the 11 years of action by the cleaners from SOAS, these disputes would not have been won. At Sports Direct, the employer's feet were never put to the fire – the industrial action that would have hit profits never materialized. It is the self-activity of workers that can win disputes – it cannot be done on their behalf.

Narrow demands and often small issues may be the tinder for long accumulated grievances, but linking disputes with wider politics has been critical. Recognizing the particular oppressions of women, Black and migrant workers is important, but the successful case study disputes were linked even more widely into solidarities in the labour movement and the politics of bigger campaigns, over anti-racism for example. The role of politics was writ large in the success of the struggles discussed here. Activists and socialists in the branches, and union organizers who supported the workers' action, played a role in shaping the terrain of struggle, but at the core of the campaign and action was the self-emancipation of workers. The future of precarity in these sectors depends on a set of complex and interrelated factors. The confidence of workers will be influenced by wider class struggles and how they play out in the politics of individual unions.

Notes

[1] The National Minimum Wage (NMW) in the UK is dependent on age and is set annually by the Government, based on recommendations by an independent body – the Low Pay Commission. From 1 April 2021, this hourly rate was £8.91 for adults over 23. The Living Wage is calculated by the Living Wage Foundation, a campaigning organization in the UK, and therefore has no legal basis. The Living Wage for the UK was set at a recommended £9.50 per hour, and £10.85 for London, in 2021. It is a more realistic calculation of how much a worker needs to earn in order to meet the basic cost of living, such as rent, food and utility bills. See https://www.livingwage.org.uk/.

[2] TGWU merged with another union to become Unite the Union in 2007.

[3] Unite the Union has 1.3 million members and the GMB has 600,000.

[4] Estimates of the number of members of the Independent Workers of Great Britain are 5,000 and of United Voices of the World range from 1,000 to 4,000.

[5] These are discussed in more detail in Hardy, 2021.

[6] Unison is the largest trade union in Britain, with 1.3 million members in the public sector.

[7] This is a broad-based anti-racism organization with trade union affiliation. See https://www.standuptoracism.org.uk/about/.

[8] The estimated membership of the Bakers' Union is 20,500.

[9] The idea of summer patrols comes from the Norwegian trade union centre LO-Norway. Every summer for over thirty years, LO-Norway has sent trade union activists into workplaces where young people are likely to be working in worse conditions. The TUC have sent delegates to Norway and have also used this strategy in the Yorkshire and Humber region.

[10] Unite the Union has a category of membership – community membership – for those not in employment. This could include workers who are unemployed or those who are retired. It is an important resource for supporting local campaigns.

References

Alberti, G., Holgate, J. and Tapia, M. (2013) 'Organising migrants as workers or as migrant workers? Intersectionality, trade unions and precarious work', *The International Journal of Human Resource Management*, 24(22): 4132–48.

Clarke, S. and Cominetti, N. (2019) 'Setting the record straight: how record employment has changed the UK', Resolution Foundation Report, January. Available from: www.resolutionfoundation.org/app/uploads/2019/01/Setting-the-record-straight-full-employment-report.pdf [Accessed 7 February 2021].

Fine, J. (2006) *Worker Centers: Organizing Communities at the Edge of a Dream*, Ithaca: Cornell University.

Fitzgerald, I. and Hardy, J. (2010) ' "Thinking outside the box"? Trade Union organizing strategies and Polish migrant workers in the United Kingdom', *British Journal of Industrial Relations*, 48(1): 131–50.

Grady, J. and Simms, M. (2019) 'Trade unions and the challenge of fostering solidarities in an era of financialisation', *Economic and Industrial Democracy*, 40(3): 490–510.

Hardt, M. and Negri, A. (2000) *Empire*, Cambridge, MA: Harvard University Press.

Hardy, J. (2021) *Nothing to Lose but Our Chains*, London: Pluto.

Harvey, D. (2005) *A Brief History of Neoliberalism*, Oxford: Oxford University Press.

House of Commons Select Committee (2016) 'Employment practices at Sports Direct', third report of session 2016–17, HC 219, London: House of Commons, 22 July. Available from: tinyurl.com/yj2wxqqq [Accessed 7 February 2021].

McAlevey, J.F. (2016) *No Shortcuts: Organising for Power*, Oxford: Oxford University Press.

Moore, S. and Hayes, L.J.B. (2017) 'Taking worker productivity to a new level? Electronic monitoring in homecare – the (re)production of unpaid labour', *New Technology, Work and Employment*, 32(2): 101–14.

Moth, R. (2020) '"The business end"': neoliberal policy reforms and biomedical residualism in frontline community mental health practice in England', *Competition and Change*, (24)2: 133–53.

Standing, G. (2011) *The Precariat: The New Dangerous Class*, London: Bloomsbury.

Upchurch, M. (2014) 'The internet, social media and the workplace', *International Socialism*, 2(141): 119–38.

Wills, J. (2008) 'Making class politics possible: organising contract cleaners in London', *International Journal of Urban and Regional Research*, 32(2): 305–23.

16

Afterword: A Pandemic of Precarity

Joseph Choonara, Annalisa Murgia and Renato Miguel Carmo

As the chapters of this collection demonstrate, we confront a world in which there are multiple phenomena – some old, some new, some still emergent – that can legitimately be examined under the headings of precariousness and precarity. Likewise, we confront a panoply of possible theoretical frameworks within which such discussions might take place. Rather than seeking to impose a convenient but unwarranted consensus on the disparate voices in this work, we seek in this chapter – an afterword rather than a conclusion – to identify some developing themes in contemporary discussions of these topics.

In particular, we highlight issues arising from the COVID-19 pandemic, which has operated both as an accelerator of important social trends and a spotlight, exposing and highlighting existing social conditions.

Ecological strains

When this collection was conceived, few people were even familiar with the term *coronavirus*. By the time it went to press, the COVID-19 pandemic was well into its second year. As several authors in this collection note, if precarious work and precarious subjectivities entail a transfer of risk onto the subject, the pandemic offers an especially salient example.

The temptation to view the pandemic as an anomaly, a chance exogenous factor, impinging on society from outside as an 'act of God', should be resisted. On the contrary, critical scholars have long warned that the likelihood of such pandemic eruptions is vastly increased by the incorporation of nature into the circuits of capital (see, for instance, Davis, 2005; Wallace, 2016, 2020). The commodification of wildlife, industrialization of farming practices and the broader processes of environmental destruction associated with late capitalism create conditions in which the zoonotic transfer of novel viruses into human populations becomes far more likely. In other words, pandemics can be viewed as part of a broader process of ecological degradation, characteristic of capitalism and tending to intensify existing societal fault lines.

Likewise, the channels through which contagious diseases spread reflect the spatial and temporal structure of production and commerce, which also constrain, condition and inform governmental responses. Britain's prime minister, Boris Johnson, has offered a particularly vulgar example of the prevalence of neoliberal thinking, arguing in the early stages of the pandemic:

> [W]e are starting to hear some bizarre autarkic rhetoric, when barriers are going up, and when there is a risk that new diseases such as coronavirus will trigger a panic and a desire for market segregation that go beyond what is medically rational to the point of doing real and unnecessary economic damage, then at that moment humanity needs some government somewhere that is willing at least to make the case powerfully for freedom of exchange, some country ready to take off its Clark Kent spectacles and leap into the phone booth and emerge with its cloak flowing as the supercharged champion, of the right of the populations of the earth to buy and sell freely among each other. (House of Commons, 2021)

In this vision, adopted by many governments across the globe, the subordination of public health provision to the economic rationality of the market implies a tacit transfer of the burden of risk – along with the burden of dealing with the consequences of the pandemic – onto individuals. These transfers operate differentially across the population. Forced domesticity, traditionally the condition of people with poor health, disabilities or legal problems, has become the condition of almost everyone, but its democratic image is only apparent because it hides significant gender asymmetries and marginalization of specific social groups (Cozza et al, 2021). The same mechanism takes place in the labour force. Some found themselves without employment or underemployed during the outbreak. Others found themselves with little choice but to expose themselves to the risks of contagion through the pandemic – this certainly constituted a majority of the workforce globally, and even in most of the relatively wealthy countries of Europe. Still others, in substantial numbers, were forced out of physical workplaces and found their job now penetrated their home, like never before. Alongside these groups were large numbers of migrant labourers forced to weigh economic pressures to seek work abroad against the risks to health, and the risks of being stranded in an inhospitable host country, entailed by crossing borders in search of work. The experience of precarity is in fact intertwined with the pluralization of discrimination and marginalization of people on the basis of intersecting and compounding differences of ethnicity, race, caste, class, gender, age, sexuality, immigrant and refugee status, and disability (McDowell, 2008).

These experiences reflect and reveal existing patterns, but also mark the way in which the pandemic has intensified and accelerated existing trends. In this sense, the pandemic can be viewed as a particular instance of the intensification of precarity through ecological degradation. As such, it joins processes such as global warming, the disruption of ecosystems upon which the reproduction of life and social relations depends, the expansion of extractivism into new geographies, and the effort to impose the economic costs of environmental degradation on wider populations. The resulting burdens and risks are unlikely to be distributed equally across society – and ecological questions will provide further flashpoints for mobilization of the precarious in response to their conditions in the years ahead.

Neoliberalism in question?

The economic dislocation accompanying the pandemic is also driving changes to labour markets and labour forces that are likely to have longer-term implications for the themes addressed by authors in this book.

One trend has been the explicit return of the state to the centre ground of economics. So, taking the example of Britain, alongside and in contradiction to the neoliberal rhetoric sometimes deployed by Johnson, and noted earlier, there was also the enactment of a state-sponsored furlough scheme that supported the income of a third of the workforce. Similar measures were enacted, and on a similar scale, in France, Germany, Italy and Spain. As a result of this state largesse, official measures of unemployment rose only modestly at the height of the pandemic. Across high-income countries, employment fell by 18 million between 2019 and 2020, but hours worked fell by the equivalent of 39 million full-time jobs, reflecting the extent to which furlough schemes cushioned the rise in formal unemployment (ILO, 2021: 22). Swelling public debt in many European countries and North America allowed further direct financial support, such as soft loans, and indirect support, such as ultra-low interest rates, to be lavished upon enterprises. In this context, in many countries firm bankruptcy and default rates *fell* at the very moment at which contemporary capitalism was witnessing its sharpest ever recession.

The tendency to deploy states and central banks in the face of crises was already evident during the 2008–9 crisis but the pandemic has radicalized and extended this trend. Future research will be required to explore how far-reaching this renegotiation of the relationship between the state and capital is, and what consequences it has for studies of precarity. Elements of the prior neoliberal policy regime – the attempt to insulate markets from democratic control, support for outsized financial systems or the preference for workfare over welfare – are unlikely to disappear. However, the evolution of policy suggests a further shift away from neoliberalism's 'heroic era' in the Global North, roughly from the early 1980s through to the early 2000s. This poses the question of whether state managers will be tempted to mount further interventions to restrict the free play of the market in employment relations. It also raises the prospect of movements contesting precarity, choosing, as a result, to orientate on the state, reinforcing a tendency, already present among some European trade unions, to push for 're-regulation' of employment relations (Carver and Doellgast, 2020).

There were also, at the time of writing, signs of deep-seated dislocations in labour markets. In the short term, the recovery from the economic crisis associated with the pandemic was accompanied by shortages, not simply of goods caught up in overextended just-in-time supply chains, but also of labour power. The issue has achieved particular prominence in the haulage industries but has also featured in areas such as food and accommodation services, manufacturing and construction (Cribb and Salisbury, 2021: 411). There is evidence that in some countries much of the 'bottom' of the labour market simply fell away at the height of the pandemic, with workers reluctant to return to low paid or gruelling jobs they might once have occupied, or to risk migration in a suddenly not-so-borderless world.

As a result, conditions within the labour force that once passed unnoticed have suddenly emerged into the light. For instance, the *Financial Times* recently asked, not unreasonably, why a young person might want to work in the haulage industry, where they could look forward to 13-hour days of driving, punctuated by mandatory breaks in inadequate rest-stop facilities (Thomas, 2021). *Time* magazine reported on the 'Great Resignation' in the US, as 4.3 million people quit their jobs in the month of August 2021. Robert Reich, former US Labor Secretary under the Clinton Administration, suggested in response that employees 'don't want to return to backbreaking or boring, low wage, shit jobs. Workers are burnt out. They're fed up. They're fried. In the wake of so much hardship, and illness and death during the past year, they're not going to take it any more' (Vesoulis, 2021). In this context, neoliberalism also affected the production of subjectivity (Boltanski and Chiapello, 1999; Gill and Kanai, 2018), which has been trapped between conflicting expectations. On the one hand, efforts are made to maintain high standards of competition; on the other hand, subjects experience this pressure as a form of self-abuse. In this context, we should consider the argument that quitting a job does not simply mean resigning from a working position but perhaps also represents an act against the neoliberal model and an attempt to construct different visions and life and work trajectories (Coin, 2017).

The public debate has thus far focused on the potential for increased wages and improved conditions to draw workers back into the workplace, though it is likely that the whip of economic necessity, in the context of welfare retrenchment and the removal of whatever emergency support accompanied the pandemic, will also play a role in their return. Given the deeper structural shortages of labour across the European Union prior to the pandemic (Weber and Adăscăliţei, 2021), it is likely that the promotion of migrant labour will also feature during the recovery. As critical scholarship has long recognized, the development and regulation of migrant labour is precisely the institutionalization of categories of precarious labourers (Anderson, 2010). Indeed, during the pandemic, a disproportionate number of the 'essential' workers who maintained basic services in areas such as healthcare, social care and food supply were migrants, and mostly women. This has further highlighted the tension between their 'essential' character and a precarious nature that renders them relatively 'disposable' when their services are no longer required (see Anderson et al, 2021).

A digital future?

Another phenomenon widely discussed during the pandemic, with the potential to carry over into the post-pandemic world, is the digitization of work. This topic has long been interwoven with discussions of precarity. Forms of work categorized as either 'crowdwork', which entails 'completing a set of tasks through online platforms', or 'work on-demand via apps', consisting of 'traditional working activities ... channelled through apps managed by firms' (De Stefano, 2016), grew in prominence during the pandemic. As other forms of work became less tenable, these forms, typically taking place outside the traditional framework of employment, with its associated protections, came to the fore.

Even for many of those remaining in formal employment, there was an increased use of information and communication technology to transfer work to the household during the pandemic. A shift to widespread 'teleworking' has been forecast for decades, but had, prior to 2020, made only a limited impression on the labour force in most countries. In the UK, for instance, 'it had taken almost 40 years for homeworking to grow by three percentage points, but its prevalence grew eight-fold virtually overnight as people were instructed to work at home if they can because of the pandemic' (Felstead and Reuschke, 2021). Around a third of the workforce across Europe and in the US worked from home in early 2020 (Felstead and Reuschke, 2021). It remains hard to generalize about the effects on both employees and employers. Overall, impacts on productivity appear to balance out, with some firms reporting deterioration or improvement but most suggesting a broad continuity. Yet the impacts of home working depend both on the nature of home life – in particular, there are highly gendered impacts of childcare responsibilities – and the nature of the work being undertaken, as contributors to this collection have noted. Many workers also report feeling drained and isolated, or working longer hours than before (Felstead and Reuschke, 2021).

It is not simply the antipathy of workers towards working solely in their own home that is likely to limit the use of teleworking post-pandemic. Aside from the impracticality of shifting many jobs in areas such as manufacturing, or service sector jobs such as food serving, into the home, many employers fear that informal collaboration, both within and between firms, may suffer and, perhaps more importantly, that managers will lose their ability to 'exert direct control over and to supervise remote workers' (Hurley et al, 2021: 59). A norm is emerging at many larger firms in areas such as finance and business services with an expectation that employees will be in the office two to four days a week (FT reporters, 2021).

Regardless of the eventual redistribution of work between the home and the traditional workplace, it is necessary to recognize that the digital technologies deployed during the pandemic are not neutral with regard to their social content. Information and communication technology is not simply about changing the *location* of work; it is also about measuring and enforcing its intensity, duration and effectiveness. Technologies that monitor the location of formally self-employed Uber drivers can also be deployed to monitor the movement of warehouse staff. Techniques to quantify work rates in call centres can also, in principle, be extended into the domestic sphere through invasive monitoring of home workers. Future research on precariousness will be forced to explore what Phoebe Moore and Simon Joyce (2019) refer to in these contexts as 'platform work managerialism'.

Precarious agency?

Finally, it is possible to detect in recent discussions of work and employment modest signs of a revival of collective agency in challenging conditions in the workplace. Among the wealthier nations, this has been most noteworthy in the US, where, amid the tentative post-pandemic economic recovery, unions were celebrating an uptick in strike activity – hitting industries such as manufacturing, logistics, food processing, transportation and healthcare. Unionization drives have been launched at firms such as Starbucks and Amazon, and within the airlines, transit firms and universities (Allen, 2021).

While these events are not even close to reversing the pattern of decline in union membership or struggle in the US since the Reagan era, and far from all union drives or strikes are successful, it nonetheless reinforces the message of several contributors to this collection – that workers are never entirely without agency. As the examples cited within this book show, these struggles certainly extend to areas associated with high proportions of workers on precarious contracts or subject to precarious conditions. The processes of precarization, in fact, have not only intensified the structures of domination but have also led to new forms of disruptive agency, or disruptive subjectivities (Neilson and Rossiter, 2008; Bailey et al, 2018), confirming the fact that there is always a capacity for refusal, even on the part of those in an asymmetrical power position (Tronti, 1964).

In Europe, it remains to be seen whether, as the typically more thoroughgoing furlough schemes and other supports to labour markets are withdrawn, these countries witness the emergence of different struggles, thus also allowing for political invention. Nonetheless, recent scholarship has noted the persistence of precarious workers' struggles throughout the history of capitalism. In particular, national and transnational struggles against precariousness have proliferated since the early 2000s and were carried out by collective actors capable of mobilizing subjects belonging to the most diverse categories of workers (Foti, 2017). In a recent study of British labour struggles from 2015 to 2020, Jane Hardy notes that recent outbursts of activism have encompassed many such groups. She highlights equal pay strikes among mainly female council workers in Glasgow and care workers in Birmingham, who were predominantly on permanent contracts but subject to poverty pay; strikes by mainly migrant cleaners in London, who secured the 'living wage' and, in some cases, reversed outsourcing after a decade-long campaign; and a series of small-scale but remarkable battles in Scotland by restaurant and club workers who were often subject to zero-hour contracts and many other markers of extreme precariousness (Hardy, 2021). In this outlook, whether precariousness is viewed as a label for multifaceted forms of insecurity faced by workers or as a condition experienced by specific parts of the labour force, there are good grounds for doubting a rigid line of demarcation separating a putative 'precariat' from the broader working class.

Conclusion

In the late 1990s, the sociologist Pierre Bourdieu (1998) published a short text where he identified, in the context of liberal economies, the tendency for precarity not only to spread to multiple sectors of the labour market but also to extend to other spheres of society. Precariousness would thus spread everywhere, affecting objective elements, such as contractual relations, wage levels and social protection, but also subjective elements. The latter process has implications for, among other things, the way life is lived, how one perceives the present being experienced and how the future is projected. In this regard, several studies have drawn attention to the impact of employment precariousness on the capacity of individuals to plan and to establish relatively stable and predictable time horizons (Leccardi, 2005; Carmo et al, 2014).

In this sense, precariousness can be viewed as an increasingly broad phenomenon that tends to reproduce itself from the past to the present and to condition expectations and aspirations for the future. In this approach, it tends to become a total phenomenon with multiple ramifications and implications for the social and economic life of workers and the societies in which they are inserted. However, viewed this way the concept runs the risk of becoming too broad, exhibiting a ubiquity in which almost everything related to the processes of marginalization and the deterioration of living conditions could be included. This leads to growing difficulties in the theoretical problematization of the concept as well as its empirical operationalization.

This collection aims, on the one hand, to capture the tendency of precariousness to incorporate a certain social totality, insofar as it is not reduced to labour conditions and reaches other social, economic and cultural spheres. On the other hand, it recognizes the risks resulting from this theoretical amplification or overextension of the concept, warning of the analytical and interpretative consequences. Thus, precariousness may be everywhere, but this does not necessarily mean that it explains everything or that it is the producer of all social weaknesses and fragilities. On the contrary, it must be repositioned and considered from the most pertinent theoretical angles which, in turn, do not stretch too far away from the relational contexts and frameworks of social interaction. This balance is not easy to establish. It represents an immense challenge in the field of social sciences, with this book representing a small contribution to the deepening of multidimensional analysis, duly grounded and anchored in the critical analysis of social reality.

Authors in this collection duly approach the concepts of precarity and precariousness from different theoretical and methodological perspectives, considering their analytical multidimensionality. Being broad concepts, they allow for the constitution of a field of discussion that crosses and relates the processes of reconfiguration and deregulation of labour markets, especially in the weakening of labour and social rights and the proliferation of atypical contracts, with the wider social dynamics of the *life world*, namely the impact on everyday experience and collective action practices, the social construction of subjectivities, and on the production and reinforcement of social inequalities.

References

Allen, J. (2021) 'Striketober', *Tempest*, 3 November. Available from: https://www.tempestmag.org/2021/11/striketober/ [Accessed 3 November 2021].

Anderson, B. (2010) 'Migration, immigration controls and the fashioning of precarious workers', *Work, Employment & Society*, 24(2): 300–17.

Anderson, B., Poeschel, F. and Ruhs, M (2021) 'Rethinking labour migration: covid-19, essential work, and systemic resilience', *Comparative Migration Studies*, 9(45): 1–19.

Bailey, D.J., Clua-Losada, M., Huke, N., Ribera-Almandoz, O. and Rogers, K. (2018) 'Challenging the age of austerity: disruptive agency after the global economic crisis', *Comparative European Politics*, 16(1): 9–31.

Boltanski, L. and Chiapello, E. (1999) *Le nouvel esprit du capitalisme*, Paris: Gallimard.

Bourdieu, P. (1998) 'La précarité est aujourd'hui partout', in *Contre-feux*, Paris: Liber-Raison d'agir, pp 95–101.

Carmo, R. M., Cantante, F. and Alves, N.A. (2014) 'Time projections: youth and precarious employment', *Time & Society*, 23(3): 337–57.

Carver, L. and Doellgast, V. (2020) 'Dualism or solidarity? Conditions for union success in regulating precarious work', *European Journal of Industrial Relations*, 27(4): 367–85.

Coin, F. (2017) 'On quitting', *ephemera: theory & politics in organization*, 17(3): 705–19.

Cozza, M., Gherardi, S., Graziano, V., Johansson, J., Mondon-Navazo, M., Murgia, A. and Trogal, K. (2021) 'COVID-19 as a breakdown in the texture of social practices', *Gender, Work & Organization*, 28: 190–208.

Cribb, J. and Salisbury, A. (2021) 'Employment and the end of the furlough scheme', Institute for Fiscal Studies Green Budget, chapter 9. Available from: https://ifs.org.uk/uploads/9-Employment-and-the-end-of-the-furlo ugh-scheme-.pdf [Accessed 3 November 2021].

Davis, M. (2005) *The Monster at Our Door: The Global Threat of Avian Flu*, New York: The New Press.

De Stefano, V. (2016) 'The rise of the "just-in-time workforce": on-demand work, crowdwork and labour protection in the "gig-economy"', International Labour Organization, conditions of work and employment series, 71. Available from: https://www.ilo.org/wcmsp5/groups/public/ ---ed_protect/---protrav/---travail/documents/publication/wcms_443 267.pdf [Accessed 3 November 2021].

Felstead, A. and Reuschke, D. (2021) 'A flash in the pan or a permanent change? The growth of homeworking during the pandemic and its effect on employee productivity in the UK', *Information Technology & People*, https://doi.org/10.1108/ITP-11-2020-0758.

Foti, A. (2017) 'The precariat for itself: Euro May Day and precarious workers' movements', in E. Armano, A. Bove and A. Murgia (eds) *Mapping Precariousness, Labour Insecurity and Uncertain Livelihoods*, London: Routledge, pp 137–48.

FT reporters (2021) 'UK employers plot return of office workers', Financial Times, 6 September.

Gill, R. and Kanai, A. (2018) 'Mediating neoliberal capitalism: affect, subjectivity and inequality', *Journal of Communication*, 68(2): 318–26.

Hardy, J. (2021) *Nothing to Lose but our Chains*, London: Pluto Press.

House of Commons (2021) 'Global Britain', debate pack. Available from: https://researchbriefings.files.parliament.uk/documents/CDP-2021-0002/CDP-2021-0002.pdf [Accessed 3 November 2021].

Hurley, J., Fana, M., Adăscăliței, D., Ortolani, G.M., Mandl, I., Peruffo, E. and Vacas-Soriano, C. (2021) 'What just happened? Covid-19 lockdowns and change in the labour market', Eurofound. Available from: https://www.eurofound.europa.eu/sites/default/files/ef_publication/field_ef_document/ef21040en.pdf [Accessed 3 November 2021].

ILO (2021) 'World employment and social outlook trends 2021', International Labour Organization. Available from: https://www.ilo.org/wcmsp5/groups/public/---dgreports/---dcomm/---publ/documents/publication/wcms_795453.pdf [Accessed 3 November 2021].

Leccardi, C. (2005) 'Facing uncertainty: temporality and biographies in the new century', *Young – Nordic Journal of Youth Research*, 13(2): 123–46.

McDowell, L. (2008) 'Thinking through work: complex inequalities, constructions of difference and trans-national migrants', *Progress in Human Geography*, 32(4): 491–507.

Moore, P.V. and Joyce, S. (2019) 'Black box or hidden abode? The expansion and exposure of platform work managerialism', *Review of International Political Economy*, 27(4): 926–48.

Neilson, B. and Rossiter, N. (2008) 'Precarity as a political concept, or, Fordism as exception', *Theory, Culture & Society*, 25(7–8): 51–72.

Thomas, D. (2021) 'A day in the life of the British trucker', Financial Times, 1 November.

Tronti, M. (1964) 'Lenin in England', *Classe Operaia*, (1), January. Available from: www.marxists.org/reference/subject/philosophy/works/it/tronti.htm [Accessed 3 November 2021].

Vesoulis, A. (2021) 'Why literally millions of Americans are quitting their jobs', *Time*, 13 October.

Wallace, R. (2016) *Big Farms Make Big Flu*, New York: Monthly Review Press.

Wallace, R. (2020) *Dead Epidemiologists*, New York: Monthly Review Press.

Weber, T. and Adăscăliței, D. (2021) 'Tackling labour shortages in EU member states', Eurofound. Available from: https://www.eurofound.europa.eu/sites/default/files/ef_publication/field_ef_document/ef21006en.pdf [Accessed 3 November 2021].

Index

Note: References to figures appear in *italic* type; those in **bold** type refer to tables.